Ayurvedic Nutrition

AYURVEDIC NUTRITION

Vaidya ATREYA SMITH

MOTILAL BANARSIDASS PUBLISHERS
PRIVATE LIMITED • DELHI

Reprint: Delhi, 2015
First Indian Edition: 2011
Parts of this book first appreared in 2001 under the title
Perfect Balance *published by Avery Publishing, USA*

ISBN: 978-81-208-3537-5

MOTILAL BANARSIDASS
41 U.A. Bungalow Road, Jawahar Nagar, Delhi 110 007
8 Mahalaxmi Chamber, 22 Bhulabhai Desai Road, Mumbai 400 026
203 Royapettah High Road, Mylapore, Chennai 600 004
236, 9th Main III Block, Jayanagar, Bengaluru 560 011
Sanas Plaza, 1302 Baji Rao Road, Pune 411 002
8 Camac Street, Kolkata 700 017
Ashok Rajpath, Patna 800 004
Chowk, Varanasi 221 001

Cover by: *Tanya Schild-Signes*

FOR SALE IN ASIA ONLY

Printed in India
by RP Jain at NAB Printing Unit,
A-44, Naraina Industrial Area, Phase I, New Delhi–110028
and published by JP Jain for Motilal Banarsidass Publishers (P) Ltd,
41 U.A. Bungalow Road, Jawahar Nagar, Delhi-110007

Dedication

I wish to acknowledge the help and support of my teachers in India. I am deeply indebted to Dr. Robert E. Svoboda for the excellent foreword, feedback and support during the writing of the original manuscript in 1999 and 2000. Additionally, I wish to thank the many patients who have been my best teachers over the years and I wish to give my deep appreciation to my wife, Girija, who has continuously supported me in every way possible.

Contents

Preface to the 2010 edition xi

Foreword by Dr. Robert E. Svoboda xv

Introduction xix

1. Why Use an Individual Approach to Nutrition? 1

2. What Type of Person Are You? 9

   Simple Questions to Help You Determine Your Type 12

3. The "ABC" of Ayurvedic Nutrition 23

   The ABC of Nutrition 24

   Physiological Profiles 27

   Psychological Profiles 37

4. The Principles of Constitutional Nutrition 43

   Your Genetic Code and How it Affects the Food You Digest 50

   The Six Primary Combinations 53

5. Avoid Disaster – Learn How to Eat 63

   How You Eat Begins the Digestive Process–for Good or Bad 64

6. How to Avoid the Dangers of Dieting and Food Fads 89

–The Myth of Labeling 93

–Dangers of Dieting 95

7. Food According to Your Metabolism 101

Eat According to Your Metabolic Capacity 104

Raw vs. Cooked / Liquid vs. Whole Foods 110

8. Descriptions of Food Groups 115

–Fruits 115

–Vegetables 118

–Grains 121

–Beans (legumes) 124

–Nuts and Seeds 126

–Dairy Products 128

–Oils 135

–Animal Products 141

–Seafood 142

–Sweeteners 143

–Spices 146

–Beverages 149

–Vitamins and Minerals 155

9. Why Eat a Low Protein Diet? 159

–Protein Content of Common Foods 165

–The XYZ of Ayurveda 170

10. Poisoned Food 177

How Environmental Pollutants in Food Affect Hormone Function in Men and Women 179

11. How to Lose Weight Permanently by Increasing Metabolic Function 187

Explanation of Digestive Problems and Metabolic Malfunctions 188

How to Correct the Metabolism 190

Eliminating Fatigue and Increasing Performance through Food 194

12. Lifestyle as Nutritional Support 197

13. Dietary Supplements – Myths, Facts and Traditions 219

Myths of Marketing Supplements 224

Supplements That Your Body Can Actually Assimilate 230

14. Increasing Immunity through Diet 235

–Dietary Support to Immunity 239

15. Descriptions of Foods by Constitution 247

16. The 21 Days Plan to Feel Better 279

-Plan for the Vata People 280

-Plan for the Pitta People 284

-Plan for the Kapha People 287

-Plan for the Dual Type People 292

17. Improve the Quality and Length of Your Life 295

Appendix :
The Difference between Biochemical and Ayurvedic Nutrition 301
Biochemical View Follows a Mechanical Model 304
Ayurvedic View Follows a Mind/Body Model 314

Bibliography 325
Index 329

Preface to the Revised 2010 Edition

It is now over ten years since my agent sold this manuscript for its first publication in 2001. The resulting first edition in July 2001 was in many ways extremely disappointing, even though the edition was truly beautifully done and it is always exciting to have a book published. My primary disillusion was over the one-third of the manuscript that was cut out in editing, 80% of footnotes were removed and all Sanskrit terms were "translated" – in other words the book was "dumbed down" so it would make money. I became so disillusioned by the modern publishing industry that over the last ten years I have stopped writing books for the general public and instead have written three textbooks on Ayurvedic medicine for Western people.

I feel that this book does not need to be "dumbed down" and that the public is sincerely searching for real information on nutrition that is not "fashion" or "fad" orientated. I also realized that I would rather write for one-percent of the population than for the public at large if I need to remove or water down the very information that will help them. I revised the manuscript in 2006 by re-inserting the original text and up-dating the text in general. I was ready to bring out an illegal edition due to the refusal of the first publisher to either give back the author's rights or make the book available. Fortunately, my agent, Rosalie Segal, managed to have the rights returned to me in 2009 after six years of the original book being listed, but for all practicality, un-available. Since 2009 I have once again gone through modern studies for updates and changes for what I had written in 1998-1999.

Unsurprisingly, very little has really changed. There is some superficial satisfaction to say "I told you so". However, that is much less satisfying than seeing what I wrote over ten years ago now becoming commonly accepted in both the media and public. The bottom line is still that, *a balance diet based on plant foods, that respects seasons, environment and the individual eating them* leads to good health.

The studies since 2000 have continued to show the same results as in the 1980's and 1990's. There are several noticeable differences however. People are getting sicker, fatter and so are our children. "Fashion" diets are as popular as ever, even when they contradict science and common sense. In spite of all the evidence very little change from the government or the "health" industry has occurred in changing the fundamentally wrong way in which people eat in developed economies.

The other notable difference in the 1990's and the first ten years of 2000 has been the switch from enzyme based studies /medicines to genetic studies /medicines. In spite of the fact that studies often indicate that the expression of genes and genetic tendencies are primarily rooted in diet and lifestyle, the media is still trying to sell people on a "magic genetic pill". Only the form has changed, they are still selling a "magic pill" that does not exist. We see that science also has its fashions and fads that ultimately use the public as their guinea pigs.

The sudden realization that an animal based diet is destroying the environment by producing more CO^2 than all of world-wide transport combined is welcomed. If you truly wish to help the planet, stop consuming animal products. Reducing driving may have a small effect – basing a diet on plant foods will have a huge effect.

And lastly, in spite of repeated studies that indicate little or no effect from the use of vitamins, anti-oxidants and other pills on our health, world-wide sales are ever increasing. The urban myth that dietary supplements are the basis of good nutrition will never die so long as people can make money from it. And make money they do, which is why multinational pharmaceutical companies own a major share of the dietary supplements industry.

To give up the illusion that you can be healthy, happy and contented without cooking and eating real food remains the message of this book. In spite of more than ten years – or because of it – the timeless message of Ayurveda and a whole food diet is more important than ever. Thus, this book, in its entirety for the first time, will find a happy home in the hands of those who wish to find health in an individualized approach to nutrition and diet that empowers rather than victimizes.

VAIDYA ATREYA SMITH, BSc.
South of France, January, 2010.

Foreword by

Dr Robert E. Svoboda

There is really nothing like a good chuckle, particularly when traveling in India, which I was when I first read *Ayurvedic Nutrition.* Laughter makes such annoyances as traffic jams, train delays, and the depredations of monkeys easier to bear, while stimulating the circulation, encouraging good breathing, improving immune function, and generally promoting all the while active, positive states of health in the mirthful.

Humor is particularly valuable when trying to advise or teach, for it lightens subjects like Ayurveda that may otherwise sit heavily on their recipients. As recently as twenty years ago Ayurveda was practically unknown in the West, and even now the majority has yet to hear its name. Many folk have however begun to slowly adapt to thinking and speaking Ayurvedically, and some of these are attempting to present their findings in print.

But one can learn a lingo without being able to teach it, and mere study of the language of health and healing that is Ayurveda does nothing to prepare the student to be able to edify others. Wrongly concocted, Ayurveda becomes a dense, nearly-indigestible study; to present it accurately is to walk the tightrope between what should be and what is, between tradition and innovation. Ayurvedic theory can be abstruse, with its complex proclamations, and its arcane references to Indian cultural tropes. Its practice can be equally mystifying, for all its rules are subordinated to the dictates of common sense. What cures the patient is always the right medicine, whether it reinforces the theory or violates it, and one of the most difficult things to convey to a student of Ayurveda is how to know when to embrace theory, and when to ignore it.

This is particularly the case when one is attempting to translate Ayurveda from its natal Indian idiom into a tongue that Westerners will find lucid and topical. The West differs so dramatically from the East that I often wonder how the two can share the same planet. The water and air, flora and fauna, customs and rituals of the one often have so little in common with those of the other that it becomes no mean task to extract from the details of an Ayurveda that developed in India a system that will function well in Canada, Italy, Argentina or Australia.

Even when the process of translation proceeds well, there is no guarantee that the final product will be readable. Which is why it is always a pleasure for me to find a work on Ayurveda that eschews pomposity, and seasons its prescriptions with the levity of wit. I enjoyed *Ayurvedic Nutrition* for its topicality, for its focus on providing readers with tools for transformation, and above all for its tone. Even on topics where his convictions are decided and deeply held, such as the wisdom of eliminating meat from one's daily diet (a view that I endorse heartily), Atreya's tone remains measured and clear. Even serious matters, like the "expectation of violence as normal" that has contaminated our society, he introduces without bludgeoning the reader with them. He advocates without preaching, suggests without insisting, and garnishes his arguments with refreshing drollness.

Atreya turns his subject into a light, delectable confection, into an info soufflé that goes down easy, digests agreeably, and leaves its consumers well-fed but hungry for more. Read his words, and try them out in your own life. Experiment with his suggestions, and find which ones agree with your body and mind. Make small changes, and let them accumulate into life-enhancing reorganizations. Let the book's playfulness awaken in you the spirit of rejuvenation, that it may return to you some of the vigor and lightheartedness that you had as a child.

Sample the treats that *Ayurvedic Nutrition* has to offer, and taste the difference that Ayurveda can make in your life and your living.

Introduction

A woman client came to me several years ago complaining of feeling bloated, heavy and depressed. She was under high levels of stress in her profession. She said that she had gained an extra 11 pounds during these last six stressful months. Jenny had good reasons to feel stressed and concerned about her body as she owned and managed a company that worked in the fashion and advertising industries. Several years ago we had worked together on her diet and achieved good results. However, this last period of time had been very demanding and stressful and she was feeling "out of sorts". I gave her nutritional advice and some natural herbal supplements to help her digestion. Soon after, she came into my office looking great and feeling relaxed.

"I'm back to my normal weight and feeling good", she said. "Thanks!" It took Jenny nine weeks to lose 11 pounds permanently without dieting or taking drugs. As she had been a fashion model herself she was very happy to be back to her normal healthy weight without drugs or strict diets.

How did she do it? What advice did I give her? I advised simple changes in her lifestyle and diet to match her changed environment of higher stress. I followed the 5000 year old holistic medical system named Ayurveda.

As a culture in poor health we need to question some basic facts about our whole approach to food and nutrition. It is estimated that 97 million American adults are overweight today. The number one killer of all people in the United States is heart disease. This is a disease that can be prevented through diet and lifestyle more effectively than any drug.

The state of our ill health becomes more alarming when we note that child obesity has increased by 54% in the last 38 years and that half of all children from the ages of 7 to 12 have elevated blood cholesterol. It is also estimated that 98% of all children (ages 2-18) now have at least one risk factor for heart disease. The news gets worse – 67% have three or more risk factors. The American Heart Association views three or more risk factors as highly favorable for hardening of the arteries (atherosclerosis). It is estimated that 70 million people currently suffer from heart disease in the United States.

If the current scientific model of nutrition was working why are Americans becoming fatter and unhealthier than ever? Why is the rate of heart disease deaths not affected when we lower our cholesterol and watch calories and fat intake? Why are Americans spending 27 billion dollars on alternative medical treatments each year? Why are 40% of people in the United States using alternative medical or nutritional methods? Nearly 60% of these people are using alternative methods to prevent disease or maintain their existing state of health.[1]

There are two primary reasons for this – one of which this book will address. The first reason is that the food industry as a whole is profit oriented. This industry is supported by a pharmaceutical industry that is also profit oriented. Both of these industries have an arm lock on your doctor – one on each side. Unfortunately, a segment of our doctors are also

---

[1] *British Medical Journal*, 1998; 317:1408 (21 November), quoting various reports from the *Journal of the American Medical Association* (JAMA).

profit motivated and this adds to the complexity of the whole distortion in our basic cultural approach to nutrition and eating. Doctors are now even taking recruiting money to send pharmaceutical company's patients to test drugs on – without the patients' knowledge. Some doctors make an additional $500,000 to 1 million dollars in extra money from this practice.[2]

Money is, in itself, a neutral medium of exchange. Unfortunately, money in the health and food industries are dominating not only our health, but the health and, perhaps, very life of our children.

It is striking that when we read any information on a medical study in the papers or media the second thing mentioned after the subject matter is the cost of the study. Does a $50,000 study have less validity than a 5 million dollars study? Is a study of $200,000 less important that one that costs 2 million dollars?

The sad fact that is now becoming known publicly is that any study – even the infamous randomized double blind placebo study – can be twisted to meet the author's biases. Or more importantly, the biases of the company funding the study. As 90% of all 'scientific' studies are funded by profit oriented companies (whether food or pharmaceutical) one wonders if there really is such a thing as an objective view in modern science. Unfortunately, fraud is rampant in the scientific community, which adds to the problem. "More than one-quarter of the scientists surveyed by the American Association of the Advancement of Sciences admitted that they had personally encountered at least two instances of research that they suspected was falsified, fabricated or plagiarized in the previous decade."[3]

---

[2] "Doctors on the Take", editorial in the *International Herald Tribune,* May 27, 1999, quotes the work of two *New York Times* journalists, Kurt Eichenwald and Gina Kolata.

The other fact that is seldom spoken of is that of how we study the body. Modern chemistry is based on the study of non-living systems. In other words, all our medical and nutritional information is coming from a system that studies things out of their original context. Substances are removed from their original habitat and studied in a test tube or glass slide. This approach fails completely to account for the interrelationship of the substance within the living organism of its origin. Whether the substance is a food cell or body tissue the actual context of origin is completely lost or changed. Modern science is based on the study of dead objects, not living substances interacting in their normal environment.

In contrast the Ayurvedic system works with living humans and has observed the effects of food and nutrition on the body for thousands of years. They have also had the opportunity to obverse the effects of nutrition on the mind and emotions – Ayurveda is a mind / body system of health that works with living people, not dead objects.

Looking in my Concise Oxford dictionary I see that the definition of science is: "*1. a branch of knowledge constructed on objective principals involving the systematized observation of and experiment with phenomena, especially concerned with the material and function of the physical universe.*" This brings to mind numerous questions as to the real objectivity of modern science and the studies that come through the medical media. An example of this questionable objectivity is the opening topic – obesity.

The Washington Post service released an article – in early October of 1998 – about the profit motivation in the treatment of obesity. There are currently 45 different companies trying to develop an "anti-obesity" drug. If this drug were sold to only one fourth of the overweight

---

[3] *British Medical Journal,* 1994; 308:283-84.

Americans its revenue would account for over $26 billion dollars per year. The article states "if a company developed a truly safe, effective weight-loss drug (they would make a fortune)". There has never been and there probably never will be any drug that does not cause some side effects. Modern drugs by their very nature cause effects and secondary effects (see appendix 1 for a discussion of this subject). Drugs are considered safe if they only cause a few minor problems – like water retention, depression and sexual dysfunction. What then is the scientific standard for safety? That it doesn't cause cancer? That it doesn't destroy your liver function? Will profit determine the degree of safety? What percentage of physiological damage will be allowed as a "safe level"?

The Concise Oxford continues to say: "*2. a systematic and formulated knowledge especially of a specified type or on a specified subject.*" Hence, the term science, by definition, is not limited to the material universe. The whole of the psychiatric and psychology profession have been trying to clarify this situation for over 100 years – to what extent they have succeeded in relation to the physical sciences is questionable.

I believe that the American public is very concerned by the obvious contradictions in modern medical and nutritional science. Fortunately, there is an alternative scientific medical and nutritional system – Ayurveda or "the science of life". As a medical system it is many thousands of years old. The age can vary from 2500 to 6000 years depending on the historical bias of the person. This system has been in continuous use for this whole period and still treats a large segment of the world's population (approximately one fifth according to the World Health Organization, which recognizes Ayurveda as a valid system of medicine).

The word "Ayurveda" is a very old Sanskrit word that is composed of two words – Ayur and Veda. The word ayur means "life", or more specifically, the length of your life.

Veda means understanding or knowledge obtained in a logical manner, which is why it is usually translated as "science". The Ayurvedic medical system is a system that is concerned with how long you live and the quality of your life while you are living it.

This system is not interested in suppressing symptoms or even in adding a few years to your life through medication. The whole approach is different. First, Ayurveda only treats people, individual people like you and your family. Second, Ayurveda seeks to find and cure the cause of disease. Of course symptoms can be helped in this process, but the focus is on curing the individual person not treating the symptoms through the lifetime use of chemical drugs.

The result of this approach is not only long life, but more importantly a high quality of life. Using the Ayurvedic system to add years onto your life sounds more like marketing to me than fact. However, in years of practicing Ayurveda I have seen people living disease free their whole life when they follow the guidelines for their individual types. Many of these people have also been able to stop taking drugs once their body begins to function normally.

Ayurveda stresses the importance of living a balanced life. It emphasizes nutrition and lifestyle as the basis of health. Medicine is given a secondary place next to these two pillars of health – eating right for your individuality and living a life style that has exercise, creativity, joy, challenges and a routine that optimizes your personal performance or creative ability.

Ayurveda came from ancient India and is rich in its scope of understanding the mind and body. It is the original mind/body or holistic medicine. There is also an important understanding of the soul and human being's desire to know some divinity in life. Yet, Ayurveda is a science of health and is not associated with any one religion. This is obvious in that Ayurveda is practiced in different forms in Buddhist, Hindu and Muslim countries in the East. Ayurveda is just as suited for Christians as any other religion because it stresses the health of the body, the health of the mind and the needs of the soul. It is not a system that is advocating any one approach to fill the desires of the human soul; simply that it is an important factor in health.

Ayurveda is truly a logical system that one can actually call scientific as it is based primarily on observing nature in all its forms. Unlike modern nutrition and medicine Ayurveda has always observed the effects of foods and medicines on human beings. This is vastly different in that the whole effect of any substance can be observed or experienced by living people in their normal environment.

In contrast to the holistic approach of Ayurveda we have modern science that is continuously studying substances outside of their natural environment. What we currently call science is questionable. Actually, what we have today is the brilliant marketing of science and very little of real objective observation of nature – beginning with your individual response to different foods. The proof of anything is to try it and see if it works. Ayurveda is based on a long history of observation and experimentation on living human beings. By following it one is taking advantage of the oldest medical system and the contribution of countless doctors and patients over thousands of years.

This book will answer the questions raised in this introduction and early chapters and will present a clear, logical and objective method as an alternative to modern nutrition. The alternative is the Ayurvedic nutritional system, which we know from more than 5000 years of experience to work.

1
Why Use an Individual Approach to Nutrition?

Jenny had success in looking and feeling good for two reasons. Most importantly she was motivated to change her health through natural means. This allowed her to follow the suggestions I gave her. Secondly, she actual did what I suggested. Ayurveda is a system that requires your participation; in fact, Ayurveda is a system that empowers you as a person. If you want to run away from taking control of your life, to give up your personal power then Ayurveda is not for you.

For Jenny this meant making several small changes in diet and in lifestyle to account for the changes in her work environment. She also took several digestive herbs religiously. The combination of all of these factors – mental and physical is what gave her success. Any one of the suggestions that I made alone would not have done the trick. This is because Ayurveda is concerned with all aspects of your life and has a completely different vision of health and living.

If we accept the theory stated in the introduction that there are two primary reasons for the poor health of our nation, and we acknowledge that the commercial motivations of the food and medical industries may be partly responsible – what could be the other reason? Well, for a moment let's assume that all food companies, pharmaceutical companies and medical professionals only have your health in mind

What could be the other cause of the failure of modern nutrition? Every book on nutrition and dieting fails to really address the most fundamental possibility – that the whole basis of modern nutrition is wrong.

This means that in spite of the best intentions of researchers, doctors and the millions of others involved in this industry everything they do will be of limited worth. There is great honesty in the medical research community. Read any book written by a Ph.D. scientist or by any serious doctor and they will readily admit that we, as scientists, do not fully understand the complete functioning of the body. This is not a question of debate but is factual. And this is the fundamental problem of nutrition that this book addresses.

Professor of physics, David Bohm, questions the basic assumptions of science and humanity in general in his book Wholeness and the Implicate Order. He clearly states the most fundamental problem with science is its tendency to view things out of their context, or from a fragmentary point of view:

> "Of course, the prevailing tendency in science to think and perceive in terms of a fragmentary self-world view is part of a larger movement that has been developing over the ages and that pervades almost the whole of our society today: but, in turn, such a way of thinking and looking in scientific research tends very strongly to re-enforce the general fragmentary approach because it gives men the picture of the whole world as constituted of nothing but an aggregate of separately existent 'atomic building blocks', and provides experimental evidence from which is drawn the conclusion that this view is necessary and inevitable."[4]

---

[4] Bohm, David, 1980 p. 15.

Dr. Bohm goes on to say that the present world view of perceiving things from a fragmentary model, e.g., one of differences and sameness, is a fundamental question for our survival. He states that using the intellect to divide or fragment something to understand it is normal, but that to then apply this same methodology to life as a whole is fundamentally wrong and inapplicable. He goes on to say:

> "Evidently, it is important and indeed extremely urgent to clear up this deep and pervasive kind of confusion that penetrates the whole of our lives. What is the use of attempt at social, political, economic or other action if the mind is caught up in a confused movement in which it is generally differentiating what is not different and identifying what is not identical? Such action will be at best ineffective and at worst really destructive."[5]

The view of Ayurveda has always been based on a vision of wholeness and not one of fragmentation. This is why we use the word "holistic" when speaking about Ayurveda – because it is looking at a whole or non-fragmented world. Modern medicine and nutrition are based on a faulty mental conception of wrong division, or fragmentation and separation. We are seeing the results today of this approach in our national state of poor health and nutrition.

It is time that the public seriously looks at some very fundamental questions about nutritional beliefs. I believe that if one objectively looks at the facts one cannot say – with any conviction – that modern nutritional views are working. In order to justify the "progress" of the modern view we are often told that we are living longer than ever before. Every American will tell you, "yes, thanks to modern medicine and nutrition we are living longer than ever before in history". Is this statement really true? Or does it change when looked at objectively – scientifically.

---

[5] Bohm, David, 1980 p. 16.

We have numerous records of people living into their eighties and nineties throughout ancient history. When we look at the actual factor used to determine life span we find two things – the total average life span of the whole population is used, and that life span itself is not accounted for separately. This means that if there is a plague, natural disaster or high infant mortality the whole average changes. If New York or Los Angeles suddenly dropped into the ocean it would play havoc with the "average life span" of the population of the United States. Using high infant mortality with an eighty year old average time of death the "average life span" will be low. If the average age of death is 60 but there is little infant mortality the "average life span" will be higher.

This is a game of math used in all branches of modern science to justify whatever their point of view is. The fact is that people are living the same number of years, but infant mortality has been greatly decreased world wide. Unfortunately, the United States is not a leader in low infant mortality rates in spite of all the high tech medial array of equipment and procedures. In fact, it is this very array of high technology that may be killing more babies in childbirth than more traditional practices.[6]

People are not living longer now than at any other time. Possibly we may be living shorter life spans and in worse health. But who will fund such a study? Who does not want to believe in the current medical and nutritional belief system? If we probe into the nutritional concepts of modern medicine what will we find? Will the model hold up under our experience? Do we listen to the "experts" and adjust everything from cholesterol to calories? Does this approach really work?

---

[6] Robbins, John, 1996, see Ch. 3, p., 35 for a good discussion of this topic.

Fundamental questions need to be asked. Why are we told to do one thing and then fifteen or twenty years later are we told to do another thing? Often the exact opposite from the first. Why is there so much conflicting information on diet? Is everyone wrong or are they right - but in a limited way? Is there any method or model that fits everyone's individuality and uniqueness? Does modern science provide this model? Are you the same as the person in the million-dollar study? Do they have your level of stress? Your medical history? Your attitude on life?

It is apparent that the modern fragmented nutritional views do not give satisfying answers to these questions. Something is wrong with the whole approach. The whole view of nutrition and nourishing the body is wrong. What are we missing? This book is about an alternative vision of understanding nutrition and the body as part of an organic whole. It is not the latest fad diet or nutritional gimmick. I am not going to try to sell you the latest energy bar or cassette tape series. I am not opening an institute or clinic to reap the profits of this system. I have already been using this system in my professional practice since 1994 and have been achieving excellent results.

On the surface much of what is presented in this book may look like the work of Dr Dean Ornish and his program to treat heart problems. Or it may resemble any program that is based on using whole foods and common sense (remember "common sense"?). It includes not only dietary information, but also basic lifestyle information for major kinds of individuals. The Ayurvedic view is to treat the individual, not the disease or symptoms. The work of innovative doctors like Dean Ornish demonstrate that good nutrition consists of a multitude of factors apart from food itself. However, the constitutional approach of Ayurveda carries lifestyle and nutrition a step further in that it understands the differences of individuality in people. These differences, we can say, reflect themselves through metabolic function.

Additionally, Ayurveda's understanding of the psychological uniqueness of individuals is a dimension away from any existing system. How the mental and emotional states relate to consumption, digestion and assimilation of nutrients is not known or even addressed by other systems, yet Ayurveda has made a special study of this over thousands of years.

When the word "constitution" is used in this book it is in reference to the traditional Ayurvedic word "Prakriti" or nature and not other nutritional programs popular in the United States. The book, *Eat Right 4 your Type,* has done a tremendous service to modern society in that it has made a large group of the population aware that not everyone can eat, or needs, the same diet. However, the use of blood types is too general a field to base nutritional needs on, but time will help to either prove or disprove the theory. From the Ayurvedic point of view it is more accurate to base your nutritional needs on the function of your metabolism than on your blood type. In Ayurveda there are seven main categories of types that give a better possibility to focus a diet to an individual. It would be very interesting to see if there was any kind of correlation between the systems, perhaps some doctor will peruse this point in time.

One primary thing that the popularity of the 'blood type' program shows is how ready people are for an individualized nutritional program. The problem, from my point of view, is that the system has been in use for only 20 years or so. In contrast the Ayurvedic system has been in use for at least 3000 years and more likely closer to 6000 as even the Chinese based much of their medicine on Ayurveda, indicating that it is the older of the two.

People today want an individualized approach to nutrition. Ayurveda is the best system to provide a working methodology for individualized diets. Hence, this book is not about a mechanical, fragmental, biochemical approach to nutrition. There will not be an attempt to put the traditional Ayurvedic system into biochemical terms and then try to back it up with modern biochemical studies – simply because it is impossible. The approach is completely different and it would be a disservice to Ayurveda to try and make it fit into the current fragmented nutritional model.

Modern doctors will scream that this is not scientific or even relevant in today's world. However, the discriminating reader should really look at the track record of the current medical and nutritional belief system and see if it is actually working. The current medical and nutritional system is really a belief system and is not based on science, but rather on the marketing of science. This makes sense when we consider that two-thirds of modern medical practices don't have any scientific proof to support them.[7]

In order for us to adjust nutrition to the individual we must have a clear and logical methodology. The advantage of using the Ayurvedic methodology is tremendous. First of all, it is the oldest continually used medical system in human history. The foundation of the system is good nutrition as it is the basic source of energy for the body (along with pure water and air).

The second advantage is that it has been used successfully for some five thousand years. Oral traditions place it at a much greater age than this and Victorian historians have placed its age less, around 3000 years ago. Modern archeological finds in India are now tending to support the older dates and history is being re-written according to modern dating methods. The British Victorian era that wrote much of our history – and all of India's history – was decidedly racist. It was based not on science, but on the politics of a colonial power trying to dominate its colony.

[7] Mctaggart, Lynne, 1996, p. 12.

While there is currently a popular movement to liken the modern man to the prehistoric man in terms of his nutritional and biological needs, Ayurveda has been working successfully with human nutrition for thousands of years. We can really only speculate what ancient man was eating – not to mention the when and how of his eating habits. In contrast to this Ayurveda has been using the same model of nutrition for some 5000 years. This is not speculation but a practical approach.

The final, and perhaps most important point, is that the system works. Any system that has been used successfully for such a long period of time deserves to be considered. There are many other reasons as well, but this is best one and the easiest to prove to yourself. However, in order to eat according to Ayurveda you need to know your individual type, or nature, according to the system.

These individual differences are called Vata, Pitta, Kapha (VPK), the individuality of a person being the most fundamental concept in Ayurveda. The three main types of people can then be divided up into seven main categories or mixes. The percentage of "pure" types and "mixed" types is roughly the same in the industrialized Western world. The following chapter helps you to "discover" or understand your personal nature.

2
What Type of Person Are You?

This chapter helps you to determine your type, or constitution, according to the Ayurvedic system. When responding to the following test it is important to keep in mind the two possible categories. Answer according to your lifetime tendencies in the left-hand column and then how you are presently in the right-hand column. They may be very different as we all experience changes in our life.

The reason for this is that we all undergo changes that give the effects of the different types. An example of this could be that today you have a cold and so your body would exhibit the signs of a Kapha type of person. This is also true when we are under stress, or have prolonged periods of tension – as most people do today. When this happens we usually exhibit some signs of a Vata type of person. Therefore, you must look back over your whole life and try to remember your lifetime patterns, as well as your present patterns.

Ayurveda recognizes these two different states. The first state is fixed for the whole lifetime and is similar, but not exactly the same as your genetic make up. This reflects your "type" or birth constitution. In this sense, the word constitution is something like your individual homeostasis, or overall metabolic function. The second state that

Ayurveda recognizes is a changing state, or a temporary state as described above in the example of a cold, stress or disease. In fact the Sanskrit word that describes this state means "to cover up the birth constitution" or "an unnatural state". The second changing state is the beginning of disturbances in the body that leads to disease. All illness happens in the second state. The first, or lifetime constitution, is health. Ayurveda takes the point of view that the body strives to return to, or maintain this lifetime birth constitution in equilibrium.[8]

Ayurveda also notes that any type can increase beyond a healthy level and cause disease or problems. This also reflects the second state – the changing state. It does not have to be a different type (e.g., Vata, Pitta, or Kapha) to show a changing state. A classic example of this could be the Pitta type who has a powerful digestive system. But when too many hot spicy foods are eaten, or too many acidic foods are eaten, or too much stress is present in the workplace, this type will have Pitta problems like heart burn, acidity, and possibly ulcers. Thus, the Pitta lifetime constitution ends up being disturbed and becoming a Pitta present or disease state. This is why Ayurveda gives specific diets for each constitutional type – to prevent your birth constitution from increasing to a level that is problematic.

Sometimes you will find that the answers for the "lifetime" and "present" categories are the same and sometimes you will find them to be different. It is extremely rare to find a person who has the same answers in both columns – this can reflect good health or an increase in your lifetime constitution that is giving you problems. If the answers in both columns are very different it reflects either a mistake on your part or the beginnings of the disease process – the more the differences the more probable the disease is to be serious. However, it can be normal for half of your answers

[8] In Ayurveda these are called 'Prakriti' (lifetime or birth constitution) and 'Vikriti' (present or changing constitution).

to differ from the "lifetime" column to the "present" column.

One reason for this is that our culture and society demand a certain kind of behavior in order for us to live. For example, our society likes competitive, aggressive types in business. In order to succeed today you need to be better than other – either smarter, cheaper, faster or in some way better. These all reflect Pitta type of qualities. This means that I may be a more laid back Kapha type, but be forced to take on more Pitta qualities in order to survive. In the following test these social pressures may show up in the "present" category.

It should be noted that the United States, as a culture, likes a kind of Vata/Pitta combination. As all stress and tensions tend to increase Vata, many of us will show Vata type qualities in the "present" category. Things like insomnia and erratic, vivid dreams are typical of Vata disturbances such as constipation, nervous digestion, colic pain, most allergies, poor nutrient absorption, increased worry, nervous problems, hyperactivity, headaches, PMS, depression, and anorexia.

Look over the questionnaire below and choose either V, P, or K for each category. You may only choose one per category, do not choose two answers. For each answer you have two answer columns – your lifetime tendencies and your present tendencies. This means for each category you will have one response for "lifetime" and one response for "present". An example of this could be for the category of "Body Weight" I might put Pitta as the answer for the "lifetime" column and Kapha as the answer for the "present" column if I had suddenly begun to gain weight in the last 3 or 4 years.

When you finish the questionnaire total up the numbers of V, P and K. Whatever letter has the highest score will be your type or constitution. If two types are very close to being the same amount consider yourself to be a mixed or dual type. An example of this could be a score of 14 – Vata, 12 – Pitta, and 5 – Kapha. This would show a dual or mixed type of Vata/Pitta. Good luck!

Simple Questions to Help You Determine Your type

CATEGORY	LIFETIME (Prakriti)	PRESENT (Vikriti)
Body Frame		
V-tall or short, thin; poorly developed physique		
P-medium height; moderately developed physique		
K-stout, stocky, big; well developed physique		
Body Weight		
V-light, difficult to gain weight		
P-moderate weight		
K-heavy; gains weight easily		
Skin Texture		
V-dry, rough or cracked; prominent veins		
P-moist, pink, freckles, slightly oily		
K-pale, moist, soft, oily		
Skin Temperature		
V-cold		
P-warm		
K-cool		
Hair Quality		
V-coarse, dry; split ends		

P-fine, soft; can gray or bald early

K-abundant, oily, thick, lustrous

Face Shape

V-small, thin, long

P-medium sized, oval, angular

K-large, round

Teeth

V-small, sometimes crooked

P- medium-sized

K- large, very even

Gums

V-dark, receding gums

P-red; gums bleed easily

K-soft, pink

Tongue Width

V-narrower than teeth, long and thin

P-same width as teeth, oval or pointed tip

K-wider than teeth, thick, round front

Quality of Hands

V-fine, dry, cold; long fingers

P-symmetrical; pink, warm

K-large, cool; thick and short fingers

Finger Nails

V-thin, rough, fissured, cracked, darkish

P-strong, pinkish

K-thick, smooth, white

Digestive Strength

V-variable or weak; often has allergies

P-strong; able to digest most anything

K-medium or slow but steady

Digestive Disturbances from Problem Foods

V-intestinal gas, constipation, colic

P-acidity or burning, diarrhea

K-bloated feeling or heaviness, nausea

Food Cravings

V-dry, sweet or salty; crispy snack foods

P-spicy, salty, hot

K-sweet, creamy, cold

Eating Habits

V-binges, snacks; forgets to eat

P-likes regular, plentiful meals

K-eats constantly; overeats regularly

Food Sensitivities (more than one indicates food allergies or imbalance)

V-beans, cabbage family

P-onions, tomatoes, fried foods

K-dairy, salt

Urination

V-two to four times per day

P-four to six times per day

K-three to five times per day

Feces

V-dry, hard, difficult or painful, gas; tends towards constipation

P-abundant, loose, sometimes yellowish; tends towards diarrhea

K-moderate, solid; sometimes pale in color or can have mucus in stool

Sweat and Body Odor

V-little sweat with no smell

P-strong sweating, strong smell

K-moderate sweating, neutral smell

Blood Circulation

V-poor, variable, cold hands & feet

P-good, warm hands & feet

K-slow but steady, cool hands & feet		
Appetite (Agni)		
V-variable, erratic; easily satisfied P-strong; eats large amounts		
K-constant but low		
Activities		
V-quick, fast, erratic, hyperactive		
P-motivated, purposeful, goal seeking		
K-slow, steady, methodical		
Strength and Endurance		
V- poor endurance; starts & stops		
P- moderate level of endurance		
K-strong, good endurance, slow in starting		
Sensitivity to Environment		
V-dislike of cold, wind, sensitive to dryness, seeks warmth		
P-dislike of heat or direct sun, likes coolness		
K-dislike of cold, damp, likes wind and sun		
Resistance to Disease		
V-poor, variable, weak immune system		

P-medium, prone to infections

K-good, consistent, strong immune system

Disease Tendency

V-nervous system diseases, pain, mental disorders, insomnia, eating disorders, arthritis

P-febrile diseases, ulcers, infections, inflammatory diseases, heart attacks

K-respiratory system diseases, mucus accumulation, edema, obesity, benign tumors

Speech Habits

V-quick, talkative, inconsistent, erratic

P-moderate, argumentative, convincing

K-slow, concise, not talkative

Mental Nature

V-quick, adaptable, indecisive, impulsive

P-factual, penetrating, critical

K-slow, steady

Emotional Response

V-quick but soon over

P-hot, irritated or defensive; holds grudge

K-slow but lingers for a long time

Emotional Tendencies

V-anxious, fearful, nervous, worries

P-frustrated, irritable, angry, dominating

K-calm, attached, greedy, sentimental

Psychological Tendencies

V-creative, intuitive, inquisitive

P-helpful, independent, dynamic

K-caring, kind, family oriented, stable

Social Relations

V-relates easily; can be superficial

P-relates well; can be dominating

K-relates with difficulty

Mental Relations to Objects

V-not very important; erratic

P-to know about, purposeful

K-important to have or own; practical

Relationship to Money

V-not very important

P-useful to gain control or respect

K-very important

Relationship to Spending Money

V-spends easily

P-spends for a purpose

K-spends with difficulty

Friends

V-has many, but not deep

P-has close or several

K-has few, but very deep

Love Relationships

V-tends to have many partners, erratic

P-tends to marry for position or looks, passionate

K-single partner; very faithful

Neurotic Tendencies

V-hysteria, anxiety attacks, depression

P-extreme temper, rage, tantrums

K-sorrow, unresponsiveness, depressive, grief

Life Goals

V-change frequently; not so important

P-determined, very important

K-fixed for life early

Sleep

V-light, tends towards insomnia; restless

P-moderate, may wake up but will fall asleep again K-heavy; difficulty in waking up in the morning		
TOTALS	**V_ P_K_**	**V_ P_K_**
Your Lifetime Constitution -Prakriti **Your Present Constitution** -Vikriti		

Add your totals up for the different categories and list them under "Totals". Next write your "lifetime" and "present" constitutions down in the appropriate columns for future reference.

Generally, you should follow the diet plan for your lifetime constitution. This will normally keep your digestion and metabolism functioning in a way that prevents diseases, or rids you of those problems that you currently have. It is possible to fill out the test incorrectly because, often, we do not have an objective view of ourselves. If this happens you can come up with a wrong type for yourself. Usually this will reflect the "present" state or the state that is overpowering your birth constitution.

However, even if you confuse the two and use the present state – or the type that is not your birth type – it will still work therapeutically for your nutritional needs. But only for a temporary period of time. Hence, it may be a good idea to take the test again in six months to see if you still have the same answers. This is a good idea for everyone as we often have the least objectivity with ourselves.

The result of using a diet type other than your birth type will work to balance the type that is dominating at that time. Presumably you have come up with a type other than your birth type because it is dominating your metabolic functions at the present moment. In this way the diet will work as a therapeutic agent to correct the metabolism. One should stick to the chosen diet for a period of six months – not less. The reason for this is that it takes at least three months for a diet to begin to work and six months to really realize the full effects. The worst thing you can do is to jump around from one diet to the other. This is true for the different diets in this book as well as any other diet that your friends may want to push you into while you are trying this way of nutrition.

It is important to understand that the body cannot loose more than one pound per week; it is metabolically impossible for the body to lose more fat accumulation than this in seven days. The body can lose water at a higher rate, however. Therefore, if you want to help your body to run as efficient as possible and to lose weight permanently, and not just water weight, you must stick to the chosen diet for six months before changing. This is the best thing for your body and the correct way to approach nutrition. But as I understand that everyone wants things immediately I have included a 21-day plan in this book. This is to give you results and encouragement – it may not be sufficient to permanently correct digestive or metabolic problems – but 6 months usually is sufficient.

Most books on Ayurveda have tests similar to the one above. It can be confusing to take a number of different tests or it can be helpful. These kind of constitutional tests do not normally make a distinction between your birth and present constitutions – hence people tend to become confused between the two possibilities. This test is unique in that respect. I suggest that you use the results from this test to determine your dietary needs even if you get different answers from other tests.

If you are really in doubt, then it can be helpful to get a consultation from an Ayurvedic practitioner or doctor. The price of this consultation should be between $60 to $125 dollars for an hour. For this price you should also have dietary, lifestyle guidance, some therapeutic advice, and your two constitutions clarified. This information you can use for your whole life, it is not limited in its value as far as time and health are concerned.

3
The "ABC" of Ayurvedic Nutrition

Many of my clients have questioned the validity of using such an old method of nutrition and health care over the years. Some have wondered if the system is still working and still others say that it is only suited for the tropical climates of India. I explain that India is a very large country that has every kind of climate possible – from desert to tropics to high mountains. Moreover, the system still exists because of its validity, not because it lacks it. Still other clients go to India expecting to find the same information that I present here in this book.

Unfortunately, the Western dominance in India today is so extreme that it is hard to find an Ayurvedic doctor practicing Ayurveda from a "mind/body" or holistic perspective. The medical training in the Ayurvedic Government University system consists of six years and a half–four years of Ayurvedic theory and two years and a half of biochemical theory – and one or two years of internship. For the last generation the universities have been educating doctors according to the Newtonian Mechanical model of the material world – the Western view (see appendix). Ayurvedic doctors in India need all the trappings of the allopathic doctor (modern medical doctor) to get clients.

One friend of mine went to India recently and saw an Ayurvedic doctor for some advice. During the consultation my friend asked why the doctor had a stethoscope on his desk. He replied, "If I don't have that in my office then my clients don't respect me". However, due to the current interest of Ayurveda in the West there is an increase of interest in both students and patients in India. The next decade will see even a greater renaissance in both Ayurvedic knowledge and practice.

The best way to combat disease in any country in the world is to improve sanitation facilities and the quality of the food. This has been proven to eliminate disease faster and more effectively than any medicine ever developed. The ancient cities in the Indus valley of northern ancient India that are currently being excavated have attached bathrooms and indoor plumbing. These sites are well over 5000 years old.

It is interesting to note that the numbering system we use, the concept of "0", the decimal point, and the mathematics concept "?" – which was calculated to minus eight digits thousands of years ago – are all from ancient India. Why do we accept these ancient innovations unquestionably in our science and not the medical and nutritional insights? I have found from my own professional experience that the Ayurvedic nutritional model is as valid and effective as their mathematical insights are.

The ABC of Nutrition

Each of us is different. Each of us has a different metabolism and response to foods. In order to adjust our diet according to our individuality we must have a method. This method we can call the ABC of Ayurveda (Vata, Pitta, Kapha).[9]

The ancient people that developed this system observed nature closely for hundreds of years. The outcome of their

---

[9] This is the "Tri-Dosha" theory which forms the basis of Ayurveda as a system.

observations was as follows: the physical universe is composed of four primary states of matter – a solid state of matter; a liquid state of matter; matter in a state of transformation; and matter in movement. These four states of matter exist in a field or space.[10] The ancients also observed that some force or principle controls these different states of matter – what we are calling the principles of Vata, Pitta, Kapha. It is the three principles, Vata, Pitta, Kapha (VPK) which govern nature as we know it. These principles can be seen, or their actions observed, by anyone.

As everything occurring in nature is different – as you and I are both humans, yet different – so is the composition of the principles, VPK, different. Hence, if we understand which of the principles is dominant we can understand a lot about the nature of the person or object. This is the basis of nutrition in Ayurveda. First, it is necessary to understand what principle of nature is dominant in your metabolism. Then a dietary plan can be formulated – again using the same three principles. You have already established your dominant principle, or constitutional type, in the previous chapter.

When we apply this system to people we have a system to understand the different metabolic functions of individuals. Each letter, "V", "P" or "K", represents a primary type of person. These three combine to make four more types or seven types in total. They are: V, P, K, VP, VK, PK and VPK.

The purpose of these distinctions is not to classify people. It is rather a way to understand how your metabolism functions. In Ayurveda, the idea is not to use one type as a comparison to another type. Actually, it is against the precepts of Ayurveda to compare people in any way shape or form. No type is better or worse than any other. Nor, is any one mix or combination better than any other. Each

[10] This is called the Pancha Mahabhuta, or five great states of matter, in Ayurveda.

type or combined type has its pros and cons. Actually, everyone has all three principles – this is just a distinction of which one is dominating.

Occasionally, you will find people using these metabolic distinctions as a means to manipulate, criticize or "put-down" others. Please note that this has nothing to do with the Ayurvedic system. People who feel the need to dominate or criticize others do so from their own insecurity and neurosis – these people will twist any system or means for their own ends. (This can be a psychological trait of the Pitta type in a state of disturbance.) I mention this because it is quite common today for people to judge others and, unfortunately, some people are trying to use Ayurveda in this manner as well. Be clear that there is no value judgement in regard to the different constitutional types. (Although politicians do tend to be both judgmental and strong Pitta types!)

Ayurveda uses these seven classifications in order to understand the main differences in metabolic types. The question here is not of good or bad, but of biologic differences. By understanding how your metabolism functions you can begin to work with it and not against it. Working against it brings various digestive problems and can eventually lead to diseases of both a minor or severe nature. Working with it brings good digestion and health – not just freedom from disease – but real health.

It is also recognized that there is a huge variance in each type. The main seven types are not to be seen as a final stopping point, but rather as a starting point. We can, once we know our type according to Ayurveda, begin to work in the context of the guidelines for our type. I have experienced this over and over again in my practice. People will generally already have recognized that certain foods are problematic for them and have learned to avoid them. When they see food recommendations for their type they are amazed to see the foods that they have eliminated as being problematic for them. However, they often think that these recommendations are final. In reality the recommendations in this book and any other book on Ayurvedic nutrition are the basic guidelines which then need to be adjusted and refined to you as an individual.

This is common sense. If you do not like brussel sprouts, even if they are recommended for your type, do not eat them (but then, who does like brussle sprouts?). The methodology of using VPK is to help you find a starting point, which you can, if you wish, further refine. You can also just use the recommendations as they are if you don't want to be bothered with learning the system too much. The choice is yours.

In order for us to follow the methodology of Ayurvedic nutrition we need to have a minimal understanding of the seven different types. In general, the seventh type, VPK, is considered quite rare as it indicates an equal amount of the three types. In practice this is my experience also. I have only come across several types like this in the last few years of seeing thousand clients. Therefore, most people will fall under one of the six main or combined types.

Physiological Profiles

Type Vata [11]

This person has a variable metabolism; in other words, there is no daily consistency in digestion. One day the person will digest a pizza easily and the next not at all. On still yet another day the same pizza will cause minor indigestion. This shows an inconsistency in metabolism, and as digestive function is one of the main indications of the over all metabolism we can judge that Vata people will not consistently digest the same food or dish the same way.

[11] The Vata Dosha is the biological humor of wind; the principle that governs movement.

These people tend to digest quickly when they do digest and tend to get gas when they do not digest well. When this type is disturbed they will become constipated, or bloated, or just "gasy". These people will tend to have dry skin, dry hair and it is this same internal dryness that can cause constipation.

This type will generally have a smaller bone structure – their skeletal frame. The bones themselves will be thinner rather than thicker. They will tend to be tall and thin or short and thin. However, when this type is disturbed or agitated they can become fat. This is truer in adulthood after the age of thirty. These people are usually thin by the time they enter adolescence, if not for their whole life.

This type has difficulty to gain weight. No matter how much they eat they rarely seem to gain any weight. In general they are not big eaters, but prefer to eat smaller amounts more frequently. They are the least interested in food of the seven types and will very often settle for poor quality foods like fast foods, junk foods or snacking, just because of a lack of interest.

Even though their metabolism is variable they will tend to be cool or cold most of the time. Their blood circulation is not strong and they generally have cold hands and feet because of this. They do not like cold weather much and need to cover themselves from the elements more than the other types.

The Vata type has the weakest immune system of all the types and will often come down with allergies, a cold or the flu. Yet, they usually have abundant energy, though not necessarily the stamina to keep up with it. They very often will be quite talkative, or even "speedy" in a scattered sort of way. They are known to be good at starting things and not at finishing them. They can easily be disturbed from computers or other electronic devises, as they are the most physically sensitive of the three types.

Type Pitta [12]

The Pitta type of person has a very strong metabolism. They digest quickly and have the strongest power of digestion; they can eat anything. Their metabolism runs on the hot side and they tend to be "hot blooded" in all senses of the meaning. They have warm skin, hands and feet. Their blood circulation is the strongest of the three types and they can be prone to heart or blood problems later in life.

Their metabolism is not only strong, but also consistent. Up until about forty years of age they will hardly notice the process of digestion unless it is heart burn or acidity. After forty they suddenly begin to notice that a few pounds arrived uninvited. Then they tend to become more aware of problematic foods like tomatoes or acidic citrus fruits.

When they do have problems digestively it reveals itself in the form of loose stools or diarrhea. Fried foods especially can trigger this kind of response. This is extremely true for fast foods or restaurant foods that are prepared in old or poor quality oils. The excess consumption of fried foods can also make them obese. Generally, they are neither thin nor overweight unless they eat too many fried and fatty foods. They will be the most regular in bowel movements of the three types.

The Pitta types tend to suffer from skin problems due to the acidic nature of their blood and body in general. They can also have liver problems even if they do not drink alcohol. Their eyesight may be poor or they may have trouble with their eyes at some point in their life. Generally, they will tend to have red eyes or be sensitive to the sunlight more than the other types. They often wear glasses.

They tend to be medium in build and bone structure. They are the most "average" in size of the three types.

[12] The Pitta Dosha is the biological humor of fire; the principle that governs transformation.

However, do not be deceived by this distinction. Any of the types can have an "average" build. They fall in-between the other types in both size and weight. They have an average level of endurance and stamina. Nonetheless, they have the strongest minds and so they can achieve actions beyond their normal strength or stamina through will power alone.

They have a good immune system and do not generally fall sick – unless they work too much! They tend to suffer more from frustration or over work than from physical illness. They are prone to exhaustion and burn out which leaves them open to infectious diseases. They suffer from inflammatory problems when they do fall ill.

Type Kapha [13]

The Kapha type of person has the slowest metabolism but the greatest consistency. Their digestive capacity is very regular and consistent. They can easily become congested or overloaded as their metabolism functions slowly. Of the three types these people take the longest to process what they eat. They will respond regularly to the same kinds of foods or meals.

When they have digestive disturbances they will get bloated or have a subjectively heavy feeling in the stomach or abdomen area. As their digestion reflects their slow metabolic function they can easily overeat or eat too much of heavy, slow to digest foods. Disturbances tend to be reflected in accumulation of mucus or fat as when the intake of food is greater than the metabolic ability of processing and assimilation.

These people have the least resistance to sweets. Yet, they may be the most attracted to eating them of all the types. This attraction can put an extra strain on the adrenal – pancreas function that regulates blood sugar and the processing of fats and cholesterol among other things. Their

[13] The Kapha Dosha is the biological humor of water; the principle that provides cohesion.

kidney function can also become weak from any excess fat that is accumulated. Of the three types they will hold more weight in fluids because of the inherent weakness in the water metabolism, i.e., kidney function. This can give a "puffy" look to the skin and edema in general.

The Kapha type has the strongest body and the greatest level of endurance of the three types. While somewhat prone to becoming over weight, it is by no means mandatory. They can achieve great feats of strength in certain sports and types of professions. They are the most physically orientated of the types and so have the greatest attraction for food. They have the largest bone structure of the types yet do not tend to be tall. Rather they tend to be strong, of medium height, and stocky.

Along with their physical strength they have the strongest immune function. Their resistance to disease is much greater than the other types and Kapha people will generally not become sick. When they do become ill it usually reflects poor nutritional or lifestyle habits. This includes drinking alcohol and smoking both of which cause problems for all the types. The Kapha type is prone to all kinds of accumulation in the body. This can manifest as tumors and other internal growths – of a benign nature. They can also be prone to lung problems or problems of the respiratory system in general.

All in all, the Kapha type generally enjoys the greatest level of physical health. Provided they do not indulge in extremes these people can live the longest and healthiest of the types. However, if they indulge in poor habits and nutrition they can fall ill and die from the many diseases of an affluent society.

Type Vata/Pitta [14]

The Vata/Pitta type is a mix of both the Vata and the Pitta types. These kinds of mixes are called dual types as

[14] Vata/Pitta or Pitta/Vata types.

they reflect a combination of both principles. Usually, a dual type is pretty equal in displaying the traits of their type. However, one of the types can dominate in either the body or the psychology giving a person who looks like one type but behaves like another type. This is not the typical scenario however.

Physically these types are in-between the Vata and Pitta types or following either the Vata or the Pitta type. Generally, they are thinner rather than thicker and can exhibit either the dry, nervous qualities of the Vata type or the hot, dynamic qualities of the Pitta type. As nature is infinite in her combinations so are the possible mixes of these two principles. Physical structure is less a means of determining a dual type than observing your metabolism. This kind of mix will tend to have a strong digestion but be occasionally troubled by gas, malabsoption of nutrients, or diarrhea. They will normally be free from disease and are stronger than the pure Vata type. Yet, they are not as resistant to illness as the Pitta type and can – when unbalanced – fall prey to the problems of both the Vata and the Pitta types.

On the same area, this mix can also exhibit the best attributes of the two types. This combination can make good athletes like track and field, skiing, racing or any sort, or swimming. They like to move and compete in events or activities and are perhaps more social than the pure Pitta type. They are also easier going than the pure Pitta type, yet more practical and persistent than the pure Vata type.

As the Vata type is the most innovative and creative and the Pitta type is the most practical and dynamic, this type is revered in our present society. The more developed side of this mix is a person who can achieve many things that are creative and innovative. They communicate well and are full of energy. They have the ability to actualize their ideas and dreams in concrete forms and can make good leaders in business. This is also an excellent mix for teaching in general and the pursuit of knowledge. The Pitta qualities add a good determination to the Vata qualities for the pursuit of studies and the ability to focus on one subject at a time in order to fully explore it.

In less developed types this mix can lead to intellectual indecisiveness, insecurity and frustration. They can become over mental but with a frustration or sense of irritability that can be difficult to live with. This mix can also lead to irrational kinds of behavior with a violent or aggressive flavor.

Type Vata/Kapha[15]

The Vata/Kapha type is an interesting mix that can offer great qualities or conflicts. The physical nature of this mix will tend to reflect the Kapha type more than the Vata type of body; i.e., stronger and well formed rather than thin. In a smaller percentage of people the Vata type can dominate physically, but if this is the case, the mental disposition will exhibit more Kapha type qualities.

Physically this type can suffer from some of the traits of the Vata type like constipation and colic pain. Generally speaking, this type has a strong constitution and does not become ill very easily. They do, however, tend to be troubled by many small, nagging problems in their health. These problems are usually related to the Vata principle and reflect either migrating pains, nervous problems or irregularities in the metabolism. The Vata side of the constitution can aggravate the Kapha side quite effortlessly and cause bloating, distention and edema. The lungs can also suffer from allergies or congestion.

The easiest qualities of this combination are the intuitive, quick mental attributes of the Vata type together with the stability and persistence of the Kapha type. The farsighted Kapha type counteracts the usual short sightedness of the Vata type – this combination gives many qualities for artistic

[15] Vata/Kapha or Kapha/Vata types.

endeavors. This type can be very socially oriented and can work well with people in a caring, motherly capacity. They make good service oriented people and are good at communicating and relating with others.

When afflicted they can suffer from the worst of both principles. This can be hard to deal with, as qualitatively the two are opposites. This means that the Vata side likes to move and change while the Kapha side hates change and movement. The Vata type likes all kinds of irregularity – staying up late, eating at strange hours – and the Kapha type likes regularity – eating and sleeping at the same time every day. The physical problems that can result from this are reflected in a confused metabolism. The slowness of the Kapha side is quite disturbed by the erratic behavior of the Vata side. The spontaneity of the Vata side is aggravated by the rigidity of the Kapha side.

Understanding the two sides is critical for this combination or mental and physical unhappiness results. Working with the dual aspect of your constitution brings harmony and peaceful metabolic function. Ignoring one or the other of your two sides will bring digestive, nervous disorders and mental problems – usually poor self-esteem and self-negating attitudes. This can be one of the most interesting and happy of the types when both sides of the nature are well understood.

Type Pitta/Kapha[16]

This type is very good for competitive sports and physically demanding activities. The strong will of the Pitta type combines with the strong body of the Kapha type and gives a powerful combination. Most of our sports heroes in football and basketball are of this type. The mental discipline needed to routinely exercise and practice is a quality of the Kapha type and the competitive, fighting quality reflects the Pitta type.

---

[16] Pitta/Kapha or Kapha/Pitta types.

These types physically are quite strong – the strongest in many ways – as they not as prone to become congested by the accumulation of the Kapha principle. Their metabolism runs hotter and stronger than the Kapha type, yet not too hot or acidic as the pure Pitta type. This is a good combination for physical activities. The problem can be if the people become sedimentary and stagnant in the life. This will tend to aggravate both sides of the constitution. The Pitta side will become congested by the Kapha qualities as they always increase in dormancy. The more inactive this type is the more problems they will have.

Mentally this type needs challenge or they become unhappy and discontented. However, they are not risk takers generally, but rather they plan. The Kapha type is conscious and careful, combined with the Pitta type the person can act when needed – though rarely without planning. These people prefer to work or be active in defined areas, such as their home town or neighborhood. They may travel some or go to the same place for vacation regularly. They are more habitual than the other mixed types. This type can also make a CEO executive type of person. While the Kapha type is good with people and management the Pitta type is aggressive and seeks power. To run a business the two qualities are often needed or the person may not be motivated enough, strong enough, or not be able to work well with subordinates sufficiently. Their willingness to fight over long periods of time for a goal gives them a powerful presence even if their physical body is not developed.

These two principles tend to work well together. The physical problems that can arrive are heart problems – especially congestion of the arteries and blood vessels. They are also prone to problems of the pancreas and the gall bladder – both tend to become congested or blocked from poor nutrition and eating habits. These people do have large strong appetites so it is important that they eat foods that they are capable of completely digesting. They are prone to eat overly rich and fried foods that – while young – they may be able to digest easily. Although, once in the mid- thirties they can balloon out with sudden weight gain.

Type Vata/Pitta/Kapha[17]

This person has a balanced physical and mental disposition. Traditionally these people are the least likely to become ill or disturbed. If they do become ill it can be from any of the three principles. In our modern culture the Vata principle is the most likely to become imbalanced and disturb the other aspects of the constitution. This is also a traditional understanding of Ayurveda. The Vata principle is the most irregular and unstable by its nature of movement. As our society loves movement and is less and less attracted to tradition and regularity this increases the tendency even more.

This type of person will tend to have a Pitta/Kapha type of body, stronger rather than thinner. Although thinness is attractive in our culture of top models and our worship of adolescent youth, it is not always conducive to good health. The body needs some fat and good muscle tone. Hence, the equal type, "VPK", reflects a stronger frame and tissue make-up than most of the other types. This person is said to be free of disease and unhappiness. They are said to live long and enjoy life. They are also said to be the rarest. Once again it is good to remember that one type is not better than another. Any of the types can be thrown into a state of unbalance by bad habits and poor nutrition, even the equal type. Generally, this type will have the greatest capacity to withstand disease and bad habits provided they are temporary and not part of lifetime habits.

This is due to the equilibrium that is present in the combination of the three together. It is the combination of the three that gives strength and freedom from disease, not because one is better than another is or stronger.

[17] The equal or balanced type.

Psychological Profiles

Psychological Profile of the Vata type

Type Vata can be very creative, imaginative and innovative. The Vata type is very good in all forms of abstract thinking or creativity. But they can have problems with the practical side of life. The "absent minded professor" is a typical Vata type with a scientific bend. They make good artists in all fields of creativity. They are very good in communication and generally like to talk or work in fields of communications.

They are the most spontaneous and flexible of all the types. This is one of their qualities. They like travel and change. In fact, they thrive on change and will change things just for the sake of change – even when it may be quite impractical to do so. They can be very intuitive.

These types are often brilliant intellectually with very quick minds. Yet, their memory is generally not that strong. They are more concerned with the short term and not very interested in the long term. They are the non-conformists of the three types. They may exist on the edges of society, even though they can be very social and likeable. They make poor leaders and even poorer followers. They may be a socialite and enjoy being in society though in a more superficial way with few real friends.

When this type becomes disturbed or unbalanced they suffer from worry, anxiety, nervous tension, nervous breakdowns, fear, and depression. They are the most sensitive of all the types and so suffer more from stress or nervous system problems. These type are the most prone to become perverse or distorted. They can also become addicts easier than the other types. Addiction can affect all types but is most common in the Vata type as they are the most sensitive and can easily fall under emotional or physical dominance – by a person or substance.

Psychological Profile of the Pitta type

The Pitta type is the most purposeful and goal oriented of the types. They rarely do anything without a purpose. Even relaxation or sports will have a goal attached to it in some manner. While understanding and focussing on goals is important in life these types tend to become obsessed with the process.

Generally, their motivation is not towards money, but rather power and control. A more developed Pitta type is orientated towards understanding things and knowledge. They are the most motivated of the types. If they are unable to follow a goal or purpose in life they become frustrated or unhappy. They need to have hobbies and interests outside of their profession or they risk to become consumed by their work.

As the Pitta principle in nature controls the transformation of matter these types are good at initiating events. They make good entrepreneurs and generally like positions of responsibility. In any situation these types will gravitate towards the responsible or authoritative positions. They are seldom satisfied to follow or serve unless they respect the person or system in which they work.

When disturbed they can become aggressive and controlling. They usually become frustrated over events that can turn into anger, irritability or jealousy. They have 'hot' emotions and have little difficulty in expressing how they feel. Yet, it is often not done in a manner that is constructive. Rather they tend to explode and then have to put things back together afterwards. The Pitta type normally controls the relationship in a couple – sometimes in a passive-aggressive manner.

They sometimes surround themselves with less intelligent or more subservient people in order to control others and expand their ego. In the more developed Pitta types this same quality becomes helpful and humanitarian. A developed Pitta person makes a good teacher, leader and helper. They often are found in humanitarian service orientated roles such as social workers, relief workers and the medical profession. Still other Pitta types will become engrossed in the pursuit of knowledge and understanding. In this sense they can become good psychiatrists or psychotherapists.

Psychological Profile of the Kapha type

Psychologically these people are concerned with comfort and security. This interest tends to reflect itself in every sphere of life. In a positive sense it makes a Kapha type caring and wanting to feed and provide for those around them. In a negative sense it turns a person into a controlling, greedy type who is unwilling to share a crust of bread with someone else unless they pay for it.

These two extremes reflect the basic need or desire for security. Emotionally, love is also a form of security. Hence, these people can become obsessed with the need to be loved. This can take on a very sentimental, romantic flare or a neurotic, needy quality. Remember that everyone has all three types to some extent and each of us has moments when romance is dominating our psychology. The Kapha type is the most concerned by love relationships and by love in general. It can happen through social or family conditioning that this takes on a neurotic flavor, but simply reflects the lower or negative side of this type.

One common tendency with the Kapha type is to replace love with food. When a loving relationship is absent then food becomes disproportionally important to a Kapha type. Food is also a symbolic form of love and it is a very concrete form of security. It can happen that people who feel inferior or unloved will put on large amounts of weight to give themselves more presence around others. These types can also just overeat out of a sense of need, which reflects greed for security in the form of food. As their metabolism is the least able to handle excessive amounts of food they often become fat through this psychological tendency.

They are strong and consistent in their efforts, goals and relationships and make a good mate or employee. They tend to like and be close to the people in their family and close friends. They are not very open to change in any way and take time to warm to others outside of their immediate group or friends and family. Yet, they often have the deepest relationships of the three types.

Mentally they are a little slower then the other types – not less intelligent – but slower. They like to reflect over things and think about them before coming to a conclusion about anything. They do not make rash decisions, nor can you push them. Generally, the more you try to push a Kapha person the less he/she will move. They are best communicated with through love and understanding. It can be necessary to be firm and even forceful with Kapha types in order to get them to change bad habits or to help them change. Even this must be done with love or care as they can be very resistant and stubborn.

Summary

One other point that classical Ayurveda points out is that no matter what your constitutional type is men will tend to have more Pitta traits and women will tend to have more Kapha traits. This is a generality that shows the more feminine, caring and receptive side of nature or the Kapha type. Men tend to be more aggressive and goal orientated, which reflects the dynamic aspect or nature of the Pitta type.

During the course of the day it is normal for everyone to move through the different types emotionally. Each type reflects certain aspects of human nature; hence, we will tend to have them all at some point in the day or week. What we are trying to establish is which of them is dominant in your nature. An example could be that during the day I get my children ready for school – feed them, cloth them and help them to on the bus. All of which are Kapha types of emotions and actions. Then I go to work to sell widgets and move into my Pitta emotions and actions. Perhaps I have an inspiration on how to sell more widgets, which reflects the creative side of the Vata psychology. Then I again come home to my spouse and feel romantic, or passionate, Kapha and Pitta types of emotions. And just before sleeping I have an inspiration on how to redecorate the living room, a Vata type of inspiration.

Also remember that any one of the types can be positive or negative depending on you. It is up to you if you want to reflect the higher or lower qualities of any constitutional type. This is not fixed genetically. If you want to be a criminal or a humanitarian it is up to you. By the same token, if you want to eat well or eat junk food it is also up to you. Whatever your constitution is you still have the ability to shape and control your life – only now you will be able to work with your nature – whatever it is – and not fight against it.

4
The Principles of Constitutional Nutrition

There are two different points of view on nutrition – biochemical and constitutional. We are all familiar with the biochemical model, which tells us that we need so many vitamins, minerals, proteins and carbohydrates in our food. This view is how we all have been brought up to understand nutrition and food. Few of us are aware that another model of perceiving nutrition even exists and that it has been successfully used for thousands of years. The appendix is worth looking at in this regard as it explains – at some length – the differences between the two systems.

This chapter will explain the constitutional point of view as simply as possible. This is not an easy task as the constitutional view is not less complicated than the biochemical view when it is embraced and entered into in a profound manner. It can seem simplistic on the surface or when we first approach it as newcomers. This is not the case however, and only indicates our lack of understanding. Hence, this chapter will endeavor to explain the basics that will suffice for the majority of people to structure a workable and healthy nutritional plan.

First of all, be clear from the beginning that the basis of Ayurvedic nutrition is what is commonly understood to be good nutrition by almost everyone today regardless of the system that they use. The foundation of most dietary plans is a variety of fresh, whole foods which are as close as possible to their natural state. Few people – experts or lay people – are in disagreement about the overall benefits of such a diet. What then is the purpose and need of a constitutional program?

The primary purpose of a constitutional dietary program is that it is adapted to your individual metabolism, not to a subjective average. This is how Jenny could lose eleven pounds permanently in nine weeks without drastic diets or drugs. As stated in the appendix the biochemical world has known for over fifty years that every person has different nutritional needs. Unfortunately, they have no method to cope with the facts. Hence, they are forced to average out nutritional requirements. If you fall below or above the average you will have trouble – and the majority of people will be either above or below.

The Ayurvedic system does not use the micro-nutrient model at all. In this system you can forget about how much vitamin A, B, C, D or E your body needs. This system is not in opposition to the micro-nutrient model; it just sees it as a very narrow, limited and a potentially dangerous approach. The reason they feel this way is because the body functions as a unit and different systems overlap in their functions and relationships. Therefore, trying to understand the needs of one aspect of the body, or system of the body, ignores the other relationships it has with a wide array of other functions and systems. This point of view and the relation to vitamins and supplements are explained in chapter 13 later in the book.

This approach makes a lot of sense in that scientists are still discovering the many different ingredients in food. Most people assume that we know what is in our food as far as chemical components are concerned. This is just not true – we do not know what all the components are in whole foods.

This is slowly becoming public knowledge; an issue of Newsweek ran a cover story related to this subject.[18] Even though this article is twelve years old it still is the same today. It quotes researches saying that they are still discovering many different compounds in all of our common foods. Therefore, if you begin to isolate the known chemicals and use them in larger amounts than occurs in foods you run an unknown risk of eliminating needed nutrients that are, as yet, unknown.

For this reason the Ayurvedic view does not use an isolated or micro-nutrient model for nutrition. It prefers to use whole foods that complement your metabolic and digestive capabilities. A constitutional model determines these. Once you know what your constitutional type is according to Ayurveda then you can continue to adjust the diet within the bounds of your type. The result is a very individualized diet that is safe for long term use.

Those of you who believe in vitamins and supplements must be patient until later in the book when these issues are addressed in depth. However, Ayurveda is not against the use of supplements. The idea they have of supplements can be quite different though, as are the substances that they use for nutritional supplementation. The kind of supplements that gave Jenny such a dramatic result are quite different than what is being sold and marketed as nutritional support in health food stores.

The biochemical approach to nutrition can be described as such: the totality can be understood from the individual parts. The Ayurvedic approach can be described like this: everything must be considered as a whole, the individual parts are extensions of the whole and intimately related to it. Because of this view constitutional nutrition tries to give a broad array of foods in a variety of preparations to people who can digest and assimilate them accordingly.

---

[18] *Newsweek*, November 30, 1998.

We can view constitutional nutrition as composed of these steps:

1. Understand your constitutional or metabolic nature
2. Recognize your digestive capacity
3. Recognize your capacity to assimilate nutrients
4. Recognize the signs if you are not completely digesting and assimilating what you eat

Before even approaching food choices or qualities of food the above steps must be understood and integrated into your daily lives. These four steps form the basis of good nutrition, as they are concerned with what your body is most likely to digest and use. Biochemical nutrition as a whole is not concerned with these four steps and your ability to actually use the nutrients you consume. Their view is that a molecule is a molecule and it will be treated the same by everyone.

People wrongly assume that whatever they put into their mouths will be used by the body in some beneficial way. This is far from the truth. Even the biochemical world is coming to recognize the problems that certain foods pose for the digestive process – the ultimate result of which is the actual use (or assimilation) of the micro-nutrients that constitute part of food. Modern science is also beginning to recognize the problems that agrochemicals and medications pose for the digestive and assimilation processes. These chemicals disturb the digestive enzymes that transform food into a state that can be assimilated and used by the body.

An interesting example of this happened to a client of mine. She is a professional singer and is very concerned with her voice and the general health of her body – if she cannot perform then she will not be paid. Zelda sings and teaches classical singing and opera, as one may expect she is a mixed type Pitta/Kapha. She has a large, strong body with a dynamic personality, but is not obese. She came to me because she wanted to have more energy and power in her voice and felt that her diet was not sufficient to provide those requirements.

Together we looked at her diet and made changes that suited both her constitution and work situation. I also advised her to take several herbs to promote better enzyme function in her body. She called me several months later with some further questions about diet and said, "Oh yes, I had an unexpected side effect – I lost 15 lbs. in the last three months!" Needless to say she was very happy because this weight loss happened effortlessly and without lowering her level of energy or performance professionally.

What are enzymes? They are special proteins in the body that bind themselves to other particles for the purpose of transforming them into something else. Enzymes speed up biological processes in the body. Most of them have very specific actions and roles in the body. They help to transform nutrients in the body without being altered or used up in the process. They are concerned in all digestive and cellular processes. However, they are quite sensitive and can be disabled by excess, or inhibited by, the pH quality in the body. Hence, if your digestion is too acidic or too alkaline the enzyme function will be retarded or stopped. This creates many problems and can even result in death in very extreme cases.

Enzymes are becoming a field of major study in the biochemical world. Many medicines are being made that either inhibit or accelerate different enzyme productions in the digestive process, usually the liver. The role of enzymes was almost ignored for many years in modern science and nutrition, but their possible use as medicines has opened up the coffers of the research industry. The concept and importance of enzyme function is at the root of Ayurvedic nutrition.[19] The digestive enzymes hold the key not only to proper nutrient assimilation, but your health in general.

[19] This relates to the concept of Agni in Ayurveda. There are thirteen

The importance of the primary enzyme function in the small intestine cannot be overstated. From the Ayurvedic point of view there are certain enzymes in all of the digestive organs and tissues of the body. However, the primary site of enzyme function is in the duodenum and the liver. If one or the other is affected then it causes a ripple effect that suppresses the ability to digest most kinds of foods. Ayurveda states that if this enzyme function is strong then the person will have good health because they will be able to assimilate what foods they do consume – even if it is of less than desirable quality.

It is this very principle that I used to help Zelda gain more energy and lose weight. Actually, the weight loss was an added bonus as our focus was to increase her level of energy and creative performance both in singing concerts and in teaching. This case illustrates how important it is to consider the enzyme levels of the body.

Ayurvedic nutrition begins with assessing the state of the enzyme function in the body. It is understood that each type of person constitutionally has a different strength of enzyme function. Knowing your constitution helps to understand your ability to digest and assimilate foods. The concept is that you inherited your basic capacity from your parents in the form of your genetic metabolic make-up. Your constitution is, among other things, a reflection of this enzyme capacity to transform not only nutrients, but also anything that comes into the body.

Interestingly enough, modern science has come to understand that we are born with a few basic enzymes. Yet they have found that most of our digestive enzymes come in the first six to twelve months of a baby's life in the form of

---

different kinds of Agni; the most important for basic digestion are the five elemental Agnis in the liver and the primary Agni in the duodenum. Yet there is also a whole group of cellular Agnis that work in the different kinds of tissues in the body – there are seven groups of these Agnis.

mother's milk and early food consumption. In this way it has been shown that population enzymes change according to culture and food as they are passed on by genetics and the mother's milk. Still other enzymes are acquired over time by the child as he or she grows and consumes different kinds of foods. It has been shown that highly processed and sterile foods create no enzymes or in small amounts. In contrast, whole foods have been shown to continue to help a child develop digestive enzymes into adulthood. It should also be pointed out that the majority of allergies are from a lack of enzymes. Often the source of the low level of enzymes comes from too short a period of breast-feeding as a baby. Or even a problematic pregnancy can reduce the enzymes passing into the developing child.

A large segment of the United States suffers from poor assimilation of nutrients. This is the outcome of poor digestion. If assimilation is disturbed then all of the previous stages of digestion must be functioning poorly or incorrectly as well. When the body is not able to use and assimilate what it consumes then the body has to try and get rid of it somehow. Most of the undigested or unused material is eliminated from the body by the intestines. Unfortunately, if this becomes a habitual process then the undigested foods begin to accumulate over time in the intestinal tract and putrefy. Rotting material in the intestinal tract puts an extra burden on the immune system and digestive organs. This is one of the major causes of degenerating diseases in the developed world.[20] In Ayurveda the accumulation of undigested foods is directly related to the state of the enzyme function – if one is high the other will be low.

---

[20] The concept of undigested food becoming toxic in the body is a key factor in disease prevention in Ayurveda. The undigested food is called *Ama* in Sanskrit.

Your Genetic Code and How it Affects the Food You Digest

There are four primary steps to stop or correct poor digestion and assimilation. First, understand your own metabolism. Does it work fast, slow or mixed? (types Pitta, Kapha or Vata) Are you prone to intestinal gas? Do certain foods disturb you, and if so, what are they? Do you have cold hands and feet often? Do you feel bloated after an ordinary meal? All these questions help you to understand how your metabolism works.

Next, begin to understand what is your individual capacity for food. This means the kinds of foods and the amount of food you consume. If three people eat a Chinese dinner it is likely that all three will be hungry at different times several hours later. It is also likely that each person will eat a slightly different amount of food, or if they eat the same amount each one will feel a different level of being full. All of these reflect your individual capacity for food.

Then try to understand if your body is using everything that you put into it. Normally people only assimilate 70 to 80 percent of what is possible. In many cases people assimilate less than 50 percent. When the level of assimilation drops then so do energy levels. This is one key factor behind the rise of the chronic fatigue syndrome in this country and was a factor in Zelda's case. When this is coupled with rotting food in the intestinal tract then it creates a low immunity and the person becomes likely to fall ill with chronic, difficult to diagnosis problems. If untreated then degenerative diseases take hold and eventually kill the person. Most autoimmune diseases are also due to this situation.

Recently a woman came to me with rheumatoid arthritis, an autoimmune disorder. According to Ayurveda this disease is reversible in early stages by correcting the above described problems of accumulated food in the intestines and by increasing enzyme functions. I explained to her the scenario of how the toxins begin to gather in the body and then can cause the immune system to over react and begin to inflict itself on the healthy tissues of the body – causing disease and pain.

Together we changed her diet to eliminate the root cause of the disease and then began to use herbs to increase her enzyme capacity. As she was a young woman in her forties she was highly motivated to correct the problem as soon as possible. After a six months treatment of nutrition and herbs her symptoms disappeared. I advised her to continue the treatment for another six months to cure the problem. It has now been several years and her problems have not returned because she still follows the diet according to her constitution.

The last factor is to learn how to recognize the signs yourself so that you can prevent the digestive system from becoming disturbed in the first place. A once of prevention can save your life as modern medicine has no cure for these kinds of problems. They are also difficult to diagnosis for the biochemical model because they do not recognize different capacities of assimilation and the accumulation of undigested food in the body. Both of which lead to countless problems. Therefore, learn to see what is going on in your own body and correct the problem. If nothing is wrong, great! At least you know that you are assimilating well.

In constitutional nutrition we do not compare ourselves to other people as we know that each of us is made slightly differently. On one hand this is called our "genetic makeup", yet Ayurveda also recognizes a constitutional difference that is deeper than genetics. This explains why brothers or sisters with the same parents are often very different in personality and motivations even when they both have the same genetics and behavioral conditioning.

Comparison with others brings several problems. Your body is unique and if you try to make it fit someone else's ideas or concepts then it will put an unnatural strain on your metabolism. We are not taught as children to understand our bodies. Very often we are taught to reject or ignore our closest friend, our body. Psychological implications aside – and there are many – it is physically hard to fit into a "normal" mode, which in fact, does not exist in the first place. Begin with understanding that your body is unique and observe it to understand its nature and capacity. You will feel better for it!

It is freeing psychologically not to compare your body to other people and to begin to accept yourself as you are now. The non-comparison facilities change in a way that is in harmony with your natural metabolic function – not against it. It is also liberating in that you no longer have to follow an ideal that may be causing conflicts for you mentally and physically. Accepting yourselves as you are today is a basic part of understanding your constitutional nature or type. Rather than being categorized it is freeing you to work with your body and not in conflict to what may be natural for you. If you have a real problem, like being over weight, then this also helps. Recognizing that there is a problem is the first thing to do. If you cannot see a problem you cannot find a solution. Any way that the pie is cut, it is necessary to start from where you are and with self-expectance.

A client came to me for several different health problems. However, after some conversation I realized that her primary problem was that she had a poor self image and was putting herself into difficult emotional and professional situations because of it. I spoke to her about this at some length and tried to get her to see that her present self attitudes were the most destructive factor in her health. In fact, she was a very attractive woman in her thirties who was in a very destructive – even violent – relationship. The husband also happened to be her boss. Even though she had taken steps to get out of the personal relationship the poor self image prevented her from completely leaving the destructive force in her life.

My ability to help her was limited and, in fact, failed. I have seen her several times in other contexts and know that she is still working under a dominating and controlling person who exploits her knowledge and personality. The roots of her physical problems lie in her constant comparison to others and a lack of faith in her own capabilities to live without the negative influence of her ex-husband. As she is intelligent there is still hope that she will soon see that the destructive emotional pattern is behind her problems and so gain strength to move away from self destructive patterns.

Hence, the main principle in constitutional nutrition is even deeper than that of genetic differences. Although the concept of different constitutional types cannot be compared exactly to the understanding of modern science's theory of different hereditary and genetic dispositions, they are, nevertheless, close in practice. Yet, the Ayurvedic use of constitution is broader than genetics in that it covers behavioral conditioning that brings differences between genetically similar people; i.e., brothers and sisters.

Therefore, we see that for over five thousand years mankind has been aware of hereditary and personality differences. These were, and are, explained by the word "constitution". And there is almost no more important place than nutrition to experience daily these distinctions of the metabolism, genetics and personality. By using this system we can choose foods that do not work against our genetic enzymes, psychological state and digestive system.

The Six Primary Combinations

Of course there has to be a method to classify foods and relate them to different people. This method, like others in Ayurveda, can appear simplistic on the surface. The method relies on three components:

- the immediate chemical action in the mouth and stomach from a food
- the ability of a food to stimulate or suppress the metabolism
- the transformed state and long term effect of ingesting a food[21]

These three factors relate to food through a complex system of understanding the different states of matter that dominate in that food. The same basis is used to understand food or the three types, Vata, Pitta, and Kapha, as was explained in chapter 3.

Because we are using the same basis for determining the constitutional types and the method to understand substances (foods, minerals and herbs) an integral logic is maintained. In other words we are not using one standard in a laboratory and then applying it to another situation that is not longer applicable to that previous standard. By maintaining the integrity of the system – as in consistently using the same methodology – we can achieve consistent results.

For every food that is used in the world Ayurveda has a classification for it according to the above principles. While this may seem like an exaggeration or wild statement it is not. I personally have English translations of books a thousand years old that list the effects of hundreds of different beverages and foods used today. These classifications are not the work of one person or even of one group of persons, but are rather the ongoing accumulation of knowledge over several thousand years. Nor are these classifications limited to the foods on the Indian sub-continent. Ayurveda spread from Indonesia to Europe in ancient times and so includes foods from these diverse regions of the Earth.

---

[21] These are the energetic classifications of substances in Ayurveda – Rasa (taste), Virya (heating or cooling action), and Vipaka (post-digestive effect). This is called the Rasa of substances in general terminology.

Using the five states of matter we arrive at six primary combinations. These combinations are listed according to their taste, or how they taste on your tongue. They are as follows:

Taste	**State of Matter Dominating**
Neutral (bland)	Liquid & Solid
Sour	Solid & Transformation
Salty	Transformation & Liquid
Pungent	Movement & Transformation
Bitter	Space & Movement
Astringent	Solid & Movement

The effect of these different combinations on the body is easily seen chemically or subjectively. Hence, they can be used effectively in either the biochemical or constitutional model of nutrition.

According to Ayurveda these different tastes (which are simple ways to classify chemical and enzyme responses in the body to different substances) affect the metabolism differently. Not only that, but each taste affects different people differently. In other words a Vata type of person will be affected negatively by the overuse of the astringent taste and positively affected by a small amount of the same taste. Therefore, by knowing your constitution you can understand which foods affect you positively or negatively and in what quantity they should be taken.

Type	**State of Matter Dominating**	**Taste Relationship**
Vata	Space & Movement	Astringent
Pitta	Transformation & Liquid	Salty
Kapha	Liquid & Solid	Neutral (mildly sweet)

The previous table is given to clarify the relationship explained above.

This relationship is extended to understand which combinations of matter increase the attributes of a type and so cause accumulation and disease, or which combinations decrease the attributes and so maintain health by preventing accumulations.

Type	Increases (accumulates)	Decreases (maintains)
Vata	bitter/pungent/ astringent	neutral/sour/salty
Pitta	sour/salty/pungent	neutral/bitter/ astringent
Kapha	neutral/sour/salty	pungent/bitter/ astringent

Thus, Vata types will be benefited from eating small amounts of bitter, pungent and astringent foods and from eating larger amounts of neutral, sour and salty foods. The Pitta type will be benefited from eating little amounts of food containing sour, salty and pungent tastes and eating larger amounts of neutral, bitter, and astringent tastes. The Kapha type will be best benefited by eating small amounts of the neutral, sour, and salty tastes and larger amounts of the pungent, bitter and astringent tastes.

Here is a brief description of the six primary combinations and their effect on the metabolism in general:

Taste	Effect on Metabolism
Neutral (protein, fats, carbohydrates, pure/complex)	Increases tissue development, increases body fluids, blood, muscle, fat, bone and nerve tissue. Supports immunity and growth including reproduction. It gives emotional satisfaction and pleasure; it gives vigor and strength.

	In Excess: Overuse causes obesity, accumulation of toxins, parasites, diabetes, obstructions in the bodies channels (atherosclerosis), gas, indigestion, dyspnea, cough, cold, vomiting, loss of appetite, and lethargy.
Sour (acidic)	Stimulates digestion and builds body tissues like the neutral taste exceptit has little action on growth and none on reproduction. It helps the senses to function, promotes strength and cause secretions of fluids in the body. **In Excess**: Overuse causes acidity in the small intestine, burning, itching, premature aging and light headedness
Salty	Promotes digestion, lessens accumulations of toxins and tissues, it increases saliva in the mouth, and has a mild laxative effect. **In Excess**: Overuse causes inflammation, skin diseases, impotence, and looseness of body, premature aging and retention of water.
Pungent (spicy)	This is the strongest stimulant aiding the digestion and activating the metabolism. It dispels gas and induces sweating. It is heating to the body and cleans the blood and skin. **In Excess**: Overuse causes pain, emaciation, burning sensations, fever, thirst, skin diseases and diminishing of reproductive fluids.

Bitter	This taste is the best blood purifier and cleaner of toxins in the body. It promotes all the other tastes. It has the effect to reduce tissues and fluids and relieves burning in the body. It is strongly reducing in action. **In Excess**: Overuse causes coldness in the body, nervous disorders, stiffness, colic pain, headaches and reduction of reproductive fluids.
Astringent	It is constricting tissues and channels in the body, which helps to maintain muscle tissue and tone. This makes it valuable as a medicine in that it stops bleeding and discharges. It heals the mucus membranes and the skin. In small amounts it aids the digestion of foods. **In Excess**: Overuse causes dryness of the body, constipation, cramps, emaciation, thirst, nervous disorders and decreased reproductive fluids

If these basic guidelines are followed the genetic function of the metabolism is supported and maintained. If they are ignored, then food allergies, low energy, obesity, ulcers, hyper acidity, constipation, diarrhea, malabsorption of nutrients, skin rashes, candida, vaginal yeast infections, diverticulitis, intestinal gripping, low immunity, toxic accumulation, headaches, type II diabetes, gall bladder stones, and suppressed liver function can result. The problems listed above are only an example of the problems resulting from not following a diet according to your constitution, but this is not an exhaustive list.

Fortunately, you do not have to memorize or learn these rules as the food tables in chapter 15 do all the work for you. However, it can be important to understand the basic logic of how these tables have been derived. They are the result of thousands of years of study and are not limited to one group of people; they are not even limited to the Indian culture. The Greeks, Persians and many other cultures have added their own contributions into these classifications over the centuries. Today we are also constantly adding new foods and revising the lists according to soil, climatic and other considerations of North America.

The six tastes also vary in degree of strength. In other words they can be strong or mild in action. There is a big difference between a chili pepper and a pinch of thyme, both of which are pungent in taste – but to different degrees. The table below clarifies this.

Taste	Pure Form	Complex Form
Neutral (bland)	sugars	complex carbohydrates, grains
Sour	alcohol	yogurt, lemon
Salt	table salt	soy sauce, seaweed
Pungent	cayenne pepper	mild spice, cinnamon, onions
Bitter	gentian, aloe	rhubarb, leafy dark green plants
Astringent	unripe bananas	pomegranate, cranberries

According to Ayurveda proper nutrition is the regular and balanced intake of these six different tastes according to your natal constitution. This is because each taste is responsible for different chemical responses and actions in the body. Many of these responses are directly related to enzyme function. As the digestion of all nutrients – be they vitamins, minerals, fats, carbohydrates or proteins is dependent on enzyme function, the logic and methodology is well founded. Taking high doses of multi-vitamins is worthless if the enzymes are not present to digest them. Taking enzymes supplements can help, but the number of enzymes in the body is very large. This issue is discussed in detail in chapter 13.

Yet the six divisions of taste into six primary combinations is only the first set of classifications used to understand the effect of food on our bodies. The second classification is to see whether the food builds tissue (anabolic) or reduces tissue (catabolic). This is described as stimulating the metabolism or suppressing the metabolism (*Virya*). All substances are therefore classified according to these terms as well. Below is a table describing the effect of the stimulating or suppressing functions on the different types.

Type	**Stimulating (hot)**	**Suppressing (cold)**
Vata	Balances	Disrupts
Pitta	Disrupts	Balances
Kapha	Balances	Disrupts

Therefore, the food tables in chapter Fifteen also consider these effects as well. An example of this table could be a Kapha type of person eating a lot of ice cream, which has a cold, suppressing action on the metabolism. The result, if done frequently, will be weight gain and a possible suppression of the enzyme function. This in turn can begin a complex process of the metabolism slowly breaking down and eventually causing obesity or congestive types of illness.

The third classification to understand the effect of substances on the genetically different types is the long-term effect of eating any specific type of food (*Vipaka*). This primarily means what effect the food has on the body after digestion. Yet, it also means what happens after eating a food for several months or years. This is a classification not used or well understood by modern nutritionists. However, it is a very important consideration and should not be discarded lightly by anyone. According to Ayurveda several of the initial chemical reactions triggered by food in the body change after digestion and, over the long run, begin to have the opposite effect on the body. Below a table is given to show how the six primary tastes change after digestion (*Vipaka*).

Taste	Long term change	Disrupts
Neutral	Neutral (none)	Kapha
Sour	Sour (none)	Pitta - Kapha second
Salty Neutral	(change)	Pitta - Kapha 2nd
Pungent	Pungent (none)	Vata - Pitta 2nd
Bitter	Pungent (change)	Vata
Astringent	Pungent (change)	Vata

By looking at the above table is apparent that certain foods will have a depleting or catabolic effect over long periods of time. These are the last three categories, pungent, bitter, and astringent. Foods or herbs that have these tastes in large quantities should be taken in small amounts by all of the three constitutional types – most especially the Vata types. However, in cases of imbalance or disease these same categories have the greatest potential to cure or bring equilibrium for any of the types – through short-term use.

While Ayurvedic nutrition begins with an understanding of each individual's metabolism and digestive capacity. It then extends this individuality onward towards the actual food itself. It offers us a clear methodology to discover which foods will support our nature and which foods will disrupt our natural metabolic function. This is related to, but not limited to, our genetic despondency towards digestive enzymes in the body and their relation to specific kinds of foods. The roles of enzymes, both in the digestive system and on the cellular level, are passed directly from our parents and cultural nutritional habits.

5
Avoid Disaster - Learn How to Eat

In the age of instant gratification we have lost the art – as a culture – to enjoy our food. The business lunch is a prime example of this. Fast food is another example. Where is the room for enjoyment if eating is rushed or giving a utilitarian role to other things – like watching the TV.

In what we call the "modern age" the actual process of eating has been reduced to a mechanical function, an almost disagreeable chore to perform three or four times daily. The act of eating is put behind almost every other kind of activity. This habit is now so wide spread that the above statements will raise eyebrows, cause puzzlement, or reflect some eccentric quality of the author – perhaps even bordering on insanity.

Eating in front of the TV or the radio is considered to be normal. Wolfing down your food in five minutes is considered normal. Eating food that you just add water to and microwave is considered normal. Eating a tasteless frozen dinner is considered normal. In fact, eating food that is tasteless is considered normal. Eating huge amounts of food – a serving that would normally feed two or three people is considered normal in United States.

In effect, everything that takes away your attention from the act of eating is considered normal. Everything that reduces the quality of the food you eat is considered normal. Everything that turns the art of cooking into a factory production to save time (which means energy and money in the American dream) is considered normal. I can assure you that none of this is normal or healthy.

Now the above critics are for our culture as a whole, not every individual is so busy pushing fast food down their throat and reading the newspaper at the same time that they miss the pleasure of eating. Yet, unfortunately, most of us do this at some point and many of us do it all the time.

However, there is another way to eat! And just changing the way you eat is often enough to lose weight, eliminate constant digestive troubles, stop constipation. And, yes, believe it or not, to actually start enjoying your food.

How You Eat Begins the Digestive Process – for Good or Bad

Ayurveda states that your digestion and assimilation of nutrients begins in your attitude toward food. Do you love food or do you hate food? Is food a necessary evil? Does it take up your time that could be used "better" for something else? Do you think about food a lot? Is your basic attitude to food negative, positive, or neutral?

Each of these different attitudes affects the whole metabolic function of the body's reception of your meal. While it may be possible through long days of research to find modern psychological studies to support the Ayurvedic point of view, I prefer the experiential. Try the suggestion below and see if you feel any effect or not, if you do then you will not need a scientific study because it will be your personal experience.

Buy or make a food that you are neutral with – one that you neither love nor hate. Then sit down and prepare to eat it. However, just before eating it look at it and say twenty times – "I hate this food, it looks disgusting!" After doing this – wholeheartedly – eat the food. While you are eating it tell yourself mentally how awful this food is and how you would rather be working or goofing off. This experiment is not done when you have finished eating though – this is only the beginning step. The meal, or food item, will take between 12 to 48 hours to pass through your system. Six hours is the minimum time for fruit to pass through the system of a vegetarian. A person who is eating meat at every meal can take up to 72 hours to digest a full meal. Therefore, you must now observe yourself for the one half to three days and see if you feel great.

If you can do this sincerely, wholeheartedly and not feel a difference, or be disconnected forever from the food you used in the experiment, then I suggest spending several days or years looking for studies to prove it to your mind. Most of us will be hardly able to eat the food in the first place after convincing ourselves that we hate it and it is disgusting!

I have given this exercise to some of my clients and students and the results are quite consistent. Rarely does a person question how their attitude affects their digestive process after trying this exercise.

Ayurveda says that we should enjoy our food! Eating is one of life's pleasures and is not meant to be either too important (obsessive) or ignored (disregarded as unimportant). Both extremes are disruptive, but enjoyment is very important. Eating the best, "health food" – because it is healthy – and not liking it is disruptive to digestion and metabolism according to Ayurveda. Enjoyment, in a balanced sense, is the best digestive aid. An attitude of uncaring or disregard will also tend to disregard certain aspects of nutrient assimilation. And an attitude of obsession will also tend to assimilate an excess of certain nutrients. A balanced, happy approach to food is where we must begin with all diets or nutritional programs – regardless of the system employed or failure will result.

According to Ayurveda there are several key factors in the actual process of eating. The first and most important is the mental attitude above, but here is the complete list of considerations.

1. Mental Attitude
2. Environment
3. Company
4. Attention
5. Quality of Food
6. Kind of Food
7. Preparation of Food
8. Order of Eating Food
9. Quantity of Food
10. The Act of Eating

Environment and Company

The second and third considerations, environment and company, are related. The actual place where you eat and the surrounding are extremely important because they will either be relaxing you or making you tense. By the same token, whom you eat with will be either relaxing or stressing. The environment means the room you are in, including the TV (which should be off!).

Our environment also means the climate that we live in and the season of the year. First of all, our diet should be in accord with our climate. People need to eat differently in different kinds of climates. Eating a diet that is good in a tropical climate in a cold climate will certainly bring on trouble for the metabolism. Secondly, one should adjust the diet according to the seasons of the year. The body has different requirements in winter than in summer and a failure to respect this is often the cause of disease. Many people think that this is not relevant today because of climate control in homes, offices and commercial centers. Ayurveda says it is very important because the body's intelligence is still following the climatic seasons even if we are not aware of it.

When I was young and in school my friends and I would stop at the fast food place and order through the drive in window. When we picked up our meal we would most often sit in the car and eat it. Sometimes we drove a few blocks to the beach and looked at the California sunset, or other times we ate it in the parking lot.

In this example the environment and company changes drastically. Without addressing the quality of the food (or lack of it), the company was friendly and the environment very different. Eating in the car is already not an ideal situation as the purpose of a car (believe it or not) is for transportation. Eating should be done in a place meant for eating. But eating in the car, sitting in the parking lot and looking at the industrial building next door is hardly appetizing. Going to the beach and looking at the ocean or sunset, however, is a vast improvement over the first choice and better for the mental attitude and so digestion.

In essence, the aesthetics of your environment are very important. This does not mean you have to eat in a five star environment. It means that you should be comfortable and what you see should be pleasing or harmonious. The same applies to whom you eat with. Conflict and emotional trauma is very disturbing to the digestive metabolism. Eating with people who are making you uncomfortable will cause problems if it is done on a regular basis. If you doubt this then make dinner, sit down with your family, partner or friend and begin to yell and scream at each other for ten minutes before eating. Really get into it, bring up all the past pain and hurts and start to criticize the other persons family and friends. It is best to only dwell in the past or to project into the future; avoid the present and how you feel now.

The above exercise should clarify any doubts you may have about how emotions can effect your digestive metabolism. If you are not disturbed by the above exercise then you will probably die of a heart attack at 50 from suppressing emotions! Humor aside, our environment and company can and do affect how we, as complete human beings, process our food. This is very much dependant on the fourth consideration, attention.

Attention

Attention is – what was I writing about? Attention is probably the most important factor in eating (and writing!). There is an ancient maxim that states – "where your attention goes, so you go". In other words what you think of is where you are – mentally. So if I am watching TV my attention is focussed on something other than my food and enjoying my food. It is impossible for the attention to be divided, it can flip back and forth, but it cannot focus on two things at once. Attention means your conscious focus. It does not mean the automated functions of your body, which you assume will transform and digest the food you are mechanically stuffing into your mouth.

Eating and watching TV gives mixed results because it divides your attention between your meal and something else. I am using the TV in this example, but reading the newspaper is the same thing. Any dual activity splits your attention and so your digestive capacity to assimilate nutrients from food. Yes, it is true that this kind of statement borders on insanity in our culture. However, there are many places in the world where people only eat when they eat! And these people enjoy it! How amazing!

Obviously some explanation is needed for this "new" concept of actually having your attention on your food and even enjoying doing so. To understand why Ayurveda insists on this aspect you should look at appendix 1 which explains that the human body, and all of its sub systems, cannot be isolated. The real holistic, or Ayurvedic point of view, is that your mental state and therefore your attention play a direct role in the integrity of all psycho / physical functions. This is called body/mind medicine now, but the conscious power of the mind is far greater than the automated or unconscious mind. The conscious mind has the power to open and change the unconscious programming; therefore it is more powerful.

This is one of the best ways to increase your energy, lose weight and correct any kind of chronic digestive problem. Simply focus your conscious attention on your food and enjoy it. This brings both the unconscious and conscious powers of your mind into your primary energy source – food. This is not about will power or positive affirmations. It is about a simple but important part of life called enjoyment.

Therefore, do not divide your attention when you eat as it will lower your digestive capacity and hence your overall energy. In the long run, 15-20 years you will begin to have chronic digestive problems. According to Ayurveda there is nothing stronger than the mind. Learning to use it as a positive force in nutrition is a cornerstone of constitutional nutrition.

Quality of Food

When the above factors are addressed we can begin to look at the more obvious side of nutrition. The first of these is the actual food quality itself. As mentioned in chapter 4 virtually all modern diets and nutritional systems are supporting a diet consisting of whole foods in as natural a state as possible.

In this light is it worth mentioning that genetic altered foods are considered a health risk in all countries other than the United States, Australia, Canada and three South American countries. All European countries and a group of over 130 nations consider genetically altered foods a serious health risk of unknown proportions. The USA has just recently (February 1999) undermined a global effort to regulate the production and distribution of genetically altered foods. Although the excuse has been given for the concern of global food supply, the primary motivation is money. This comes from American multinational food corporations and government supporters that have, and are, spending millions of dollars in experimenting on your health, the health of your family and that of unborn generations.

The American negotiator said in response to global criticism, "*We were just too important, too big to be ignored.*" [22] The response from the 130 different delegates was generally frustration and anger. A negotiator, Joseph Goto said, "The United States is holding the world at ransom." [23] Genetically altered foods have not been studied for the many generations needed to determine if they are safe. The primary goal of the other nations was to have the importers of genetically altered foods and seeds obtain permission before bringing in these products to other countries. In other words to give the people consuming the goods a choice in the matter. However, the health and possible devastating environmental effects to other countries was considered of less importance than profit by the food industry and their governmental allies. If you choose these foods you are experimenting in unknown territories that could, perhaps, result in serious health problems to you and your loved ones for many years to come. If you are not sure what kind of food you are eating you should find out.

How real should your concern be? Read this small caption from English newspaper entitled "Unbelievable Fact".

---

[22] "Growing Pains: Why Hopes for Global Biotech Treaty Withered", *IHT, 25* February 1999.

[23] "Growing Pains: Why Hopes for Global Biotech Treaty Withered", *IHT, 25* February 1999.

> "Monsanto's New Leaf Superior potato is, itself, legally registered as a pesticide with the U.S. Environmental Protection Agency (EPA) because it has been genetically engineered to poison any Colorado beetle that might eat even a tiny portion of it. The potatoes which are in commercial production and used by an arch-American fast food company amongst others, are considered safe for human consumption as they have no discernible effect on laboratory mice."[24]

Bear in mind that the metabolism of a mouse is not the same as a human, nor is a mouse a thinking conscious individual that may be having trouble with school or other emotional, or developmental problems as your child may be. The primary problem is that genetically engineered foods have never been tested on humans in controlled studies. This means that in 50 years we may find out that these foods are altering basic human functions like learning or reproduction. As there has been no long term (or even short term) studies on the effects of these foods on a living human there is no way that the scientists can honestly say that these foods are safe – which they continually do to the press.

The problems of food quality are not limited to genetically altered foods. Biochemical medicine often treats nutritional deficiencies with behavior-altering drugs. This is happening in epidemic proportions in the United States. The figures for total population consumption are not easily found, however, it is known that 5% of American school children daily take a prescription medication for "behavioral disorders".[25] This is alarming when studies have shown that 79 percent of hyperactive children improve when food additives, colorings, flavorings and white sugar were removed from their diets.[26] A leading Doctor in pediatrics, Ben Feingold, M.D., has found that 50 percent of his clients

---

[24] *Positive News*, No. 18, Winter 1998.

[25] Robbins, John, 1996, p. 159.

[26] Egger et al, *Lancet*, 1985, p. 16.

improve dramatically when food additives are removed from their diets.[27] Additionally, children with learning disabilities also found their "problems" disappearing with the elimination of food additives.

There are a number of very troubling chemicals added to the vast majority of foods. Many, if not all, of these chemicals pose problems for the human metabolism. This is especially true for children. An excellent book on this subject has been written by Doris Rapp, M.D. and is important reading for all parents.[28] One has to question the motivations of modern medicine and the food industry when disorders that are shown to respond to the elimination of food additives from the diet are treated with more drugs – especially in seven and eight years old children. It has to be very clear that the addition of chemicals to your food has nothing to do with your health or the quality of the food. It has to do with longer shelf life and the profits that result from that prolonged availability. Additionally, the chemical industry wants to sell chemicals – whether these end up in your food, your medicine or your car is of little consequence to the stockholders.

One should also be aware that studies exist that refute these facts. However, the companies that profit from the manufacturing of the food additives fund them. For example the American Dietetics Association is funded by the sugar lobby. Therefore, if you want to find out about the quality of your food you will have to look into it, no one will be handing you the information. Imagine this, "Buy this great food product, it takes three minutes to prepare, just add water, an egg and presto, you have a meal fresh out of the microwave. Additionally, this meal will give your child brain disorders, destroy everyone's nervous system, make you impotent or infertile and lower the immunity of the whole

---

[27] Robbins, John, 1996, p. 170.

[28] **Rapp, Doris, 1991.**

family." As this kind of advertising is unlikely to happen it is up to you to find safe foods and preparation methods.

In our day and age food quality has often come to mean food safety. In general, there are several things you can easily do to maintain food quality. Avoid buying anything in a can, box, or other container. Avoid frozen foods and instant foods. Instead buy locally grown foods whenever possible. Buy organic foods when possible and use the minimum amount of other pre-made or prepared foods such as canned tomato sauce. While this may seem extreme it is not difficult to do and guidelines will be given on how to implement this approach. Although your children may make a fuss it is better to provide the right kind of nutrition than to have them suffer emotional or health disorders because of a lack of care. A parent is in the position to know what foods are healthy or not – your child is not able to make this decision. This is part of having children, listening to them complain and grumble and then making them do what is right for their health.

Ayurveda is also of the mind that foods should be procured from your local environment and in their natural season. This is an especially important consideration if you are really ill (cancer) or have a chronic disease like hepatitis or AIDS. If you are normally healthy, which we have seen statistically most Americans are not, then you can get away with eating foods out of season to a large extent. However, if you fall into one of the above mentioned groups of diseases, or you think you may be prone to have a disease like one mentioned, eat only seasonal foods.

Culturally we have become accustomed to eating any kind of food at any time of the year. We call this progress. Ayurveda considers it to be a cause of disease. There is a reason why foods grow when and where they do. If you do not live in the same place then at the very least eat the food in the correct season. For example you like kiwis. Well then eat kiwis in the summer (or whenever they are harvested in New Zealand). Eating them in winter in the Midwestern United States will promote problems in digestion according to Ayurveda.

The most common thing that happens is that the body changes according to the seasons. To some extent the digestive enzymes change also according to the climate and season. This was a natural phenomenon until thirty years ago when we began to eat foods out of season. For thousands of years the human body naturally adjusted enzyme production with the seasonal changes in foods and climate. Do you think that this pattern of several thousands of years has suddenly changed in the last thirty or forty years?

One should also be aware that in order for foods to come from South America or other continents they must, by necessity, be harvested long before the full nutrient content is developed. It is a commonly accepted fact in biochemical nutrition that foods reach their highest nutrient content when they are "ripe", or ready for a traditional harvest. Hence, the regular intake of foods from different locations alone will lower the amount of nutrients available for your body.

It is also necessary to consider how old the food is before you eat it. This means the state of the food when you buy it and leftover meals. According to Ayurveda food should always be freshly cooked. Eating leftovers generally creates toxins or undigested food particles in the body. My personal experience is that it is better to eat yesterday's leftover homemade meal than to eat a bought prepared meal or to eat fast food. Frozen foods can be resorted to in a pinch, but it is far better to freeze some of your own cooking rather than buy it pre-made.

In chapter 10 we will look at the effect of modern agriculture methods and food quality. However, it is worth noting here that the vast majority of fertilizers and pesticides are made from petrochemicals. All of these products are harmful to the healthy function of the human body. Using foods that are grown without any chemical fertilizers or pesticides is, by far, the most important consideration in food quality.

Kind of Food

The next consideration is the actual kind of food that you choose to eat. This subject is discussed in depth later in the book and is detailed in food charts in chapter 15. Yet, it is worth mentioning that foods should first be chosen according to your natal constitution and then according to the changing constitution or disease state. In serious disease the food choices should be according to the changing constitution or disease state. If this confuses you just follow your natal constitution as we tend to come down with diseases related to our natal constitution.

Unlike biochemical nutrition the method of choosing food is based on the genetic tendencies of the person, not vitamins and minerals. Ayurveda uses the system of food qualities (explained in chapter 4) to get the correct amount of micronutrients for each type. As mentioned earlier Ayurveda considers a balanced diet to consist of all six different tastes as each of these tastes provides a certain chemical function in the metabolism. Also the use of whole foods is extremely important for this system to work effectively. Hence, using boxed, frozen or canned foods – even if they are correct for your constitution – will not give you proper nutrition according to Ayurveda.

Preparation of Food

The preparation of food is an art, one that I personally do not possess in great quantities. But even if you are unskilled (as I am) in cooking there are certain things that must be understood for proper nutrition to happen. Ayurveda lists the most important of these as the state of the person actually preparing the food. They say that food should be cooked with love. If the food is cooked with another emotion than love or caring then the overall result of the food will not nourish the subtle aspects of the human being. Your muscles and tissues may receive enough vitamins, but not your mind, emotions and basic vitality.[29]

There is a good reason for this according to the basis of the five states of matter that provide the foundation of Ayurveda. The act of cooking relates to the state of transforming matter. When we heat food we change it or partially digest it for easier digestion and assimilation. During this action the state of the cook becomes part of the process of transformation. According to their logic the best feeling or emotion to have as part of the transformation of food is love. It is hard to say that you do not want love; love is mental and emotional nourishment. We all are looking for love in one form or another and as it is the only truly nourishing emotion it is natural that it be associated with nutrition of the body. It is understood that other emotions than love will bring on digestive problems or lowered nutrient content – especially over time.

This is one reason why eating regularly in restaurants will create chronic health problems. Restaurants are impersonal and the cook rarely takes a personal interest in the act of feeding others. This is, of course, less true in five star restaurants where the cook is only interested in making the best food possible and will even go each morning to buy the ingredients to insure the taste is correct. However, this is less common in the United States than on mainland Europe (we all know about English cooks!). Fast food is at the bottom of the spectrum as it is not only impersonal, but

---

[29] The concept of Prana is used in Ayurveda to explain this point. Prana is the life force and link to the body / mind / soul. When food is cooked with love the Prana of the cook passes into the food and the Prana of the food is enhanced. Thus, the subtle link that binds the soul to the mind-emotions and the body is nourished – creating an integrated human being. If the person cooking is in another state then the reverse is true.

also factory like. People who make and serve the food are badly paid and often hate what they are doing. On some level this emotion is coming to you through the preparation of the food.

The best way to prepare food is to use an open gas flame as it is closest to fire. However, electric cooking can be used as there is not much difference. Ovens are usually a very good way to cook foods. Microwave ovens are to be avoided for all kitchen uses including defrosting, warming up things and boiling water. This is the point of view of all natural medical systems, not just Ayurveda. The point of view is that the quality of life is diminished with the use of microwaves. According to Chinese medicine these ovens destroy the "Chi" or "Ki" that is in food. Ayurveda also has the same opinion. This is another factor in eating fast foods. The point here is that a principle in food that is not measurable by modern instruments is deranged by microwave ovens.

There is information – not readily available to the widespread public – about the negative action of microwaves to the human body. One of the leaders in this field is a Swiss scientist named Dr. Hans Hertel. Below are some of his comments on Microwave ovens:

> "There is extensive scientific literature concerning the hazardous effects of direct microwave radiation on living systems. It is astonishing, therefore, to realize how little effort has been made to replace this detrimental technique of microwaves with technology more in accordance with nature.
>
> Technically produced microwaves are based on the principle of alternating current. Atoms, molecules and cells hit by this hard electromagnetic radiation are forced to reverse polarity 1 to 100 billion times a second. There are no atoms, molecules or cells of any organic system able to withstand such a violent, destructive power for any extended period of time, not even in the low energy range of milliwatts.
>
> Of all the natural substances, which are polar, the oxygen of water molecules reacts most sensitively. This is how

microwave cooking heat is generated-friction from this violence in water molecules. Structures of molecules are torn apart, molecules are forcefully deformed (called structural isomerism) and thus become impaired in quality.

This is contrary to conventional heating of food, in which heat transfers conventionally from without to within. Cooking by microwaves begins within the cells and molecules where water is present and where the energy is transformed into frictional heat.

These athermic effects are not presently measurable, but they can also deform the structures of molecules and have qualitative consequences. For example, the weakening of cell membranes by microwaves is used in the field of gene altering technology. Because of the force involved, the cells are actually broken, thereby neutralizing the electrical potentials - the very life of the cells - between the outer and inner sides of the cell membranes. Impaired cells become easy prey for viruses, fungi and other microorganisms. The natural repair mechanisms are suppressed, and cells are forced to adapt to a state of energy emergency: they switch from aerobic to anaerobic respiration. Instead of water and carbon dioxide, hydrogen peroxide and carbon monoxide are produced."[30]

Dr. Hertel has been in court for the last several years because of his statements and published studies. In spite of the political pressure Dr. Hertel has continued his studies and won the support of many other scientists in Europe for his findings and methodology. In Dr. Hertel's studies the conclusion is reached that people who eat microwaved food have their blood chemistry altered. The manufacturing companies are trying to keep this information suppressed through court orders and intimidation tactics. Yet, he is not the only scientist to find problems with microwave ovens.

An article in a reputed medical journal[31] stated that there appeared to be a reduction of vital nutrients in

[30] *Acres*, April 1994.

[31] Quan, Richard, M.D., *Pediatrics*, April 1992.

mothers' milk heated in microwave ovens. This study and others have prompted medical universities and their hospitals to stop using microwave ovens to warm baby bottles. In another mishap a woman patient died when given a blood transfusion that had been heated with a microwave oven.[32] Apparently the microwaves changed the blood enough to kill the poor women who had only gone in for hip surgery.

Given the above information and the modern point of view of Ayurvedic medicine I believe it to be important to review the use of microwave ovens in the preparation of your food. The effect microwaves have on food cell structure could be one reason we are seeing such a huge increase in cancer in this country. It should be pointed out that manufactures have never tested the actual safety of the food after microwaving them. Rather they are only required by law to make sure as little as possible of the microwaves escape the oven because they are known to be dangerous to humans over periods of prolonged exposure. Strange to think we would use something that is known to be so dangerous to cook our food.

What we cook our food in is also very important. Stainless steel is the best material for most people to use. Cooking with aluminum is very bad as it gives off poisons to the food in the process of cooking which the body then ingests. These metal poisons can then be found in liver and other tissues throughout the body. Many non-stick pans are also known to be carcinogenic and best avoided. There are a number of points on cooking and cooking materials that are relevant; however, these are the most important.

Order to Eat Food

The order in which we eat our food is one of the most over looked, yet important factors in nutrition. This is based on the logic that whatever enters first will either be digested first or block the way for other foods to be digested. The

---

[32] *Acres*, April 1994.

understanding is that foods should be eaten in the order that the body digests them.

A student of mine in Switzerland brought the simple truth of this home. She is an MD who has worked for fourteen years as the co-director of a woman's clinic. One class she came with the following story. "A client of mine has had digestive problems for the last five years. She has been to all of the specialists and taken a number of different medications and still has no relief. She has come to me for a few other problems, but mentioned this chronic digestive problem as well. I told her not to change her diet but to change the order in which she ate it. Within two weeks her chronic digestive problems where completely gone."

The order in which foods should be eaten can change from constitution to constitution.

For the Pitta and Kapha types it is generally as follows:

- Fruit
- Green Salads
- Cooked Vegetables and Whole Grains
- Beans
- Raw Vegetables
- Dairy Products
- Fish and Poultry
- Red Meat

For Vata types the lists changes a little:

- Fruit
- Cooked Vegetables and Whole Grains
- Green Salads with oil based dressings
- Dairy Products
- Fish and Poultry
- Raw Vegetables
- Beans
- Red Meat

The basic rules are that fruits should be eaten alone and not with other foods. This is also true of all melons and for all constitutions. The Vata type should not eat any kind of raw foods before cooked vegetables or grains. Before meat is OK if the person eats meat.

Without changing the diet each person should begin to eat in this way as it makes it easier for the different digestive enzymes to work on the foods that they relate to. This is especially true with fruits, as they require a completely different set of enzymes than other foods. There are also certain food groups that we should not mix together when eating. This is true for all constitutions.

It is worth noting that liquids generally pass solid foods in the stomach and go directly to the small intestine. Hence, the kind of liquid you drink has the capability to enhance or suppress the digestive process. Liquids do need to be taken to help lubricate the digestive tract. If they are cold they suppress completely the digestive enzymes. If they are too hot and mixed with the wrong food (e.g., food that is already generating heat like meat) then they can over activate the digestion.

One of the worst cultural habits in the United States – as far as nutrition is concerned – is drinking ice water with meals. This is an extremely bad practice. Obviously it is good business for the makers of ice machines – which is how the practice started. Drinking ice water alone can be OK, but it is completely opposite to the digestive process of food and so should be avoided with meals. The body is busy trying to heat up the food with digestive acids that are hot, putting ice cold liquids into the stomach suppresses or stops this process. Drinking warm or hot water with a meal - in moderation – is not a problem and can even assist in digestion. A step further is warm water, which is considered to be the best liquid to consume with meals.

Most vegetables and grains go well together and have few, if any, contraindications. Mixing different kinds of proteins together is very hard to digest and so is best avoided – like meat and milk. Vegetarians are better off in this respect as there are few major contraindications except that of fruit and melons. If you take dairy then be careful what you mix it with. In general it is more important to eat foods according to how fast they digest rather than anything else as then the correct enzymes can process the food efficiently.

Food or Food Group:	Does not mix with:
Ice Cold liquids	Anything
Complex carbohydrates (whole grains)	Dairy, fruits
Eggs	Red meats, fish, milk, cheese
Fruit	Anything
Honey	Ghee
Hot liquids	Meat, fish, dairy
Lemon	Yogurt, milk, cucumbers, tomatoes
Melons	Anything
Milk	Red meats, fish, eggs, sour foods, yeast breads
Nightshades (potato, tomato, eggplant, etc.)	Milk, yogurt

Quantity of Food

Another prime factor of Ayurvedic nutrition is the actual amount of food consumed by the person. The best way to start with any kind of dietary plan is just to eat less. The amount that people eat in this country is staggering. In contrast to mainland Europe where people eat roughly half the amount of food – in normal food portions – than in the United States. Interestingly enough the percentages of obesity are much less in France than in the United States where people spend hours every day eating rich foods and enjoying it! This is not to say that they do not suffer from other problems, but the rate of obese people is a fraction compared to the United States – the main reason for this is the quantity of food consumed.

The stomach is a muscle and it can be stretched or contracted with training. If you over eat regularly you are "training" your stomach to stretch out. If you eat less you will train your stomach to shrink to its normal size. Ayurveda says that your stomach should be filled with 1/3 solid food, 1/3 liquid, and 1/3 empty. This is the ideal proportion for the stomach to perform its job, which is to mix up everything that you have chewed with digestive acids. If this mix is not done well then the food and acids proceed on to the small intestine in a "half baked" state.

If the stomach is too full then this process cannot happen well. Sometimes the ratio is given of ´solid food, ˇliquid, and empty. You can use this if you are beginning or if you are a pure Vata type. However, I prefer the first ratio given. Stuffing yourself will impair your digestion. It has long been known that a secret to long life is eating small amounts of food at meals. The body does not really need that much food to run – unless you are an athlete or working in a very physical job. However, this is also much misunderstood. When I was young I had a construction job, in which I was eating a fresh piece of fruit, then nuts and dried fruits and herbal tea for lunch. I did this for months and worked with as much or more energy than my companions who ate anything normally associated with construction workers.

If you want to lose weight the best way is to eat less of everything, not just one kind of food. Good nutrition is a balanced mix of several different kinds of foods in sufficient amounts. As a culture we eat far more than we need. As you cut down on the amount of food you eat you may feel a little hunger, do not worry about it, ignore it, and slowly it will go away as the size of your stomach changes. This is not advocating starvation diets or extremes in any way. This is just an obvious place to start in a culture that overdoes everything.

The Act of Eating

At last we come to the act of eating itself. As already mentioned in the beginning of this chapter eating should be a pleasure. The guidelines above are not meant to take away the pleasure of eating but are to help bring some consciousness to the whole process of food and its consumption.

When the other factors have been considered then we can begin to contemplate the mouth which is where we derive the actual pleasure from our food in the form of taste. Chewing our food fully is very important in order to taste it well and gain the full pleasure from it. Chewing also allows the saliva to mix in with the food and prepare it for the stomach. While certain groups advocate to chew your food until it becomes a liquid mass Ayurveda does not consider this to bring enormous pleasure or enjoyment. Nor does it feel that chewing your food a hundred times is more effective for the digestive process. Chewing and tasting your food is very important, but there is little need to become obsessed by turning everything into a liquid before swallowing it. The exception to this is if you are sick or seriously ill. Then following a very strict form of eating and diet is an important part of the healing process.

The "middle path" of thought is important in all dietary matters. Moderation in thought and action is not limited to Buddhism. It is interesting to note that the greatest physician of the Buddha's time was an Ayurvedic doctor and the Buddha's personal doctor as well. Excess in any form is to be avoided and chewing is one of the places where it is very important. By chewing well each mouthfull you will feel more satisfied and need less quantities of food. Wolfing your food down as in a cartoon will fill your stomach yet not satisfy your desire for food.

After eating you should not lie down, nor should you do any heavy physical exercise for at least an hour. Fifteen minutes after eating a short, casual walk of ten to fifteen minutes can be very helpful to help stimulate digestion. If you really do not feel like moving after eating then you have eaten too much and you are exactly the type who needs to get up and walk. This is very important for the Kapha type of person, but also relevant for all three.

One of the most important issues according to Ayurvedic nutrition is when we take food during the day. This relates to the different times of the day when we eat and the quantities of food that we eat during the day. The rules change for each constitution.

According to Ayurveda the body needs no more than three meals a day. This does change slightly for each type of person. The Vata type of person should eat three meals a day, however, if they are imbalanced or disturbed they may need a snack at four-ish in the afternoon. The Pitta type needs only three meals a day, but once again, if imbalanced they can eat fruit between meals. The Kapha type should defiantly not eat any snacks especially in the evening after dinner. The only exception to this is when the Kapha type eats no breakfast – which is often beneficial for them – and then they can eat fruit between 10 – 11 am in the morning.

Eating between meals – other than fruit occasionally – is fatiguing on the digestive system and so should be avoided. The digestive system works in three basic stages:

- Liquefaction and mixing of the food (mouth and stomach)
- Transformation and assimilation (stomach and small intestine)
- Assimilation and elimination (colon)[33]

[33] In Ayurveda these three stages are controlled by Kapha, Pitta and Vata doshas respectively and are called the 'three Stages of Digestion'. Disturbances in the doshas can been seen according to the stage of digestion

Eating between meals does not fully allow the stomach to digest and move the food on towards the next stage. If you are always eating then the stomach is always working, the small and large intestines are also constantly processing something. According to Ayurveda this causes premature aging as well as poor assimilation of nutrients as the food never really has time to be completely prepared.

The body just does not need to have food all the time, in fact, it causes problems. One of the most common problems in the United States is weight gain or obesity. This illustrates the Ayurvedic point of view that constant intake of food eventually breaks down the body's ability to metabolize fats, proteins and carbohydrates. Once this inability to metabolize nutrients happens then a person begins to gain weight – even when they reduce food intake or go on diets.

For simplicity we will divide meal proportions into three sizes – small, medium and large. From the Ayurvedic point of view wealthy people (as in the United States) tend to eat far too much. Therefore some idea of what these sizes refer to is needed. My own personal view is that this translates to ¼ of a dinner plate, ½ of a dinner plate, and ¾ of a dinner plate. I do not ever say a full plate because if the plate is full it is possible to mount it so high as to add an additionally full plate of food on top! With a ¾ plate one can mount it up to a full plate size if one wants to fool oneself.

Of course, if you do not want to lose weight, stop diseases from forming, correct menstrual difficulties, eliminate chronic digestive problems, then you can cheat on the serving sizes. You should just be honest though and not fall into the trap of hypocrisy that is socially acceptable in our society. Facts and rationales will not make you eat less unless you consciously choose to feel better by eating less. Whatever you choose, be honest about it.

---

involved – e.g., bloating located in the stomach relates to Kapha, acidity in the small intestine to Pitta, gas in the colon shows an imbalance of Vata.

Therefore, a table is given below to simply explain the best times to eat and the amounts of food needed for each person during the day. Remember that these are general guidelines and should be adjusted to you lifestyle, work and family situation.

Type	Break -fast	Snack 10-11am	Lunch	Snack 4-5pm	Dinner	Snack +10pm
Vata	Medium	If needed	Medium	Yes, if needed	Medium	No
Pitta	Large	Fruit	Medium	No	Large	No
Kapha	Nothing of Fruit	Fruit if no breakfast	Large or medium if dieting	No	Medium or small dieting	

The desire for food in-between meals indicates two possibilities:

1.) old habits of constantly eating which can be learned again through good habits; and

2.) metabolic malfunction, which is physiological and needs treatment to restore proper function.

If you cannot do this 70 to 80 percent of the time then you probably have a metabolic imbalance between organ function, bile secretions, enzyme function, or all of the above. In this case it is worthwhile to work with an Ayurvedic practitioner to correct the problem.

This guideline does not mean that you can never have a snack again or that you can never have a dessert again. This is the optimum choice, but it does allow a person to have a snack once in a while. If "once in a while" exceeds thirty percent of the time then it becomes problematic. This means three snacks in ten days, not three snacks a week. Snacks are not needed if the food is nourishing to the body, the taste and the mind. If you need snacks you are not eating the right kind of meals to nourish yourself at the right times of day according to the seasons and your climate.

In conclusion, the whole act of eating should be a pleasure in one's life that is consciously enjoyed and participated in. This begins from the choice of foods, to the preparation of foods and to the consumption of foods. While Ayurveda does not traditionally support the idea of eating in restaurants they are part of our society. When eating in restaurants, follow as close as possible the best food choices for your constitution. More importantly though is eating the foods in the right order and combination so that whatever you do eat you are able to process fully and benefit from. The whole question of eating is to be present mentally when you eat and have fun! Enjoying your food is a powerful digestive aid, especially when ice cold liquids are avoided!

6
How to Avoid the Dangers of Dieting and Food Fads

Lisa is a painter living in Paris. She is married, in her thirties and has two young children. Since the birth of her second child she has not been able to lose the extra weight she gained during pregnancy. She came to me for advise about nutrition and because she was under more stress professionally than normal. Lisa is a Pitta type person and so was not used to carrying extra weight around. Normally she could lose weight easily and so she was somewhat baffled by her present situation. She had tried several diets and nothing was helping her, actually she was slowly gaining weight in spite of her efforts.

A diagnosis reveled that her metabolism was disturbed. The problem began after the birth of her second child as a hormone disturbance, but was further aggravated by the diets she tried. I gave her advice on nutrition and also recommended an herbal formula to balance her digestive metabolism. The results were normal from my experience – in six weeks she was almost back to her normal weight. In two and a half months she was feeling better than she had in years and had stabilized at her normal weight.

Lisa is a typical case where dieting only aggravated her metabolic imbalance. Not all cases respond so quickly, but Lisa was also a very determined woman. She followed all my advice to the letter and received results accordingly. In most cases diets change like fashions, yearly. This however, poses problems for your digestive functions.

Good nutrition is not based on the latest fashions. Fashionable things are good in which to make money (for the producers) and to impress other people (for the recipients). While this may be appropriate in clothing, cars or computers it is absolutely not appropriate for health and nutrition. The primary reason for this is that the body does not like sudden or frequent changes. The metabolism functions best through regularity.

The physiological fact and the social / mental reality for us – as a culture – are in opposition. This conflict arises from a culture that wants the best, wants it now, wants it to impress others, wants it bring pleasure or satisfaction, and wants all the same things tomorrow-when it changes its mind or taste. This is the culture we live in; this is our reality.

The problem is that the human metabolism wants the opposite, especially regarding diet. The body wants to have regular meals without too many conflicting tastes, at regular times of the day, every day year after year. The body has an internal clock whose function goes far beyond allowing us to wake up regularly at the same hour (unless you are an imbalanced Vata type who is generally never regular!).

This was exactly the case with Lisa. Although she was a Pitta type she had a disturbance of the Vāta principle which was affecting her whole digestive process. One of the primary changes I suggested to her was to bring regularity into her diet and times of eating. This alone made a huge difference in her response to the treatment.

This regularity extends beyond simple timings of meals. It also means the kinds of foods we eat – not only food groups but also solids, liquids, raw and cooked kinds of food. This also means those little packages of protein powder, which are not only hard to digest, but leech calcium from your bones. This distorts the body's systematic function of enzyme metabolism. The use of foods out of season also distorts the enzyme function to some extent as we learned in the last chapter.

In other words, the more regular our diet and times of consumption are, the happier our body is and the better we will feel. Unfortunately, this poses a problem for the mind which is only interested in the latest fad and changing as quickly as possible. Many people are beginning to use Ayurveda in this way today – because it is the latest health fad. The problem here is not the diet, car, or health system but the psychological addiction to change. This is a conditioned behavior pattern of our society. As it is learned behavior one can choose to unlearn it as well.

Your health and personal power, your personal freedom, begins with a choice to go beyond your destructive social conditionings. Once more it must be emphasized that buying a new car or dress every year or week may be appropriate, but for diet and nutrition it will cause severe health problems that can lead to chronic disease and even an early death.

Following a destructive mental conditioning is long term suicide as far as diet is concerned. Your empowerment can only come through choice, not through unconscious habits that are manipulated by large companies for their profit. Dieting is a huge business and so is the production of diet foods. In fact, it is worth noting that this whole psychological pattern of our society comes from greed and the consumer society.

The consumer mentality is a fairly recent mentality that has been created by companies for profit. This in and of itself is fine, but when it has gone to the extremes of today's society in the United States it needs to be reviewed carefully by each individual for the potential consequences. When we are being fed, on a mass scale, with foods that are registered as pesticides it is time to wake up. This is not a light subject, but it is the main cause for nutritional plans failing for individuals. Even if you throw Ayurveda out the window as an arcane system the same mental conditions will either allow you to succeed or fail regardless which system you choose.

Start by becoming intelligent to the market manipulations that want every women to look 20 and thin and every man to be 25 and have rippling muscles all over his body. These manipulations – even if you acknowledge them as being silly – control your food choices and more importantly the perception you have of your body.

Freedom, and so health, can only come with knowledge. We must all begin to inform ourselves to the present cultural forces, which are destructive, and consciously choose an alternative. This may be a choice to use biochemical nutrition or it may be a choice to use Ayurvedic nutrition. Regardless of the outcome a conscious choice has been made for yourself, by yourself. This is the beginning of self-empowerment and this is why most people fail in diet plans. They either buy into the concept that they need to look differently and know it's impossible from the start to look like a top model or they buy into the concept of 'have it now' diet marketing.

In either situation the person is a loser. Buying into an image created by the market to sell products will, at best, only fit a small percentage of the total population. Buying into the concept that it is possible to lose 5 Lbs. a week is also not only metabolically impossible, but also setting up the person to fail before they even start. The majority of diet plans promise things that are physically impossible for the body. This gives the illusion to the dieter that 'they' have failed and have done something wrong. In fact, the marketing was wrong, not the dieter.

In addition to this our consumer society is encouraging us to eat 24 hours a day. We are even told by "experts" to eat between meals, to "graze" like animals, to function like animals. The sheer availability of food is a problem. I was recently confronted with this problem when I was visiting my family in the United States last summer. I went to the supermarket to buy some ice cream for desert – a simple task I thought. My French wife signaled to me to come over to a 30-yard long avenue of freezer doors. I asked innocently, "Which one has the ice cream?" With awe in her eyes she replied, "All of them do!" After picking myself up off the floor it took us twenty minutes to choose a "natural", sugar loaded, ice cream. The sheer volume is overwhelming.

Everywhere you turn someone is trying to sell you a food or drink product, which is most likely detrimental to your long-term health. Will power is important, far more important according to Ayurveda is understanding. Every time you look at any diet cola ad understand that they are trying to push you to buy a product that is purely chemical in nature. This kind of product damages your digestion, your urinary system, the pH value of your blood and plasma, disrupts pancreas and blood sugar levels with long term use, and is simple being sold to make money. Clarity and understanding is important in any endeavor in life, but most importantly in nutrition.

In general one can assume that food manufacturers do not have your health in mind, they have the health of their balance sheets in mind. There are a few small companies that are hearing the needs of the consumers and are beginning to produce convenient food that is healthy, but these are few and far between.

The Myth of Labeling

Basing your diet on what the manufacturer writes on the label is like putting your head in the mouth of a lion. Maybe you can get it out in time, maybe not. The government has made steps to standardize labeling in recent years yet there is still huge discrepancies in product labeling.

In the first place if it has a label, do not eat it. If you have to go through the nightmare of trying to find real food in a supermarket then forget the nutritional information on the labels as they are often more confusing than informative. The primary thing to look for on any label is something other than food inside. If it has something else, do not buy it. Again, for most of the foods you buy in cans or boxes, you can buy also buy in a natural form. This is by far the best choice. Why buy tomato sauce when you can just put in two or three tomatoes? You will benefit from not having the extra sugar, salt and chemicals that are used to preserve the product. What is the problem?

Canning and preserving food could have made sense in the past when food was not available in a fresh state. It may have made sense before everyone had a refrigerator, but now your fresh vegetables will keep for several days, even a week, in the fridge – why buy cans and boxes? The nutritional value of these foods is far below the same food in a whole state.

However, if you need to go through the label drama avoid the nutritional facts. One, it is based on a biochemical model, and two, it is based on the concept that a calorie is a valid unit of measurement for human nutrition (see Appendix for an explanation on this point). Instead choose foods that only contain food and that are as close as possible to their natural state. Avoid foods that have sugar in them – which is ninty percent of prepared foods. Salt is also important to avoid in prepared foods, especially for Kapha types.

By all means laugh when you read the word "natural". Warning bells should go off when you read things like "100% natural" or other creative marketing slogans. Wake up to the fact that if the food was really 100% natural it would still be on the vine or tree – and even that is a myth now as it could have been sprayed, injected or genetically altered.

Simple look and see if the ingredients are food or if there are long names that sound like a contagious disease in Latin.

Labels are the advertising person's way to convince you to buy their product, nothing more, nothing less. If you want to have nutritional information it's available free in the library. Manufacturers are not going to tell you that you get as much protein from an artichoke as from a pork chop – with one major difference – it is healthier. An artichoke has 22% of its calories from protein, 3% from fat, and 75% from carbohydrates. A pork chop has 23% of its calories from protein and 77% percent from fat – there are no percentages of carbohydrates at all.[34] Perhaps a better name would be "fat chops". Chapter 9 has a table comparing foods in a biochemical manner for your reference.

While this example is using the biochemical model to explain foods – which have far more nutrients and chemicals in them than what is implied by these figures - it does make a point. Labels tell you what you want to hear (that it's OK to eat) and what the manufacturer wants you to hear (buy it, it's good). Labels do not necessarily tell you what benefits the food will actually have for your metabolism. Labels are best avoided, as are foods that have them!

Dangers of Dieting

The danger of dieting is that you will disrupt the metabolism to the point where it is hard to have any kind of decent health. This à very common situation today in the United States. Far more widespread than you may imagine. The story of Lisa was just one example of this. Fortunately, she came to me before her body was completely disturbed by trying too many diets.

There are several important points about dieting. The first is that many diets are not suited for long term use and are only meant to be used to lose weight. When these kinds

[34] Figures derived from, Agriculture Handbook No. 456.

of diets are used for any length of time, say more than 6 weeks, the body begins to have serious problems. These problems begin to manifest as digestive sensitivities to some foods, colic, constipation, poor skin quality, lack of luster in the hair and eyes, enema, and either bloating or intestinal gas to name a few.

Another point with diets is that they, from an Ayurvedic point of view, often damage enzyme function.[35] This was the case with Zelda who had poor enzyme function due to several reasons – one of them was constant dieting. Any diet that is using very concentrated foods like protein powders or handfuls of supplements will lower or destroy enzyme function in time. Diets that use large amounts of fruits, fruit juices, or vegetable juices will also tend to weaken enzyme function. The liquid and raw diets must be adapted to each person's constitution in order for it to work – for some people it will never work.

A general problem with people who diet is that they move from one diet to the next without long term consistency. This is very disturbing as many diets have little in common with each other. Thus the metabolism is forced into a very difficult situation to try and adapt continuously to different kinds of foods and preparations. This in itself is disruptive and in time will lower enzyme function and assimilation.

Not eating or eating very little in order to lose weight is also problematic for the Vata type and somewhat the Pitta type of person as well. Note that intelligent fasting is very beneficial to restore enzyme function, but used indiscriminately it will disrupt the metabolism to a point that it can be hard to restore proper function.

[35] Remember this is the principle of Agni in Ayurveda. Ayurveda is of the opinion that low or deranged Agni is behind all metabolic problems as it allows us to digest and assimilate our food. However, if the principle digestive Agni is disturbed then the other Agnis in the tissues and cells begin to break down, leading to chronic and major diseases.

The starve-binge syndrome is also extremely unbalancing to proper metabolic function. Or eating "organic", "natural" foods and then bingeing on tons of sweets is disrupting. That which brings regularity has nutritional benefit for the human body. What is irregular is disruptive to the human metabolism and ultimately the inherent intelligence of the body.

Ayurveda understands that there is an intelligent principle in the body that allows it to function in a state of health. On one hand disease can be viewed as a disruption of this intelligent principle.[36] When this happens then the whole metabolism begins to function in a haphazard manner. Often immune disorders and cancers are the result of this kind of dysfunction. The maintenance and integrity of your body's intelligence is of utmost importance for your long-term health.

Therefore, there are several things to keep in mind when choosing a diet plan. The first is to make sure that the diet can be used for long periods of time, like your whole life. This is the most important as it will tell you if the plan is based on good nutrition or a passing fad. There should be either a historical basis or at least a generation of use before you begin a diet. One of the popular diets right now in the United States and in the United Kingdom is that of using your blood type to determine your nutritional needs. This is a good example of a diet which has not been in use long enough to warrant the popularity of the system. Even if the system is working and has validity it should be studied for at least another generation – if not more – before being fully embraced by the masses. The Ayurvedic constitutional types are far more specific because they go beyond the general

---

[36] Intelligence exists in the human in conjunction with Prana. It is impossible to separate these two in both function and action. Prana relates directly to Vata and the five Vayus and disruptions of intelligence always involve an imbalance of Vata with time. However, as Prana is disturbed first the functions that it controls directly such as intellect (Budhi) and inspiration for life are affected first.

classifications of blood, race, hereditary, psychological conditioning and environment – yet all these are also included – not ignored.

Ayurveda is not a dogmatic system. It is based on a historical use for half the world over thousands of years. It is not about any culture or belief system. It is a science that has observed the functions of nature for millennia and knows the effects of mixing different diets and foods with different types of people. That is all. This book is not even about convincing you to try to eat in an Ayurvedic manner as that too would be manipulation of your intelligence, of your individuality. It is of utmost importance that each person consciously chooses a nutritional system that benefits them personally and with long term use makes one feel even better than ever.

Hence, one can say that a nutritional program should be one that also increases your intelligence and personal power. Taking pills to block fat or nutrients is not empowering. It is another method to escape taking control of your life and understanding why you have gotten into a situation. Ayurveda does recognize the need occasionally for people to use pills or medications to temporally regain their proper metabolic function, but any kind of dependency or prolonged use is far from empowering you to be a truly healthy human being.

High protein diets are quite popular with many women to lose weight; many Parisian women use this kind of diet. There is no doubt that this kind of diet does work to promote weight loss. However, it does this by actually starving the body. Protein is not a good fuel for the body. Protein is what is used to make structure in the tissues and cells. Hence, diets that are high in protein actually starve the body that begins to burn fat tissues (i.e., stored carbohydrates). Unfortunately, some protein is also used as fuel, which when burned, leaves toxic acids in the blood and plasma. These acids have a very negative effect on the pH of the body and the kidneys. This is not a healthy diet and I have had the difficult job of trying to restore proper digestive function to women after they have been on this diet for several months or even years.

Unfortunately, diets tend to victimize the participants and at the same time make them depend on some form of pill, supplement or even exotic Japanese plum. Ayurveda brings freedom from all forms of dogma associated with foods, nutrition and dietary programs. Educate yourself and question yourself if a program is really empowering you, educating you about your body and mind, or is it enslaving you to social conditions, high-tech products or evangelic type group meetings. Health is empowering – manipulations are not!

7
Food According to Your Metabolism

The case of Martha is a stunning example of how food affects your metabolism. Martha was a 42 year old Pitta/Kapha type of person when she came to see me several years ago. At that time she was seeing four different specialists for a combination of problems that had resulted in her taking constant medication. Her life had become a nightmare three years before when she began to get headaches, then mysteriously she began to have deep muscular pain. She was diagnosed as having a deep-tissue rheumatic condition that was classified as an autoimmune disease. Probably the most frightening for her was that her memory was leaving her at an alarming rate.

Additionally she began not to assimilate vitamin B-12 and needed weekly shots just to live her minimal existence that had become impaired to the extent that she could hardly see because of the pain in her head. She could no longer work, drive or do even minimal tasks around the house. The pain in her muscles required constant medication with anti-inflammatory drugs and she lived on over the counter pain killers for the headaches. Martha also had a long history of thyroid problems for which she had been seeing other specialists for many years. All of the drugs and stress of her present condition had also begun to cause a malfunction in the adrenal glands.

This was her state when she came – out of desperation – to see me. We changed her diet and I gave her herbs to restore digestive metabolism. The results were beyond what I had hoped for such a complicated array of problems. Her next visit four months later showed a reduction in headaches, muscle pain and in increase in memory function. When I questioned her I found that she had embraced all of the suggestions I have made for diet and had been taking the digestive herbs regularly. She was less depressive and her husband had noticed her to be less nervous and agitated. I saw her again six months after our first visit when she drove to the appointment!

She was feeling slowly better and better – no dramatic changes – but a slow regression of all the major problems she had been experiencing. After six months of dietary treatment she was taking pain killing only once per week instead of daily. Her daily headaches had reduced 80% in frequency and seldom required over the counter pain killers now. Her memory had improved dramatically and her doctors reported that for some "mysterious" reason her rheumatoid conditions were in regression.

Martha contributed 80% of the changes to diet and 20% or less to the herbs I had recommended she takes. She achieved almost instant results by eliminating coffee completely from her diet. The pain in both her head and muscles responded directly to no coffee intake. The elimination of all acidic foods and mucus or congestion provoking foods also gave a response in the first weeks of treatment.

I saw Martha one year after our first meeting and she was once more living a productive life. She was able to work again, to drive the car and function as a normal human being in her family. She religiously followed the diet for her constitution and continues to this day – three years later to improve. Not all of her problems vanished, the thyroid problem and the inability of her body to absorb vitamin B-12 are still being treated by her doctors. However, the autoimmune problem was reversed and her headaches almost completely disappeared. Her memory became normal again and she required no daily use of any drug for these problems. Martha had been told by all four of the specialists that her conditions were irreversible and that she would just have to live with them.

Martha's case is a powerful example of how a young woman in her forties did not accept the verdict of biochemical medicine but reversed her declining health mainly through nutritional changes. This illustrates that while diet may not cure all diseases it can cure or reverse many diseases – especially autoimmune disorders. Martha's case is not an isolated example. I have other similar cases in England and France. Martha happened to live in an almost pristine valley in Switzerland when I met her. Her environment was not a major factor in her disease – her diet was.

We have now become aware that each person has a different need of nutrients and a different capacity to absorb and assimilate those nutrients. A healthy food for one person can be a disease causing factor for another. Constitutional nutrition is based on this point of view. As the biochemical nutritional system does not have a working model for individual differences in humans we need to use an existing system with a long history of beneficial results. The Ayurvedic system fits this requirement in all respects. But in order to use the Ayurvedic system we need to look at food and food classifications differently than we are used to in the biochemical nutritional model.

First, we must begin to view foods not as separate categories per se. Instead we need to shift our point of view to seeing food according to the person who is going to eat it. This requires a paradigm shift in the way we normally look at food. The prime difference is looking at food according to the metabolism of the person rather than according to the nutrient content in the food or broad food groups.

Instead of saying, "Eat an apple a day because it has vitamin X", the new viewpoint is, "What shall I eat today to keep my metabolism in balance." This is an individualistic approach that requires the person to have a minimum understanding and responsibility for their own health.

It should be clearly understood that people using constitutional nutrition are doing so because they want to take control over their life and health. If this is not your desire or goal, then please give this book to someone who does want to take power over their health and life. If you are interested in blaming people or circumstances, or in giving your responsibility for your health to other people then it is best for you to use the old, outdated, biochemical model of nutrition, which requires that you surrender your experience, observations and intimately, your personal power.

Ayurveda is a patient friendly system that not only encourages participation – it demands it. Only you are capable of restoring your own health because it is you who is lifting your hand to your mouth and putting in the basic supply of health (food) into your body. No one is force feeding you food. True, we are all being force fed food advertising, but we can choose to accept it or not.

Eat According to Your Metabolic Capacity

The first thing in actually choosing food is to understand the basic foods that agree or disagree with your metabolism. Generally, the Vata type of person will have a variable digestive capacity. This means that foods that are concentrated and hard to digest should be avoided or taken in small amounts. The Vata type is also sensitive to gas forming foods and foods that deplete the moisture content in the body. The astringency of some foods has a drying effect on the tissues and can deplete moisture content in tissues. The Vata type is the most prone to have food allergies due to their variable enzyme function. These people tend to binge and have both a variable appetite and digestion. Hence, they should consume food in moderate amounts and at regular intervals.

In the table below a summery is given on the effects of food groups on the Vata type of person. This is a general guide to show how groups of foods affect these people. Foods listed in the "Best" column indicate foods that have the greatest balancing, or nourishing action for the Vata type of person. The "Worst" column indicates foods that are very aggravating and potentially disease forming if consumed daily according to Ayurveda. You will notice that there are not really any foods in the 100% column. This is because it is possible to over eat or abuse any food. Health lies in-between the extremes. The same is true for the 0% column. No food is totally bad or without some nutritious, healing qualities. In-between the "Best" and "Worst" are indications for the frequency of those groups consumption. This means a food listed in the occasional column means no more than a consumption of 40%, the "Rarely" column at a 20% maximum consumption. The foods are grouped according to their general action on the metabolism of the Vata type and judge nutritional value accordingly.

Summary of Vata Type Food Groups

TYPE OF FOOD	Effect of food on constitution					
Percentage	100%	80%	60%	40%	20%	0%
	Best	Medium	Mixed	Sometimes	Rarely	Worst
Fruits			X			
Vegetables			X			
Grains		X				
Beans					X	
Nuts & Seeds		X				
Dairy		X				
Oils		X				
Animal Products			X			
Sweeteners			X			
Spices		X				
Beverages		X				
Vitamins & Minerals				X		

The Pitta type has the strongest digestive capacity and can digest most any food, junk food, or chemical food (soft drinks) for years without a hint of a problem. Around 37, give or take a few years, this begins to change. The Pitta type is the most sensitive to sour and acidic foods that increase the pH balance of the body. They also may be attracted to hot spices, but these also pose problems in the long run. These kinds of foods tend to increase the bile production in the liver and pancreas which increases the acidic nature of both blood and plasma. Human cells are very sensitive to the pH level of the body and high acidity ages cells or breaks down their normal metabolic function.

The Pitta type has the strongest enzyme capacity unless too many spicy or acidic foods are eaten. These people have the greatest capacity for both the variety and quantity of food.

In the table below a summery is given on the effects of food groups on the Pitta type of person. This is a general guide to show how groups of foods affect these people. The foods are grouped according to their general action on the metabolism of the Pitta type of person and judge nutritional value accordingly.

Summary of Pita Type Food Groups

TYPE OF FOOD	Effect of food on constitution					
Percentage	100%	80%	60%	40%	20%	0%
	Best	Medium	Mixed	Sometimes	Rarely	Worst
Fruits		X				
Vegetables		X				
Grains		X				
Beans			X			
Nuts & Seeds				X		
Dairy		X				
Oils					X	
Animal Products					X	
Sweeteners		X				
Spices					X	
Beverages		X				
Vitamins & Minerals				X		

The Kapha type of person has the slowest digestive function. These people will be the most prone to weight gain and obesity due to the slower rate of metabolism. They will have to pay the closest attention to the quantities of food consumed and will have the most restrictive diet accordingly. They are the most sensitive to carbohydrates especially in simple sugars, yet all excess tends to clog and further slow down the transformation of food. Dairy products due to their mucus forming properties and congestive qualities can also trouble them. The enzyme function of these people is lower than the other types, but is consistent. Hence, they can have stronger digestive power than the fluctuating Vata type. The Kapha type has the most restrictive diet in both quantity and variety of foods.

In the table below a summery is given on the effects of food groups on the Kapha type. This is a general guide to show how groups of foods affect these people. The foods are grouped according to their general action on the metabolism of the Kapha type of person and judge nutritional value accordingly.

Summary of Kapha Type Food Groups

TYPE OF FOOD	Effect of food on constitution					
Percentage	100%	80%	60%	40%	20%	0%
	Best	Medium	Mixed	Sometimes	Rarely	Worst
Fruits			X			
Vegetables		X				
Grains			X			
Beans		X				
Nuts & Seeds				X		
Dairy					X	
Oils					X	
Animal Products					X	
Sweeteners						X
Spices	X					
Beverages				X		
Vitamins & Minerals					X	

The above information gives the general metabolic capacity for each of the three main types of people. Dual or mixed types should be put together. Generally dual types will tend to have some of both types and not have any clear-cut distinction between the two The traditional way Ayurveda worked with these types was to have them change the kinds of foods they eat according to the seasonal changes in year. In chapter 16 clear information will be given for dual types trying to follow a yearly plan.

Raw vs. Cooked / Liquid vs. Whole Foods

Before looking at different food categories and how they affect each type of person we must look at the form the food is in, i.e., cooked or raw; liquid or solid. Each different state of the foods has different actions on the metabolism of each type. This means that a banana milk-shake will have different effects on each of the three types. So the final question will not be the milk-shake, it will be the person receiving the drink into their body. Nevertheless, the form of the food has effects for all types.

The basic rule is that raw foods are more difficult to digest than cooked foods. The process of cooking acts like a form of pre-digestion in that it makes the food easier to be broken down in the stomach. Juicing foods – fruits or vegetables – also helps to make them easier to digest than just raw. Cooked food is considered to the best way to take food in the long term for all constitutions. Here are some of the actions – pro and con – for each preparation.

Raw Foods – Raw fruits are best for the Vata and Pitta types of people. Fruits commonly have a cooling (lowering internal body heat) and cleansing action, which is best suited for the hotter Pitta type. The Pitta type cannot eat only raw fruits in the morning for breakfast or they will tend to become irritable or have too much acidity in the digestive system. The moistening action of fruits makes them good for the Vata type – who tends to be dry – and not for the Kapha who tends to be too watery or congestive. However, the Vata type can become too light, or undernourished from large amounts of fruit. They do better with cooked fruit for long-term, or daily, consumption. The Kapha type will do well with certain fruits in the late morning if breakfast is missed. If the same fruits are taken at other times of the day they can cause the body to retain weight in the form of water. However, unless in excess fruit will generally help the Kapha type by its cleansing action.

Raw vegetables can be taken best by the Pitta type who has the strongest digestive powers. The Kapha type has the second greatest capacity to handle raw vegetables and the Vata type the least. In general the Vata type should avoid all raw foods unless they are antidoted with spice, sauces or oil. The concept of antidoting food is new and will be discussed a little later in the book. It is worth noting that most foods can be consumed by anyone if the foods or spices that antidote them are known. The Kapha type can eat raw vegetables in the late spring and summer, but should avoid eating them in the fall, winter and early spring. Even the Pitta type – who has the greatest capacity for raw foods – should avoid them in the late fall and winter.

Ayurveda states that raw foods require more metabolic energy and body heat to digest. Hence, people living in cold countries should eat less raw things – especially in the cold seasons. However, people living in warm climates can eat more raw foods – possibly year round. The exception to this is for the Vata type of person. They should not eat the majority of their foods in a raw form even in the tropics or they can become ungrounded and "spaced-out". The point here is to adjust the intake of raw foods to the warmer and dryer months of the year.

Nuts, seeds and oils should be taken raw and not cooked. Although nuts and seeds are often hard to digestion, as they have more concentrated forms of proteins than other plant foods, they are still quite good for the Vata type, less so for the Pitta type, and almost never for the slow and congestive Kapha types. Oils vary from type to type, but tend to be slightly warming. They are best for the Vata type and can make problems for either of the other two types. The main point is the oils must be taken in a raw from and never extracted by heat or chemical; see the section on oil in chapter 8 for a full explanation.

Other foods should generally not be taken in a raw form. Dairy products can be taken in a raw form. Meat is not to be taken raw nor is seafood generally; see the following sections on these foods for explanation. However, the Pitta type has the greatest capacity to digest any kind of raw food and the Vata the least; the Kapha type falls in-between.

Cooked Food – Ayurveda says that cooked food is good for everyone as it is the easiest to digest and assimilate. There are no real contra-indications on eating cooked food for any of the types. The Vata type does better on cooked fruit than on raw fruit. Cooking itself is a kind of antidote as it changes the quality of many foods that would be uneatable otherwise. Some foods are not good to heat or cook. One of the most important in this respect is honey. When heated the enzyme structure is changed and the normally healthy honey becomes poison. Oils also fall into this category; they are best raw and should not be heated in the extraction process or used in cooking.

While some people point out that cooking the food eliminates some vitamin and nutrient content Ayurveda states that cooking still is better. This is because the cooking generally allows whatever nutrients are left to be absorbed quite easily. They say that if the food is not cooked the same amount or less of nutrients is absorbed because of the extra work expended by the body to digest it. And the body is often unable to break down a food as completely as cooking it – thus releasing more nutrients. There are two important factors in this – one is to not overcook food or cook it with very high levels of heat. The other point is to adjust everything to your individual capacity of digestion. Steaming food is often sufficient enough to make the food more usable by the digestive enzymes, acids and bile.

Liquid Foods – Almost anything can be put in the blender and turned into a drink or juice. While it is very popular in many diets to only take raw or slightly cooked foods in a liquid form it is problematic over long term use according to Ayurveda. The human colon needs solid matter in it to maintain its tone, if long periods of liquid foods are taken the colon will begin to prolapse. Fiber is important for a number of reasons and one of them is to maintain the tone and strength of the colon and lower body. According to Ayurveda the colon is also a major site of nutrient absorption. A liquid diet does not allow the colon time to fully absorb the available nutrients before elimination. Another problem with liquids is that they can actually diminish the digestive capacity through lower enzyme function.[37]

Nevertheless, a period of liquid diets can help any of the constitutions at times. Liquid diets are generally cleansing to the digestive system and can be of great benefit to any type of person for this purpose. The Kapha type usually does very well on vegetable juice fasts one day a week or for several days a month. This has the effect to increase the enzyme function if done correctly and according to individual capacity. However, fruit juices have the potential to aggravate the Kapha type by their cooling and moist properties. The Pitta type does well with either fruits or vegetables and can do liquid diets twice a month for a day each time. The Vata type does better with a mix of liquid foods and solid foods during the day. For example, a solid lunch and a liquid breakfast and dinner will be far better for a Vata than a total liquid diet. Both the Vata and Kapha types need to have some spices added to liquid diets to antidote them. Once more, it is important to avoid this kind of diet in the cold times of the year, as the liquids are normally drunk cool or at room temperature – never take beverages ice cold.

[37] It is known in Ayurveda that long periods on a liquid diet will generally put out the digestive fire, Agni. This is very much a problem for Kapha as they generally have low Agni to begin with, and for Vata who may or may not be able to keep the fire going with their variable Agni. It is better for these types to avoid liquid diets for more than a day or two without guidance.

Solid Foods – Solid foods should form the basis of everyone's diet. Without solid food the digestive organs can collapse. In Yoga there are special exercises to prevent this from happening if the Yogi wants to eat a purely fruit or liquid diet. However, this requires special training and is not applicable to most people. For the average person cooked food is a necessary part of life. The following chapter gives specific information on actual foods now that we have seen the general effects on the different constitutions.

8
Descriptions of Food Groups

The following descriptions give an idea about different foods in general. Use the charts in chapter 15 to find out exactly which foods are more specifically beneficial for you. Remember to use the lists as starting points and adjust the foods according to your own experience and to your unique constitutional make up – including any allergies or genetic tendencies.

The six primary combinations that were discussed in chapter Three describe how food affects the body in Ayurveda. Foods are also described according to their effect to warm or cool internal body heat. For example, black pepper warms up the body very quickly and an apple cools it down. Also within each food group there are foods that are more or less heating or cooling than others. The food lists in chapter 15 are arranged according to these traditional distinctions.

Fruits

Fruits are generally good for all types in moderation and they are mildest in action. They are best suited to the Pitta type, second to the Vata type and third to the Kapha type. Fruits are the lightest food group and digest the fastest. Therefore, they should be eaten alone or before other foods. If they are combined with other foods they tend to ferment in the stomach and cause bloating and gas. Some sweeter fruits like apples can be mixed with yogurt or milk, but sweet fruits in general do not combine well with other foods. Sour tasting fruits can be mixed on occasion in small amounts with grains, but this too is risky if a person does not have enough information.

Fruits are best fresh, sweet and ripe for Pitta types who should avoid very sour fruits. The Kapha type can take fruits that are mildly sweet or sour. However, either very sweet or very sour fruits will aggravate them. Additionally, fruits that are high in water content should be avoided as they tend to increase body weight for Kapha people if eaten in too great a quantity. Eating dried fruits avoids this problem and the Kapha person can often substitute fresh fruit for dried fruit. The Vata type does well on sweet and sour fruits provided they can digest them. Often the Vata type will have low enzyme function and fruits will cause gas and bloating. Cooked fruits are good for all constitutions but especially so for Vata types. They should take fruits in small amounts and avoid dry fruits.

As mentioned before a diet consisting of mainly fruits will tend to unbalance the Vata type of person and is best suited for the Pitta type. Yet this kind of diet will not provide enough mass or bulk for the body if the person is living in urban areas and /or doing much physical labor. This kind of diet is also not very good for mental labor and is not stimulating to the mind or intellect. A diet based mainly on fruit is also not suited for cooler climates and should be avoided in the winter by all constitutions. Fruits should be eaten when they are in season and ripe, not at other times as they tend to promote poor digestion that then results in undigested foods accumulating in the colon. In this respect the idea that one needs to eat fruit every day is false if that fruit is not in season. This is an example of looking at foods by groups – as in the mythical "four food groups" that we were brainwashed with as children – or using foods according to your constitution and environment.

Generally all fruits can be antidoted by either cooking them or using warm, sweet spices like cinnamon, cardamom, nutmeg or ginger root. All constitutions should only eat fruit in season, but can eat them regularly. The amount of fruit consumed and the preparation is what changes for each constitutional type. Sour fruits are better to eat in the morning and sweet fruits are better to eat in the afternoon. Fruit should never be eaten after meals in any circumstance by any constitution.

Fruits have a lightening and cleansing action on the body and can promote a detoxifying effect in the body provided the fruit is ripe and chemical free. Beware that most fruit in the United States is heavily sprayed with chemicals – frequently over a hundred different kinds of chemicals – this eliminates the benefic action of removing toxins from the body. For any kind of fasting or cleansing diet organic fruit must be used. Studies have shown that 44% of produce has pesticide residue and that 42% have more than one kind of pesticide.[38] Many of these chemicals are carcinogenic in clinical tests.

There is one reoccurring theme in this book – the quality of foods and how they are prepared before we buy them. When we consider that an apple often contains the residue of 110 different pesticides it adds a new meaning to the old axiom, "an apple a day keeps the doctor away".[39] In fact, today an apple a day could put you in the hospital or deform your children or your grandchildren. Chapter 10 will go into more detail on this subject. It is not a laughing matter, however, but one of grave concern. Few of us are really aware of the vast quantities of poisons that are left on our food before we eat them. Fruits represent a special danger in that they are often eaten raw. The wax that is used to preserve and present a shiny product also binds the pesticides into

---

[38] Murray, Micheal T., 1993, p. 26.

[39] Quillin, P., 1990.

the fruit and prevents them from being washed off with water.

The importance of eating organic fruits cannot be stressed enough. The chemicals used in modern agriculture are ones that do not break down easily and very often remain in your body for the duration of your life. The argument that has been used for the last several generations was that the amount of chemicals stored was too small to pose a problem. This has turned out to be a wrong theory. While it may have some relevance in the formation of cancer it has been proven to be wrong in relation to endocrine and nervous function.[40] There is now ample proof that small amounts of certain chemicals can be more dangerous than large amounts.

Nothing is better than fruits eaten in season and grown organically. Although, taken in any other way they may be acting as agents of disease or metabolic disturbance. This point is true for all foods, but especially relevant for foods that we eat raw.

Vegetables

Vegetables are good for all constitutions and are also mild in action, though less so than fruits. Vegetables combine well with all the food groups (except fruit) and so can be used in a variety of ways in meals. Vegetables tend to be more complex in their composition and so make for a very balanced action in the body. This same complexity gives a broad range of nutrients – many of which are still unknown to modern biochemical nutrition.

Vegetables come in different groups – roots, green vegetables, nightshades (potato, tomato, eggplant and bell peppers), and pungent vegetables. The cabbage family (cabbage, broccoli, cauliflower, Brussels sprouts, kohlrabi and kale) falls under the green vegetable category. Each of these

---

[40] Colborn, Theo et al, 1996, Ch. 7 & 10.

groups has a different effect on the body and with the different constitutional types.

Root vegetables are the most nutritious of the four kinds, followed by green vegetables and nightshades. Pungent vegetables are the least nourishing to tissues, but have many other properties. Often pungent vegetables act as catalysts for different actions in the body. While green leafy vegetables may have less ability to nourish body weight and mass as roots can they provide a large array of vitamins and minerals. Hence, a balanced diet for all constitutions should include a variety of all of these forms. Root vegetables should be well cooked before eaten and are good to use in soups and oven baked dishes. Leafy green vegetables can be steamed or lightly sautéd in ghee or oil. Some of them can be eaten raw in salads such as the many different kinds of lettuce. Nightshades and pungent vegetables should be cooked although the Kapha type can benefit from eating small amounts of raw, pungent vegetables before or during meals.

Vegetables should form the basis of everyone's diet along with grains and cereals. Many vegetables have shown themselves to be anti-carcinogenic and to help actually repair the natural functions of the body. This is because each kind of vegetable is functioning in a complex manner and as a whole. It is erroneous to try and separate out different chemicals from a vegetable and say that this chemical "Z" is the responsible agent behind the anti-carcinogenic (or whatever) action of the plant. As long as nutritionists and doctors approach food in this way they will never understand what is actually happening.

The total action and relationship of all of the components of vegetables are responsible for the health giving benefits of any plant. The reality is that there may not be any rational mechanical explanation of this process. The health giving and protective qualities of plants may be closer to a quantum model of physics than a mechanical model of physics.

However, this is frightening as people want to have some kind of linear concept of the physical functions of the body. Eat vitamin "X" and you will not get disease "Y". This is not possible according to Ayurveda who views life as a dynamic force that "moves" in often unpredictable ways and is affected by the involvement of the environment and the observer or person eating. In this sense the quantum model of non-linear movements is closer to the Ayurvedic understanding of nutrition.

If we adapt a more multi-dimensional view of eating and consuming vegetables we find that things like the freshness and preparation of the foods is of utmost importance. Using the mechanical model of viewing vegetables we can eat canned, frozen or microwaved foods and view them as being the same as steaming fresh vegetables. In fact, there is no substitute for fresh cooked vegetables in the human diet. The fact that this single item has been disappearing from the American diet over the last seventy years is perhaps one of the reasons why one in five people now have some form of cancer.

The Vata type of person can have problems with certain vegetables. The nightshade family can pose problems for the Vata type particularly if they are suffering from Vata type diseases like arthritis. Other vegetables that can pose problems are very astringent plants like the cabbage family. This whole family can cause gas or bloating for the Vata type of person. They can be prepared best by cooking and spicing them to reduce their gas forming qualities. As this family has many beneficial effects on the body it is good to learn how to cook them correctly so that they do not disturb the Vata person. Thus, the Vata type may have less choice or have to consume less quantity of vegetables than the other two types of persons.

The Pitta type of person do very well with all kinds of vegetables, but can have problems with the nightshade group (tomatoes, potatoes, eggplant and bell peppers). This is due to the acidic nature of the nightshades. If someone is having problems with food sensitivities then start by eliminating the nightshades. Other foods that are problematic are very pungent vegetables like garlic and onions.

No doubt garlic has many medicinal qualities. However, it is wrong to assume that garlic – or any other substance – is good for everyone across the board. I frequently come across statements exalting the benefits of garlic. While these claims are usually true garlic can be very disturbing to Pitta types. If a Pitta type has any kind of skin inflammation, ulcers or internal burning sensations then garlic should not be taken at all. All hot spicy foods are aggravating to the Pitta type and should be taken in small amounts or not at all. The over use of these foods can cause an imbalance in the pH of the blood and disturb both liver and gall bladder functions.[41] Therefore, more mild, bland and astringent vegetables are better for the Pitta type.

The Kapha type also does well on vegetables and actually has the greatest freedom to eat the full variety of vegetables of the three types. All of the vegetable groups are good for the Kapha type and a person can adjust according to their personal tastes or sensitivities. The primary rule for the Kapha type is the same in all food categories – eat in moderation.

Grains

Grains along with vegetables should form the basis of everyone's diet. Each constitution will have to use the grains that are best suited to them. Whole grains are gaining popularity in recent years with biochemical nutritionists because they are finding out how important they are for health. There is a huge difference between whole grains

[41] According to Ayurveda overuse of spices by the Pitta type will cause a kind of toxin to develop in the intestines which will – in time – move into the blood. This Pitta/ama can cause a number of diseases including the aggravation of the other doshas (principles).

and the normal preparation of wheat, corn and other grains that we commonly get today. The refining of flour for example removes all of the portions that have nutrients in them – the life. The large food companies found this out earlier in this century when they first began to introduce white flour in the market. Many people began to be deficient from the lack of B vitamins that were normally found in whole-wheat flour. This prompted the government to require that white flour be "enriched" with vitamins and nutrients. The only reason wheat flour needs to be "enriched" is because it is now dead from the processing procedure that makes it last an almost indefinite time on the supermarket shelves.

If you are using any kind of refined cereal or grain then you will not benefit from the nutrients normally found in that grain. It must be understood that refining has a monetary reason behind it and not your health. Whole grain flour lasts a very short time before it begins to rot. You should understand that if something is NOT rotting it is because it is not alive or it has been treated with enough chemicals to preserve an elephant. If you want to eat a diet based on plant foods it is imperative that you eat whole grains and not refined grains – the failure to do this will be that you will end up with some form of malnutrition. If you are eating meats or other animal products then this becomes less critical, but still important.

However, if you are eating animal products you should know that the use of refined grains with meat is responsible for many modern diseases like cancer of the colon, diverticulitis, colic and many others. The refined grains coat the intestinal walls with a glue-like substance that prevents correct absorption. When this is combined with meat and the high fat content in animal products it makes an environment perfect for the breading of disease, clogging or congesting the channels or arteries, increasing blood pressure and contributing to the formation of cancerous cells in the body. In short, you may be getting enough nutrients to live but this combination is a recipe for chronic health problems.

Grains in general are a very balancing food and are good for all constitutions in moderation. The Kapha type can be affected from the overuse of grains, but rarely the other two types. The more building or strengthening a grain is the better it is for the Vata type and to some extent for the Pitta type too. But, any very building or strengthening grain will be aggravating to the Kapha type. Wheat falls into this category as does brown rice. This same distinction is true for the warming and cooling effects of the grains also. Some grains have a diuretic action and so are better suited for the Kapha type as they help to remove excess water from the body and tissues. It is important to understand that using a grain that is not really indicated for your type is far less damaging than using other kinds for foods that are listed as disturbing your constitution.

Some people have allergies to certain grains – especially wheat. There are several interesting reasons for this, and several possible solutions. Wheat allergies have been traced to the early eating habits of babies when their mothers gave them wheat before six months or even twelve months of age. For new or expecting mothers one should know that giving a child dairy or grains before six months of age can cause allergies later in life. This is because the baby does not yet have the enzymes necessary to digest these kinds of foods. I advise my clients not to feed their babies dairy, most grains (rice is ok), and meat (if they eat it) before one year of age. Fruit, vegetables and mothers milk are more than enough for a child under the age of a year.

Another cause is that children were not nursed or nursed for too short of a time. I am of the opinion that 12 to 24 months is the average time to nurse a child. Unfortunately, the majority of mothers in the USA have high levels of DDT,

PCB's and other poisons that are consumed in animal fats. Interestingly only 8% of mothers who are vegetarians have the same levels of these poisons in their milk. What the effect of these poisons will be in relation to enzyme function and normal growth is not yet known for our future generations.

However, people who do have allergies to wheat can be cured of them by increasing enzyme function in the intestine and by following a re-education program to change previous habits of digestion. This process is individual and should be structured and advised by an Ayurvedic practitioner. It is also interesting to note that people switching to whole grains from refined grains often find their allergies disappearing altogether. Whole grains are whole foods and so have a broad action on the body, one of which is to clean out the intestines from build up of undigested foods.

Grains can be taken in the form of breads and pasta very effectively. People who are sensitive to yeast or candida should not take yeast breads, but use instead sourdough breads. Pasta made from refined white flour should be thrown out the window as it will not provide you with any of the benefits of whole grains. However, there are many good types of pasta made from whole grains or whole grain combinations. These are very beneficial and are an easy way to get whole grains without having to eat brown rice or other longer to prepare dishes. Also pasta made with eggs can be problematic for some people, it is not a necessary ingredient and so can be left out.

Beans (Legumes)

Beans are a good staple food if prepared correctly. They are disturbing to Vata types and are mostly contraindicated for these people. They are the best for Kapha types for whom they have many beneficial qualities. The Pitta types fall in-between these two. In general, beans make a good source of building, nourishing food when taken in small amounts and when mixed with whole grains.

According to Ayurveda there is one bean that is considered to be the most nutritious and easiest to digest – the mung or moong bean. This bean is small and green in color and can be purchased in a split form (called dal) which is even easier to digest than the whole form. This is staple food in Asia and India and is the bean used to make oriental bean sprouts. In Ayurveda this bean is mixed in equal parts with white basmati rice to form the simplest yet nourishing food – kicharee. This mix – which looks like a kind of gruel – is given to people recovering from illness or those just breaking fasts. It is also a balanced staple food for all constitutions.

A good way to benefit from soy – which is hard to digest – is to use soy products. There is a kind of movement – especially for women – to use a soy product, such as tofu, every day. This can be very disturbing for the Vata type of people. The Vata type people do better with tofu and soymilk than pure soybeans, but still find them difficult to digest. If they are taken once to three times a week in preparations Vata types usually will not have problems. My professional experience (and personal as I am a Vata/Pitta type) is that taken regularly in small amounts they are a good food. For regular use though Vata types will do much better with mung beans than soy. Some Vata types do better with Adzuki beans than either soy or mung.

Tofu and soy products are very good for the warmer Pitta type of person as soy is cooling in nature. The Pitta type also has enough digestive capacity to process the dense soy products. They can eat these products daily if they wish. The Kapha type may find that soy products are congestive to some extent; they can actually do better with the beans themselves. All beans tend to be good for the Kapha type as they are astringent and most are diuretic in property – thus helping to prevent water accumulation in the tissues. Soymilk is an excellent substitute for cow milk for the Kapha type of person. In this light soymilk is a good milk substitute for all constitutions although the Vata type may do better with rice milk or almond milk.

It is very important that all beans be cooked with an antidote to balance out their problematic qualities. The main substance used to antidote is spice. These include the following: onions, cumin, asafoetida, cayenne pepper, black pepper and salt to some degree. Asafoetida is the best spice to use to counter the gas forming action of beans. It smells a bit like rotten eggs, but loses this smell and taste when it is cooked with beans.

Beans need to be very well cooked. One other method to reduce their irritating action is to soak them over night and throw away the water the next morning before cooking. Additionally, while cooking throw away the water – you can throw away the water several times; each time replacing it with clean water. This reduces the gas forming qualities of any bean. Still another method is to cook them with hard forms of dried seaweed which also have some balancing effects. Care should be given to the source and quality of the seaweed however – see the section on seafood below for more information on this aspect.

Nuts and Seeds

Nuts are a good source of plant proteins and fat. They are an important food and can be prepared in a number of ways. They are a little heavy to digest and so should not be taken in large amounts. They are best for the Vata type of person and lest beneficial for the Kapha type of person. The Pitta type falls in-between these two. The oil in nuts can disturb the Pitta and Kapha types, while the Vata type is benefited by oil – provided they can digest it.

Seeds are lighter to digest provided they are ground or very well chewed. Some small seeds like sesame are very difficult to chew and often pass through the whole digestive tract undigested. They can even cause gripping or colic pain due to their roughness. Hence, small seeds, like sesame, are better taken in butters (tahini) or in oils. In general, all seeds and nuts need to be chewed very well to prevent problems of digestion and to aid good absorption.

The preparation of nuts is very important as it changes their effect on the different constitutions. Today, one needs to be especially alert when buying nuts or seeds as it has been estimated that most are rancid. From the biochemical point of view this is caused by free radicals oxidizing the oil in the nut or seed. This creates a bad effect in the human body and can actually contribute to the disease process. Hence, the Ayurvedic guideline is that one should eat fresh foods. This needs clarification as fresh nuts and seeds have valuable disease preventing attributes.

Lightly roasting nuts and seeds makes them easier to digest and it releases more nutrients, it also helps to preserve them longer. Overcooking them as in full roasted nuts brings out more oil and damages the oil itself (see oil section below). This also tends to make them very aggravating to the Kapha type of person who is, by nature, sensitive to oil and fat. Taking them raw is better for the Pitta and Kapha types, but the problem of putrefaction is a draw back. Vacuum-sealed packages are better but do not retard the oxidation of the oils in nuts or seeds. Normal plastic bags are the worst choice to buy them in, while nuts and seeds in their shell is the best choice as they can last up to a year in this manner. Probably the best is to not eat them at all if the quality and freshness cannot be determined.

This would be a great loss however, as they are valuable source of many vitamins, minerals and omega "what-do-you-call-it". It is unfortunate that I feel the need to add the positive qualities from a biochemical point of view – even when I know this view to be very narrow and inherently limited in scope. However, I am aware of our social conditioning that immediately thinks differently about nuts and seeds if someone says, "They are high in omega-3 fatty acids, increase the production of prostaglandins, prevent many diseases by increasing immune function and by regulating brain and nervous function." While these statements are true for most nuts and seeds from a biochemical view they limit the quantum paradigm of the total inter-relationship of a fresh food to the intelligent organism as a whole. The real effect of nuts and seeds on the body and mind is far greater according to Ayurveda.

Traditionally, Ayurveda considered nuts and seeds to be able to rejuvenate the whole body and to support the mind through increasing function and memory. Nuts and seeds are used in many medical preparations to help convalescing people recover their strength and for older people to prevent degeneration. It should be noted that both nuts and seeds were thought to be extremely powerful as a food source and were taken in small amounts daily. Eating large amounts is considered to be potentially harmful to the body and can cause weight gain and congestion – especially for the Kapha type of person.

Once more it is necessary to point out that nuts and seeds are the final product of the reproductive action of plants and trees. This makes them a powerful food, but also makes them susceptible to pesticide accumulation. Agrochemicals tend to accumulate in both nuts and seeds and can render them potentially harmful to people. Therefore, it is necessary to buy them from an organic source or not at all. Often using the oil of seeds and nuts can be the easiest way to receive their benefits (see the oil section).

Dairy Products

There is a major conflict around the use of dairy products for people today. Traditionally Ayurveda enjoyed the use of dairy and noted many benefits from the *moderate* use of milk and milk products. Unfortunately, today we no longer have the same kind of dairy products that were available in the past. Our dairy products are nothing short of poison unless a person is buying certified raw organic milk, or its by-products.

While this may seem like a strong statement – that modern diary products are poison – it is backed up by substantial evidence from the biochemical research community. It is also very strongly supported by traditional Ayurvedic precepts. An example of this happened just recently when one of my teachers from India stayed with me in Paris. My wife served him a glass of warm milk. He was very excited and happy as he said that this was the first milk he had tasted outside of his hometown that was not poison – in other words – it was real milk. The milk we served him was delivered the day before by the farmer in as certified raw milk and was given by cows that were not feed hormones, antibiotics or other chemicals in their foods nor by injection.

People are not generally aware in the United States that the milk and dairy products they consume are illegal in almost all other parts of the world. The primary reason for this is the massive and widespread use of hormones in animal feed and through, often daily, injections. Research scientists in other countries are very concerned by this habit to promote extra weight gain and milk production in cows. The reality is that the effects of this procedure are unknown. The facts are clearly pointing to major endocrineal disruptions in the consumers of such products – often after the second or third generations.

This situation is not new. The European Community has outlawed all meat and dairy products coming from the United States that contain hormones for the last ten years. Additionally, in Europe, all the meat that was tested as hormone free did, in fact, contain large amounts of hormones and even hormone products that are illegal in the USA. This has lead to a complete ban on all beef exported from the USA.[42] The only reason that this practice exists is

[42] James, Barry, *IHT*, May 13, 1999.

to increase profit of the framers and the pharmaceutical companies. The Beef and Dairy lobbies are shouting unfair trade and have the World Trade Organization (as well as the US government) pushing for millions of people who do not want hormones in their food to have them.

This is a serious matter as the United States dairy and beef communities have never studied the effects on humans of using these growth hormones in our food sources. On the other side there have been numerous studies that show the effects of these estrogen-like hormones on developing boys and the increase of un-descended testicles. And perhaps the most frightening fact is the huge number of women suffering from breast cancer and other tumors that are clearly estrogen dependent. This may cause one to question why the United States has the highest rate of breast cancer in the world. Researchers in both the United States and Europe point out that American children and adolescents are receiving as much as hundred times the amount allowed of estrogen by the US government.[43]

This is a very serious problem that has only one cause – greed. Are the profits of the Beef and Dairy industry worth the life or your children or grandchildren – or even your great grandchildren? This is a horrible practice that should be stopped by consumers uniting and boycotting all animal products that contain hormones. No other major country in the world is using hormones in this manner and there is no need to continue doing it at the risk of breast cancer and the deformation of your son's testicles and his ability to reproduce.

Another problem with dairy is the use of antibiotics in animal feed. It is now a major concern worldwide that virus, bacteria, and parasites are all growing more and more resistant to antibiotics. This poses a huge problem for doctors

---

[43] James, Barry, *IHT*, May 13, 1999, and Colborn Theo, et al, 1996.

as there are not many things left in which to combat infectious diseases. Some researchers state that there are now bacteria proliferating in the "disinfectant soap" trays in hospitals. This may present a situation for super strands of viruses and bacteria to grow which are completely immune to antibiotics. Some researchers fear mass epidemics on huge scales because of the abuse of antibiotics in food and medicine.

There is a primary way to prevent this from happening to you and your family – stop consuming animal products that have been fed antibiotics in their food. Simply break out of the chain of events. By not consuming second generation antibiotics you will have a much better change to respond to them when and if needed. Antibiotics are meant to be used to save lives in extremely grave circumstances. The wonton use – such as in France where the doctors give antibiotics to "prevent infection" when one has a cold (caused by a virus which does not respond to antibiotics anyway) – of these drugs will definitely cause major health problems for all of the Western cultures that rely on them. I often wonder why medical doctors in France go to school for six years, have an internship for two years, only to ask you what is wrong with you (diagnosis seems to have been left out of the curriculum) and then prescribe the same antibiotic regardless of your problem. It should be supposed that this would happen in the country that consumes more pharmaceutical products per capita than any country in the world. Unfortunately, this same scenario is ramped in all industrialized Western countries and is not limited to France.

So in returning to dairy products no discriminating individual can recommend them as a source of nutrition in the United States. The exception is certified organic products which will benefit the Vata and Pitta type the most and should generally be avoided by the Kapha types altogether. Milk should never be taken cold, it should always be taken warm and if it was not part or your childhood foods it can be mixed with cardamom and cinnamon to increase its assimilation, or avoided altogether. It is a good idea for Vata types to mix the above spices in milk as it always will benefit them. If milk is taken cold it is very mucus forming and it suppresses the digestive enzymes that normally can digest it. This is one of the main reasons why many people are lactose sensitive as they either have in the past, or in the present, consumed milk in an improper manner.

Milk should not be pasteurized or homogenized as this renders the milk into a form which the body cannot digest. Hence, it turns to poison in the body and creates toxins. The long conservation milk is dead (as described with any food that does not deteriorate in a normal time). Low-Fat products of all kinds are to be avoided like the plague. I know that this is surprising after hearing for the last twenty years that they are healthy. Tragically, research in Switzerland (and perhaps in other places I am not aware of) has shown that low-fat dairy products are supporting a carcinogenic environment in the body and directly precipitate pre-cancerous conditions. No one at this point is sure why this is happening in the biochemical world, but in Ayurveda this process renders the dairy product indigestible which makes it into a burden on the immunity and elimination systems. If you wish to reduce the fat content in your dairy product simple mix it with water. This effectively cuts the fat in half without creating more problems. This is easy with milk, yogurt, sour cream and other soft or liquid products – cheese presents a problem for this method so one is advised to simple eat less or avoid it if fat content is a major concern.

Aside from all the gloom and doom (which happens to be factual) I personally take dairy and certain dairy products like butter. Please note that I buy my products directly from the farmer whom I know and trust – an older couple who have a personal relationship with their cows and customers. The body needs fat and organic butter is a good source of many nutrients and provided you do not cook with it, is not harmful in small amounts. Butter is less likely to oxidize than most oils and therefore is a more stable form of fat to use than almost any other. It is by far much, much safer than margarine which is the cause of many modern diseases' (see oil section).

The favorite dairy product in India is ghee. This is usually translated as "clarified butter", but in fact ghee is not traditionally made from butter in India, but from a kind of yogurt. My teachers from India laugh at our ghee (but they also acknowledge that it works) as the traditional method is quite more complex and time consuming – though yielding a higher quality product. Personally I was quite hesitant to believe in "cooked butter" as being of real benefit. It actually took me some years before I got the courage up (being stubborn) to make it, and worst still, to use it in cooking and as medicine. This is strange because when I lived in India I only cooked with ghee and found it to be quite good in all respects. However, I relate this because my own resistance may help you to actually try it out for yourself. My wife (who is French) only cooks with ghee now (which is a major social reconditioning!).

Why should anyone use ghee? Because it is said to have the following properties: it is a rejuvenator; it is nutritive (it contains the same amount of nutrients as butter but without the harmful solids); it increases and protects bone marrow and nerve tissues; it promotes fertility; it increases immunity; it is said to improve intelligence and mental functions; it increases or improve vision; it promotes proper liver function; it improves the voice; it enhances enzyme function in the intestines, liver and tissues; it strengthens the kidneys and brain; it prevents congestion in the blood and plasma; and it is considered to increase the nutritional value of any food that is prepared in it. Ghee is best for Pitta types although Vata and Kapha types can use it in small amounts. Ayurveda considers it to be the best substance in which to cook food.

Note that the over use of Ghee will provoke the same kind of problems as any other fatty substance. Normally the average dose to cook with is one half teaspoon per meal. If you are using more than one teaspoon you will get fat.

Making ghee is very simple, but must be made with organic unsalted butter. Here is a simple recipe:

Making Ghee

- Put a piece of unsalted organic butter in a small saucepan and melt the butter over a medium flame

- As soon as it is melted reduce the heat to low. The butter will foam on top which is good and normal. Stir it to keep it from burning.

- After about 10-15 minutes the foam will disappear and take the shape of small white balls or flakes that will slowly sink. This is good; stir occasionally so that the butter does not burn.

- Up until now the butter will have been a clear or light yellow color. Now the color will become darker and it will begin to smell roasted and it will begin to make a crackling sound. Be very careful now as it can burn. It is important at this point to keep it cooking as the tendency is to not cook it enough. If it starts to turn brown remove immediately from the heat.

- Before it burns remove it from the flame and let it cool, and let the solids sink to the bottom. After 10 to 15 minutes strain it through a metal strainer into a glass jar that has a lid that closes well. Throw away the solids that you have strained off. If ghee is cooked long enough it keeps indefinitely without refrigeration. You can put it in the fridge to help it set up faster if you wish. If it begins to mold after ten days or two weeks you did not cook it long enough. Ghee should not be kept in refrigerator.

In the Western world nutritionists have discovered that the use of olive oil actually helps to clear and clean the bile ducts of the gall bladder and liver. In Ayurveda it is known that ghee has the same affect as olive oil, but on ALL of the channels and ducts of the body. This is why it is held such esteem.

In conclusion, the use of dairy has to be done with the utmost discretion or it can be enormously harmful. The modern use of cows as material objects to make money is directly opposite to the Ayurvedic use and its understanding of life. Therefore, if you choose to use dairy then do so by supporting a small farmer who cares enough about his animals and health to farm organically. It should also be noted that dairy products do not combine well with other foods and so can cause allergies and skin problems when taken with other foods. The only foods they seem to be combined well with is whole grains (but not yeast breads) and raw sugars. Milk is especially bad when combined with fish or seafood and is known to cause a variety of digestive and skin problems (one should note that ancient fishing cultures were not dairy farmers). Therefore, dairy, especially milk, should be taken in small amounts, alone and not mixed with other foods.

Oils

Oils that are produced from nuts and seeds contain large amounts of nutrients. Ayurveda considers oils to be building and strengthening to the body and tissues. Oils provide lubrication in the digestive system and are an important part of the diet to aid and maintain regular bowel movements. The excessive use of grains or brand without some oil can create dryness in the system and gripping that contributes to constipation. Oil has many medicinal qualities as was known by Huckleberry Finn.

Fats and oils are mainly neutral but can cause congestion in the body if taken in large amounts. Oils are the best for the Vata type of person and are considered to be the most balancing substance for their normal dry constitution. Oil massage is a primary way to nourish the body – especially for Vata types – as the nutrients in oil can also be absorbed through the skin.[44] The Kapha type of person is the most easily disturbed or congested by oils and fats. Most oils and fats are not recommended for the Kapha person and should be taken in very small, infrequent amounts. Oils that are more cooling and mild are OK for the Pitta type, like olive oil. However, oil can also cause some problems for the Pitta person if taken in large amounts.

Oil is a necessary part of nutrition and is greatly misunderstood today because of the narrow biochemical view of metabolic function. Once more we are faced with products that do not normally occur in nature, and yet are called by natural names – like oil. The fact today is that we are consuming a kind of oil that is processed and refined in such a way as to change it from its original form in the nut, seed or vegetable into a problematic substance. One can even go so far as to say that hydrogenating oil turns it into poison – margarine and shortening are both hydrogenated oils. Hence, the problem lies more in the preparation of the oil than in the oil itself.

Oils and fats have many important qualities to contribute to nutrition. Without fat and oil the body becomes diseased and dies. Fats and oils lubricate the tissues and provide the basic building blocks for all hormone production in the body. Diets that are very low in fat are known to cause women problems in the proper formation of natural hormones. In the United States it is the over consumption of fats and oils that cause problems. This is mainly because of the high intake of meat and dairy products. Typically the average American has more than 40% of their total calories in fat. In contrast a normal vegetarian diet will have only 10% of its total calories in fat.

---

[44] See, Smith, Atreya, 1999 for a full discussion on this topic and the different qualities of oil from an Ayurvedic point of view.

How much these kinds of statistical comparisons are valid is a questionable point for me, as Ayurveda does not recognize the whole subjective use of calories as a valid form of measuring food intake and consumption. However, I quoted these just to bring home the fact that people in industrial Westernized countries eat far too much fat – in all forms – than what is good for them.

The problem about looking at fat and oils is that the whole diet is seldom, if ever, considered. The use of large amounts of vegetable oils in the context of a diet based on whole grains and fresh vegetables seems to be very healthy. Yet, the same oil used with a "modern" industrialized diet has been shown to directly contribute to disease. A discriminating person may then wonder at all the information in the media about the "good and bad" forms of fat. The real question seems to be that there are good and bad diets, and good or bad methods of refinement.

The main problem with oil is that it oxygenates very quickly. This means that it starts to putrefy when exposed to heat and air. Normally with seeds or nuts the shell protects them from oxidation. However, once the oil is extracted from the seed or nut it begins to deteriorate. If the deteriorating oil is consumed then the deterioration continues in the body in the form of "free radicals" and the impairment of normal metabolic function. This fact was known by some ancient cultures because they tended to use forms of oils or fats that are "saturated". This means that they are more stable and do not oxygenate like the more liquid oils that are a mix of monounsaturated and polyunsaturated fats. So the more a fat is saturated the less likely it is to deteriorate and cause tissue and cellular damage.

The exception to this seems to be oils that are balanced in polyunsaturated and monounsaturated fats. The classic oil used in Ayurveda (and throughout the Middle East) is sesame oil. Note in the chart below that sesame oil is the most stable of all vegetable oils and the least likely to oxidize and cause the proliferation of free radicals. However, the use of ghee (clarified butter) for cooking is considered to be the best as it is not too high in saturated fats, yet is stable enough to not be affected by high levels of heat in cooking. Heat changes all of the oils and creates the possibility for them to oxidize at a rapid pace. Biochemical scientists state that the oils high in polyunsaturated fats are the most prone to deteriorate in cooking and so should not be used to fry foods in. This is also the Ayurvedic point of view. The best cooking oil is ghee followed by sesame oil. All others should be avoided for cooking on a daily basis.

Even more important than the kind of oil or fat is the process of preparing it for consumption. Most of the oil used in the industrialized world is already oxidized as it has been exposed to heat as high as 600° F or more in processing. Oil technically becomes "synthetic" after 320° F when the fatty-acids become "trans fatty-acids". This kind of change in oil accounts for all kinds of nasty diseases like high cholesterol, arthritis, cancer and heart disease to name a few. In plain words when you eat any kind of refined oil, margarine, or shortening you are suppressing your immune system, blocking the normal assimilation and use of fats and destroying the normal cellular function through the increase of "free radicals". All of these products also contain many chemicals – or traces of chemicals – that were used in their manufacturing process. These chemicals also have effects on cells and tissues that are far from promoting normal metabolic function.

Biochemical Classification of Different Oils

Kind of Oil	Saturated	Polyunsa-turated	Monounsa-turated
Almond	9%	21%	70%
Avocado	18%	8%	74%
Canola	6%	34%	60%
Coconut	92%	2%	6%
Corn	17%	54%	29%
Ghee	65%	30%	5%
Olive	10%	8%	82%
Palm Kernel	83%	1%	16%
Peanut	18%	22%	60%
Safflower	8%	79%	13%
Sesame	13%	41%	46%
Soy	14%	58%	28%
Sunflower	8%	66%	26%

The worst example of heating oil is the well known "restaurant scenario". In this scenario a restaurant will keep the same oil for several days to cook things over and over again – like French fries. This kind of oil actually kills people sooner than later and Federal law prevents the extended use of cooking oil for this reason. The level of oxidation becomes so high that the oil – and any food cooked in it – becomes poison. This coupled with the potatoes that are registered with the EPA as a pesticide makes a very interesting fast food snack. This may later be named "fast grave food" as the combination of all of the above factors are leading to heart disease and most cancers from the Ayurvedic point of view.

Oils are best made by a non-chemical extraction process that does not use heat. This is normally called "cold pressed oil". In practice though this is a very costly way to make oil – using heat and chemicals can more than double the amount of oil extracted. Once more it is money and not good nutrition that is determining your food choices. It has been known in the oil industry for the last several generations that heat extractions cause the oil to oxidizes and deteriorate – this has led to the use of more chemicals to prevent further deterioration. In this process all the natural anti oxidants and nutrients are removed, so from and Ayurvedic point of view, the food is dead.

Canola oil is becoming very popular because of the biochemical classification of the different kind of fats within it. However, it cannot be considered to be a good oil from an Ayurvedic point of view because it goes through extreme refining procedures that turn it into dead oil. The refinement process uses large amounts of chemicals as well as high heat levels. Oils are best used raw with salads and pastas. You should look for oils that are extracted at temperatures not more than 100° F and are classified as cold-pressed oils.

Deep-fried foods are not recommended for any constitution. Lightly sautéd spices and onions are OK, but full fried foods are considered to form toxins in the digestive system. The Kapha type should use little or no oil in cooking as it is not needed for their constitutional health. The Vata type needs the most oil but should also stay away from deep fried foods. The Pitta type is very disturbed by any kind of fried foods and hot, heavy oily food, avoiding them is an important method of disease prevention.

In conclusion, the first thing that I do with a client is change their consumption habits of oils and fats. If they use margarine[45] or shortenings I have them switch to butter in small amounts. If they are willing I have them begin to cook with ghee and only use the oils that agree with their

[45] It should be noted that heart disease has increased proportionately with the use of margarine since its introduction as a food. This is true both in the USA and the United Kingdom.

constitution (see chapter 15) in a raw or warm manner. All refined oils should be thrown out immediately. Avoid any restaurant that you may suspect uses the oil more than the allotted two days – which is a day and a half too long already. Animal fat has its own problems and will be discussed below.

Animal Products

Animal products were used in Ayurveda for the treatment of the sick or weak as they are known to build tissues (muscle, fat, etc.) faster than any other food However, the opinion of Ayurveda is that the tissue quality is superior when built through the longer method of metabolizing plant foods. Whether animal products are good or bad is not really the issue because they certainly have nutritional benefits. Nor will the social and environmental issues be addressed in this section (see chapter 9). The real issue of this section is the actual state of meat and poultry today in the United States.

All of the same information that was given in the section on dairy applies to meat. In plan words it is pumped up with hormones, antibiotics and other chemicals all of which have a negative long term effect on your health. If you like meat then, please, for your own safety and health, buy organic. All of the chemicals that have been discussed in this book so far, pesticides, DDT, PCB's, hormones, antibiotics and many more all end up in the tissues of the animals you eat. But the levels of concentration are astounding. PCB's (like any other non-biodegradable chemical – called a "persistent" chemical) can easily concentrate up to 25 million times the amount found in the water supply.[46]

Animal fat is a prime resting place for these persistent chemicals. When you eat the animal you get the same high concentration of chemicals and are unable to eliminate them from your body. Hence, they slowly collect until a deadly or

---

[46] Colborn, Theo et al, 1996, p. 26.

carcinogenic level is reached. It is my opinion that eating commercially produced meat is a slow form of suicide due to the accumulation of toxic chemicals in the environment and in the process of growing animals commercially. The traditional use of meats in all cultures has been to use small quantities and it is the over consumption that poses a problem for the human body.

Ayurveda considers meats and poultry to be best for Vata types as they are the weakest physically. The Kapha type should take almost no animal products due to the fact that the high fat content is extremely aggravating. The Pitta type falls in-between these two with occasional use acceptable. Daily use of meat or poultry is not recommended for any constitutional type.

Seafood

Seafoods are better for the Vata and Kapha types as they are too warming for the Pitta type of person. Fish were a good source of food in the past and had many positive qualities for people who liked some form of meat in their diets. However, this is not the situation today. Fish, although promoted extensively in the media, is not a safe form of food today. Fish are recipients of the same heavy persistent chemicals in the environment as other animal products. They typically have levels of PCB's two to three million times higher than the water they inhabit.[47]

These chemicals affect the people eating them directly – there is not a long delay of years or generations – although this is also true. Within a short period of several years people consuming fish from the Great Lakes have noticed behavior changes, learning impairment, hormone disturbance (PMS, breast cancer, infertility) and more insidious things like subjectively feeling depressed or lack of enthusiasm. The learning impairments are the most easily proved and recorded through studies.

[47] Colborn, Theo et al, 1996, p. 26.

Shell fish and bottom fish have the greatest concentrations of persistent chemicals and should be avoided altogether if your long term health is of concern. There is no ocean untouched by this situation. In fact research has shown that some of the most desolate places on the planet have the highest concentration of chemicals in the water, sea animals and their predators.

By association this makes seaweed a very questionable food source. It is true that the levels of chemicals are very low in sea plants, nevertheless, it is still there. Buying algae and seaweed that have been cultivated is a better choice in today's world. This also applies for people wishing to eat sea foods. Choose fish that have been raised in a controlled environment or fish farm. These will pose less of a threat to your health than any other source. There is a lot of media hype about certain oils found in fish and their positive effects on the body. These same components can be found in flax seeds without the high level of dangerous chemicals.

Sweeteners

All forms of sugar come under fire by the biochemical and naturopathic nutritionists today. Ayurveda is not opposed to sugar and other sweeteners when they are used correctly by the right constitution. It is beginning to sound like a broken record, but it is the refining of sugar which turns it into a disruptive chemical. Natural occurring sugar in itself is beneficial for the metabolism – in small amounts.

As stated earlier the consumption of hundred grams of sugar effectively suppresses the immune system for six to seven hours. Three cans of cola provide you with more than the 100 grams of sugar needed for this suppression to take place. The average American consumed 187 grams per day in 1996. Refined white sugar has many problems associated with it that is pretty well accepted by most nutritionists. However, the extent to which refined sugar affects the health is literally staggering.

There are numerous diseases which can be linked to refined sugar consumption. These include, but are not limited to: leeching minerals from the body, hyperactivity, anxiety, learning deficiencies, kidney damage, certain cancers, interference with the absorption of minerals like calcium, arthritis, gallstones, MS, diabetes, and changes the pH of the blood and plasma.[48]

Refined sugar is absorbed very quickly into the blood stream and damages the normal enzyme function through its fast action. Normally foods have to be broken down before they are absorbed into the body. This is not the case with white sugar which is overly refined already. Therefore, the body's enzymes are disrupted by this direct action which then forces the liver, stomach and pancreas to balance the excessive amounts of blood sugar caused from the immediate digestion of the sugar. This strains the system and causes energy fluctuations, which will, in time, disrupt the pancreas and water metabolism (from an Ayurvedic point of view). The physical part of the sugar also tends to sit in the duodenum and ferment. As the fermentation of sugar is well known in the manufacturing of alcohol it should come as no surprise that large amounts of sugar ferment in the body and have an alcohol like effect on the liver and blood.

There is little doubt that refined sugar is totally detrimental to health. It has no nutritional value whatsoever and many damaging effects. But, do we need to throw the baby out with the bath water? Non-refined sugar has many minerals and is a complex food which the body can use, in most cases, without problems in small amounts. If you are a sugar addict then it is better to avoid it completely until you have reeducated your metabolism to function well without it. Honey also provides a good complex food that has a very different effect on the body than refined sugar.

---

[48] Appleton, Nancy, 1996.

As with any food you must check the quality and source of the food to be sure that it is going to be of some benefit to you. Honey and raw, non refined sugar should not be cooked or heated in the processing procedure. Cooking or heating damages the structure of the sweetener and makes them difficult to digest – Ayurveda says that honey becomes a poison when heated. The whole key to using sweeteners is to use them in moderation. It is the excessive amounts of refined sugar that are found in all processed foods (just read the label of anything in a can, box, or jar) that disrupt the metabolism. This is one major reason to eliminate refined and processed foods from your diet. Even if you never take sugar directly, but still eat processed foods your total consumption of sugar will be over a 100 grams per day.

From an Ayurvedic point of view sweeteners are best for Vata and Pitta types and are not recommended at all for the Kapha type of person. The Kapha type will be the most attracted to eating sugar and they are the ones that should avoid it completely. Small amounts of honey are acceptable for the Kapha type. The Pitta type should avoid honey altogether and use non refined sugar instead. The Vata type can use both as they choose.

It should be noted that there are many sugar substitutes available on the market. The older ones have long been shown to be carcinogenic in laboratory tests. However, as I am writing there are appearing a host of new studies linking many of the newer and most widely used artificial sweeteners to cancer. This should be watched closely as all "soft drinks" are using these sweeteners. There are many detrimental effects of carbonated soft drinks besides sugar that will be covered under the Beverage section. From the Ayurvedic point of view none of the artificial sweeteners can be recommended. In fact, they are to be avoided at all costs.

There are several books available on how to get off of sugar if you are seriously addicted to it.[49] I strongly suggest breaking this habit so that you can enjoy the freedom of a healthy life without disease and food cravings. It should be noted, however, that most of my clients find eliminating refined sugar is easy when they begin to eat a diet based on whole foods and correct their metabolism as described in chapter 11.

Spices

Spices are used in Ayurveda to antidote food or food combinations for each constitution. Spices also play an important role in enzyme production and maintenance. These are both extremely important roles and so herbs and spices perform a key role in Ayurvedic nutrition.

The use of spices is both an art and a science – the art of cooking and the science of herbal medicine. As I am not a great cook I will suggest several cook books to cover this aspect.[50] I will, however, introduce the basic spices / herbs for each constitutional type; note also chapter 15 and the individual spices recommended for each constitution. Ayurvedic medicine begins with nutrition and lifestyle. The foundation of good health – from the Ayurvedic standpoint – is good digestion. Herbs and spices play a key role in this by promoting enzyme function. Changing the spice according to the quality of food allows the enzymes additional support and improves your digestive capacity.[51] The over use of spice can have the opposite effect to imbalance the metabolism.

---

[49] Appleton, Nancy, 1996. This book is interesting and can help people break the habit of sugar.

[50] See, Morningstar, Amadea, 1994.

[51] This is called increasing Agni in the body. As stated earlier Ayurveda regards the function of the 13 major Agnis to correspond to enzyme function. Hence, most important in daily nutrition is to keep the Agni strong so that enzyme function will be sufficient to digest the food consumed.

If one is attentive to the quality of the food being prepared and the constitution of the person eating the food, then one can use spice to change the quality of the food to match the person. This is called antidoting in Ayurveda. The essence of spicing lies in the basic qualities of the three types – or their attributes as discussed in chapter 2. By knowing the basic qualities or attributes of each type, or mix of types, it is possible to adjust the quality of the food accordingly. This is possible because we have traditional classifications of both foods and spices. Hence, by using spices that correspond to our constitution we can maintain our health. Additionally, by knowing the quality of a specific food we can change that quality by using a specific spice – the result of which will be an antidote to a food that otherwise may not fit our constitution.

Some examples of this are needed. A Vata type eating dry crackers (light, dry, cold, rough) in-between meals in the afternoon will increase the dry, light qualities in their body. This will give rise to the following problems if done on a regular basis: dryness in the colon, gas, constipation, dry skin, colic pain, gripping and lowering enzyme function. This may seem extreme from a modern point of view – especially from an innocent looking cracker! But this would indeed be the result of eating crackers regularly between meals according to Ayurveda for a Vata type. An antidote could be cheese or peanut butter, both of which are high in fat and would balance the dry qualities of the cracker (by the way this combination would really disturb a Kapha type in a short time).

In another example of antidoting food the Kapha type could find cooked apples aggravating constitutionally (mildly) and so would avoid any negative side effects by adding cinnamon, clove and ginger in small amounts. These are obviously hot, warming spices that will "lighten" the "heavy" quality of the cooked apples. Extreme examples can also be given, like using black pepper on cheese to help counteract its moist, heavy, dense attributes.

The important thing with spices is to understand the principle behind their use. This principle can be applied to any kind of cultural cuisine – Italian, Mexican, French, American, and even, believe it or not, English! People wrongly assume that cooking or spicing according to Ayurveda means having to eat Indian food. This is a misunderstanding because the basic point of comprehending the individual attributes of foods has been missed. Spices are used only to adjust the attributes of food to the individual eating them.

The subject of using spices to increase enzyme function cannot be supported by biochemical studies – even if any were available. The reason for this is that it is the combination of several spices, according to the constitution, that works to increase enzyme function. Once more this is far closer to the quantum model of physics than the mechanical model because it works on multiple levels – taste, interaction with food, interaction with other spices, total interaction of food and spices, chemical reaction in the digestive system, interaction with the pleasure of eating the well spiced food, environment of eating, and finally the sum total of all of these factors. Hence, we must rely on the traditional information and use of spices. My own personal experience in professional practice backs up this approach as not only valid, but also effective. I encourage everyone to try it before coming to a conclusion. The use of spices before meals is called *Dipana* in Ayurveda and means, "that which excites agni".

Here are lists of herbs / spices that are beneficial for the support of enzyme function (agni) as per constitution:

The Vata type will find these spices beneficial:

- Cardamom
- Fennel
- Cumin
- Asafoetida

The Pitta type will find these spices beneficial:

- Cumin
- Fennel
- Coriander

The Kapha type will find these spices beneficial:

- Ginger
- Black Pepper
- Fenugreek
- Cumin

One can buy these dried spices fresh and grind them up in a coffee grinder (which you will not need after reading the following section) into a powder. Take half a teaspoon of this powder with a little warm water before (Dipana) or after eating (Pachana) – main meals are the most important. The Kapha type can also eat raw pieces of fresh ginger root – sliced into four pieces the size of a dime – just before food. However, this is a strong method for most Westerners and I have gotten good results with people using the powdered spices. The raw ginger method can also be used by Vata types who have poor digestion and appetite, but should not be used by the Pitta type.

Beverages

What you drink is what directly supports your plasma and lymphatic system according to Ayurveda. Pure fluids that we drink are turned into a subtle medium of kinetic energy that is charged with intelligence.[52] Consuming fluids that are dead, i.e., man made, will not support or create this intelligent kinetic energy. Modern science knows that the plasma / lymphatic system is a prime site of immune function and that a healthy, properly functioning lymphatic system is a key to good immune response. What they do not know is that – according to Ayurveda – your beverages (and food) directly contribute to the state of lymphatic health.

[52] Ayurveda says that what you eat becomes Ojas, what you drink becomes Prana, and what you think becomes Tejas. Prana is life itself which has intelligence as an inseparable component.

With this in mind one would question the consumption of synthetic soft drinks which, by their chemical nature would produce poor quality lymph, and contain high amounts of refined sugar (coke has about 17 teaspoons per can). This double action has strong degenerating effects on immunity and general health. Additionally, the kidneys are organs of filtration for the plasma and blood. Their health is directly dependant on the form of liquid consumed by an individual. Ayurveda views kidney and adrenal function as being interdependent. Consequently, any weakness or damage to the kidneys will affect adrenal function that – from a biochemical view – are paramount in controlling endocrine (hormone) functions of digestion, pain and many more metabolic tasks. This means that – from an Ayurvedic point of view – the consumption of manmade chemical drinks will not only have a long term negative effect on immunity, but also on digestion, inflammation, immunity, maintenance of body heat, lubrication, digestion of simple sugars and hormone function.

Probably the most important thing you can do for your health is to stop drinking all synthetic drinks. Even occasional use is detrimental as soft drinks leech out minerals from the body. The effect of these "empty foods" is not neutral. They have no food value whatsoever and remove important minerals from the body. Clean water, vegetable or fruit juices or herbal teas are much better substitutes. Everyone must have at some point tasted a hot or warm cola. And everyone knows from this experience how bad tasting it is, that leads one to guess why these kinds of drinks have to be served ice cold. Because ice numbs the taste buds and allows bad tasting substances to be passed unnoticed into the system.

Ice cold drinks also suppress the enzyme function in the body. The second best thing you can do for your health is to stop taking any ice cold drinks – especially at meal times. There is no quicker and surer way to suppress digestive function than to drink ice water or ice drinks with meals.

This is a particular illness of the United States which seems to be contagious as ice is now starting to appear in Europe and other countries where it had been unheard of before. No doubt the ice machine manufactures are doing their best to convince the world that drinking ice cold water has some benefit. The exact opposite is the truth. If you are in doubt, and you have digestive problems, just change this one aspect in your diet and see if your problems do not disappear or improve.

Drinking large amounts of liquids before or after a meal also dilutes the enzyme function considerably and so should be avoided. The best for all constitutions is to sip small amounts of warm water (Vata and Kapha types) or room temperature water (Pitta types) during the meal. The job of the stomach is to mix and liquefy its contents; if there is too little liquid then this job is difficult. If there is too much then it is also done poorly. Drinking in moderation with the meal facilitates this process.

I am shocked by the daily consumption of coffee in the United States. I can understand that people like two or even three cups of coffee a day, but when I repeatedly see half gallon cups being filled in convenience stores, gas stations and even vending machines I realized that this country has a major problem with a very addictive and potent drug. Some researchers are of the opinion that if coffee came up before the FDA today it would be classified as a prescription medicine because its effects are so strong.

Ayurveda is not against coffee in small amounts used infrequently at the right time by the Pitta or Kapha types. Coffee is rarely recommended for the Vata type and will cause constipation (or the need for coffee to defecate), dry skin and hair, insomnia, PMS, pre menopause symptoms like hot flashes, kidney problems and adrenal suppression to name a few. The other types can also suffer from the above problems of coffee. The main problem is the amounts in which it is consumed and the time of day in which it is taken.

Coffee is very astringent in action and can actually aid the digestive process when it is taken after a meal in small amounts. However, when it is taken before a meal it cuts the digestive process and suppresses appetite. But using this to lose weight or to avoid hunger will disrupt your adrenal function and, for many women, contribute greatly to all forms of PMS and pre menopausal problems. If you are a woman and you have any kind of problems related to your cycle I suggest that you stop coffee and sugar totally. It may take several months but it is the experience of many women that the majority (or all) of their problems disappear after doing this.

While men will not have this problem they will tend to have overactive mental function, insomnia, anxiety, nervousness, stomach problems, moodiness, pancreatic cancer and heart problems. Women can also have these problems coupled with miscarriages, breast cancer and even birth defects if coffee is taken during pregnancy. (The FDA has recommended that all pregnant women avoid coffee since 1980.) In many respects men are less lucky because there is no monthly warning system to alert them to the fact that they are overstressing their nervous and endocrine systems by drinking large amounts of coffee. Very often this has tragic results with a sudden stroke or heart attack that kills young men of forty to fifty years of age. All this for only two cups per day! You do not need to drink a gallon a day to have these effects, although if you drink large amounts your chances to provoke problems climb very quickly. Even two cups per day has been shown to raise cholesterol levels. Your doctor or biochemical nutritionist will most likely not tell you this, but there are ample studies in the scientific world to support these statements.[53]

---

[53] Welsch, C.W. et al, Caffeine, (1,3,7-trimethylxanthine), a temperature promoter of DMBA-in-duced rat mammary gland carcinogenesis. *International Journal of Cancer* 32: pp. 479-84, Oct 15, 1983; Williams, P., Coffee intake of elevated cholesterol and apolepoprotein B levels in women. *Journal of the American Chemical Society* 253: p. 1407, 1985; Roche, F., 1983 pp. 258-59.

If one is addicted to coffee it is best to try and get free from it as it has many negative side effects. Coffee is also prepared with many chemicals and the decaffeinated variety is even worse than "normal" coffee as the chemicals used in this process are poisonous to the human system. It would be better – from an Ayurvedic point of view – to buy your own organic coffee beans and freshly grind them each time you have a coffee as ground coffee also oxidizes very rapidly. Alternatively tea can be used as a substitute to coffee.

Tea, in small amounts, has medicinal properties. Per serving size it has 1/3 less caffeine than coffee (and of a different kind) and so is less strong in affecting the body. However, tea can be abused by all types as well. The Vata type will again be the most sensitive to tea. There is an interest of late in green tea which is the unfermented preparation of black tea. Green tea has shown antioxidant properties and can be of use in some health problems. I do not recommend the daily use of either as they also will play havoc with adrenal / kidney function over time.[54] Drinking tea or coffee with milk has been shown in population studies to reduce the rate of stomach cancers and acid indigestion from coffee or tea consumption and can help lessen the negative effects. Soy or rice milk can be substituted for cow's milk.

Ayurveda says that the best beverage is spring water. As most of us do not have springs we must find a good source of water for our health. Water quality is extremely important for long term health and any nutritional plan. There are many water filters available today and the kind you need will depend on your local water quality and your budget. Ayurveda considers bottled water to be – generally speaking – dead as it is not being oxygenated anymore. Obviously heavy metals and high contents of chemicals are to be avoided. If

[54] Coffee and tea aggravate the Vata Dosha which controls the kidney – water metabolism, of which the adrenal glands are intimately related to and dependant on.

your water is bad tasting it is a good indication that you need to do something now. Take the money that you would spend on all other forms of beverages and buy a good water filter. If water is not satisfying enough squeeze a lemon into it (for Vata and Kapha types) or a little unfiltered apple juice (for the Pitta types). Herbal teas are also readily available and can make good daily beverages.

All alcoholic beverages should be taken in moderation or not at all for obvious reasons. In small amounts wine can be a very good digestive stimulant for Vata and Kapha types, even the Pitta type can take small amounts of older, more mature red wines. Cheep white wines should be avoided by all constitutions. Beer can be taken in summer rather than winter and is best accepted by the Vata and Pitta types. The yeast in beer can disturb the Kapha types. Everyone should avoid hard liquor, as it is too concentrated. Some medical uses can be acceptable (like for the arrival of your mother-in-law!).

The occasional use of fruit or vegetable juices is good for everyone and has many beneficial effects on the health. See the individual classifications of each fruit or vegetable to know which is best for your constitution as their properties vary greatly.

One last point is that of liquid consumption. Some people advocate large amounts of water / fluids to be drunk on a daily basis. The general rule is as follows: the Vata type needs the most water, the Pitta type a moderate amount, and the Kapha type the least. For Vata or Pitta types that have dry skin, skin problems, or excessive signs of heat in the body warm water can be taken in the early morning when you wake up – about one to two quarts at a time (see a practitioner if you are unsure). The Vata type can drink a large glass of warm water first thing when they wake up. For the rest of the day on should only drink when thirsty. Exceptions can be: traveling, hot climates, direct sun or heat exposure, and exercise. The Kapha type needs little or no water and should drink only when thirsty. If you are thirsty all the time then your metabolism is not running correctly – see an Ayurvedic doctor. Adjust liquid consumption to your needs, not those of the latest theory.

Vitamins and Minerals

Supplements will be spoken of in a more specific sense in Chapter Thirteen, but here we can speak of them in a general biochemical sense. Ayurveda has a different view on this subject than is commonly understood, although it is not in disagreement with dietary supplements as a means to support health. This is especially true for people with serious dietary or health problems. It should be stressed, however, that using supplements when you are sick needs to be guided by a professional that has experience in this field. Large doses of vitamins or other supplements can derange the normal metabolic function or even further aggravate an existing disease.

Generally, the Vata type needs the most supplements, the Pitta type needs them in moderation and the Kapha type rarely. This follows the general trend that the Vata type is less physically strong and needs more nourishment than the other types. The Kapha type tends to be over nourished, often with excess, and so needs little or no supplementation. The Pitta type falls in-between but should avoid large doses of acidic supplements like vitamin C. See chapter 15 for the specific guidelines for each constitution.

Your use of vitamins and minerals will greatly depend on your diet. If you eat a "Standard American Diet" (SAD) then you will certainly need as many (probably more) vitamins, minerals and trace elements as possible. But, according to Ayurveda this will not bring you health. Following the dietary guidelines in this book will allow you take a minimum or no supplementation depending on a variety of factors covered in this book. Hence, the major question is where and what do you eat? This will decide the amount of supplements that you need.

There is a false – from the Ayurvedic point of view – notion that taking vitamins will allow you to eat in restaurants, eat junk foods, fast foods, or eat canned and frozen foods. This is absolutely wrong as there is no substitute for whole foods in their natural state. Relying on chemicals or "super foods" will not promote proper metabolic function over time. One can use supplements for short-term needs or to combat a disease, but they are absolutely not the foundation of good nutrition. I know many people throughout the world who are healthy and productive who never use vitamins. In today's world there is a real concern over the lack of nutrients in foods – this should be counteracted with eating organic foods, increasing enzyme / digestive function and then only should one can consider adding supplements to the diet, not before.

Conclusion

For those of you who feel compelled to have biochemical proof of many of the statements about food and nutrition in this book I suggest the following book by Paul Pitchford – *Healing with Whole Foods.*[55] While I do not personally agree that one can use Oriental or "energetic" nutritional systems in conjunction with a mechanical / biochemical model, Mr. Pitchford has attempted this and done an excellent job. However, the book is a good example of how instead of bringing the mechanical model up into the broader quantum model the contrary happens and the quantum ends up being put into a box of defined limits. Personally, I feel that this is a disservice to both visions of life as each has valuable contributions to make to health and, hopefully, nutrition.

---

[55] Pitchford, Paul, 1993.

Perhaps the most important book to come out on food, nutrition and health in the last twenty years is *The China Study*[56] by T. Colin Campbell. I have been following Dr. Campbell's work since 1995 and he is the single most important author on nutrition alive today. There are over 600 studies quoted in his book for people who wish to have that kind of data. He also addresses a number of current social problems on why government, and science in general, do not follow the data and conclusions that modern studies on diet, lifestyle and disease indicate.

While it may seem to the reader that I am unnecessarily dwelling on many of the negative aspects of environmental problems in the food chain, it would be, in my opinion, a false view of nutrition to eliminate this information. These pollutants are having a major effect on our health today and social awareness is needed immediately to change this situation. I am presenting only the tip of the iceberg and I am intentionally avoiding quoting the hundreds of studies that are in my files and research books. Furthermore, the purpose of this book is to introduce the Ayurvedic constitutional nutritional system to a modern society. A failure to clearly address the current state of our society, our environment and its polluted food chain would be a failure to adapt the Ayurvedic methodology and understanding of nutrition to Western culture.

---

[56] Compbell, T. Colin, 2006.

9
Why Eat a Low Protein Diet?

In order to eat a low protein diet one must eliminate animal products from the diet. This means meat, fowl, fish and dairy products. Naturally the question that arises for many people is, "why would I want to do that?" The first and foremost reason is for your health. There are other reasons as well, perhaps the very survival of the human species will depend on a majority of people switching to a plant based diet.

Albert Einstein once said, "Nothing will benefit human health or increase the chances for survival of life on earth as the evolution to a vegetarian diet." This is a dramatic statement from one of the most respected scientists of modern times. There are many reasons for this statement and they are backed by solid facts of the effects of a large consumption of animal products by humans on the environment. It is not the intention of this book to enter into this aspect of eating a low protein plant based diet; nevertheless, it is irresponsible not to mention it. For truly shocking information on this subject read the books of John Robbins[57] or contact a non-profit organization that is concerned with this matter directly.[58]

---

[57] Robbins, John, 1987; 1992.

[58] EarthSave International.

The primary concern of this book is nutrition as seen from the Ayurvedic point of view. In this vision eating animals is not necessary for good health. The twelve million vegetarians in the United States would tend to agree with that. Dr. Dean Ornish and his dietary / lifestyle plan for heart problems would also agree. In fact there are more and more health professionals that are agreeing with this point of view.

A case in point is Dr. T. Colin Campbell who led the largest study ever conducted on diet, the China-Oxford-Cornell Project on Nutrition, Health, and the Environment. Dr. Campbell became a vegetarian during the study, and when criticized for being a vegetarian his response was, "I'm just paying attention to what the data are telling me: The scientific evidence came first."[59]

The result of the study indicated that: "...whether industrialized societies...can cure themselves of their meat addictions may ultimately be a greater factor in world health than all the doctors, health insurance policies, and drugs put together."[60]

This information was not well accepted by the media, the food industry or the greater medical community – even though research scientists applauded the results. But this is only one of many studies that indicate the same thing. The editor-in-chief of the *American Journal of Cardiology*, Dr. William C. Roberts, said in an editorial, "When we kill animals to eat them, they end up killing us because their flesh...was never intended for human beings, who are natural herbivores."[61]

Once more this is not an isolated view. Dr. William Castelli, the director of the longest ongoing investigation of heart disease and diet, the Framingham Heart Study, said

[59] Robbins, John, 1992 p. 87.

[60] Robbins, John, 1992 p. 86.

[61] Robbins, John, 1992 p. 87.

this when asked about the best diet, "Vegetarians have the best diet. They have the lowest rates of coronary disease of any group in the country."[62] Actually there is so much scientific evidence in support of a low protein plant based diet that one wonders why the research community does not push it more aggressively into the media.

Some doctors have tried. During a 1991 national conference Dr. Campbell stated to his medical peers: "Why must we be reticent about recommending a diet which we know is safe and healthy? We, as scientists, can no longer take the attitude that the public cannot benefit from information they are not ready for. We must have the integrity to tell them the truth and let them decide what to do with it. We cannot force them to follow the guidelines we recommend, but we can give them these guidelines and let them decide....We must tell them that a diet of roots, stems, seeds, flowers, fruits, and leaves is the healthiest diet, and the only diet we can promote, endorse, and recommend."[63]

Even Dr. Benjamin Spock the author of the world famous book, Baby and Child Care, has promoted a diet free of all animal products. In his seventh edition he has taken a firm stance on what he calls a meaty diet. "We now know that there are harmful effects of a meaty diet. Children can get plenty of protein and iron from vegetables, beans and other plant foods that avoid the fat and cholesterol that are in animal products."[64] When questioned on the seemingly radical approach Dr. Spock replied just before his death, "that he wanted to be in the forefront of the growing awareness of the link between animal foods and disease."[65] As his *Baby and Child Care* is the best selling book only second to the Bible, it certainly gives food for thought.

---

[62] Robbins, John, 1992 p. 85.

[63] Robbins, John, 1992 p. 90.

[64] Brody, Jane E., *International Herald Tribune,* June 22, 1998 p. 3

[65] Brody, Jane E., *International Herald Tribune,* June 22, 1998 p. 3

There is a strong cultural resistance to the link of animal foods to disease. When I told a friend that I was writing a book on nutrition his response was, "I hope you are not going to write a stupid book on how everyone should be a vegetarian. People can live on anything; some tribes in Africa live mostly on drinking blood." While I am not personally aware of cultures living primarily on blood his point is well taken – the human body can live on almost anything – no matter how disgusting it is.

This argument could be used to justify living on cupcakes and donuts as easily as blood. Another point is the Eskimos who traditionally live on a purely meat based diet. Whether you are living on TV dinners, donuts, blood or walrus meat there will be a price to pay in terms of your health. There is a huge difference between good nutrition and what the body can survive on. Somehow the general public is reluctant to make this distinction.

The primary cause of this is the profit orientation of the food industry itself. They are very intelligent marketing people; never underestimate their ability to sell you anything. The unfortunate part is that their profit has little to do with your health or good nutrition.

A good example of this marketing strategy is the protein myth. People in the United States are literally paranoid about getting enough protein in their diets. Yet as a culture we are poisoned by an over consumption of protein. It is almost incredible when one thinks about it objectively. The very substance that we worry about getting enough of is the one that is killing us? This really shows the power of the marketing community.

An example of this was given already in a previous chapter – comparing an artichoke and a pork chop. If we were asked to choose which of these items has more protein we would inevitably choose the pork chop, right? Who would believe that an artichoke has as much protein as a pork chop? Well, it is true. An artichoke has 22% of its calories in protein and a pork chop has 23%. The difference here is that an artichoke has only 3% fat and the pork chop has 77%. The pork chop has 0% carbohydrates and the artichoke has 75%. Using the biochemical model of nutrition what choice would represent the best nutritional balance? If you choose the pork chop then we must all bow down to the mighty power of the American marketing machine.

Several studies and researchers have tried to construct a diet deficient of protein. They failed on every occasion except one, that of basing a diet primarily on refined sweets like cakes, donuts, jams and jellies. If a person is eating a whole food diet or a diet based primarily on whole foods then it is impossible not to get enough protein.

In fact, one of the main factors in the rapid recovery of Martha and her autoimmune disorder (see chapter 7) was due to the almost complete elimination of animal proteins. At first Martha was skeptical, but as she was desperate she followed my advice. She did not completely eliminate animal foods altogether. She did, however, reduce her intake by 80% and is still following this kind of diet years later. In her case this change not only matched her constitution but was critical in her recovering her health.

I have found it necessary to introduce some of the modern biochemical information in this chapter because I feared that a lack of "scientific data" would force many people to completely disregard this chapter. It is unfortunate that we live in an age where people use "scientific data" to promote their own products and dogma. While several examples have been given above it should be noted that this is only the tip of the iceberg. Another example is that of osteoporosis. Women are especially targeted by this effort of misinformation as they are supposedly going to lose bone mass as they enter post menopause. They are told to eat lots of calcium rich foods like meat and milk products and take calcium supplements. Unfortunately calcium supplements have never been shown to increase bone mass.[66] This conclusion was not made by a quack; it was the result of a research team lead by Dr. B. Lawrence Riggs of the Mayo Clinic. There are many other studies that have also come to the same conclusion.

The main cause of bone density loss, or of calcium leaving the bones, is an excessive intake of protein.[67] With this understanding the recommendation of eating animal products because they are high in calcium is just unbelievable. Animal products remove far more calcium from the bones than they add. Thus following the current advice will create a perfect situation for bone density loss and the onset of osteoporosis. This is perhaps why one of the leading causes of death for women sixty-five and over is from the effects of osteoporosis. If a person, man or woman, is concerned about bone density the single most important factor is to begin a low protein diet based on plant foods.

The actual protein needs of the human body are only 2.5% of total calorie intake according to the American Journal of Clinical Nutrition. The World Health Organization sets the adult requirement at 4.5% and the Food and Nutrition Board of the National Academy of Sciences puts it at 6% – adding a 30% margin for "safety". Even the level of 6% is easy to achieve by eating a few vegetables or fruits every day. Actually out of 44 vegetables listed in the Agriculture Handbook No. 456 only one, the sweet potato, is at the limit of deriving 6% of total calories as protein. The others more than exceed this requirement as do grains and legumes. Even many fruits meet or exceed these requirements. In passing it is also worth noting that allergies are a reaction to the proteins in foods. If you are having

---

[66] Riggs, Dr. B. Lawrence, *Science*, August 1, 1986.

[67] Wachman, A. et al., *Lancet*, May 4, 1968, p. 958.

food or other kinds of allergies a low protein diet should form the foundation of a natural treatment plan.

Protein Content of Common Foods

(figures are given in percentage of total calories)
Table Source: "Nutritive Value of American Foods in Common Units," USDA Handbook No. 456.

Food Type	**% Protein**	**% Fat**	**% Carbo-hydrate**
Fruits			
Apples	1	8	91
Apricots	7	4	89
Bananas	5	3	92
Cantaloupe Melon	9	3	89
Cherries	8	4	88
Cranberries	3	13	84
Dates	3	0	97
Figs	6	5	89
Grapefruit	5	2	93
Grapes	8	13	79
Lemons	15	7	78
Mango	4	5	91
Oranges	8	4	88
Papayas	6	2	92
Peaches	6	2	92
Pears	5	6	89
Persimmons	3	3	94
Pineapples	3	3	94
Plums	3	0	97
Pomegranates	3	5	92
Prunes	4	1	95
Raspberries	8	16	76

Food Type	% Protein	% Fat	% Carbo hydrate
Strawberries	8	12	80
Watermelon	8	7	85

Food Type	**% Protein**	**% Fat**	**% Carbo hydrate**
Vegetables			
Artichoke	22	3	75
Asparagus	32	6	62
Avocado	5	81	14
Beets	15	2	83
Bell Peppers	22	8	70
Broccoli	45	6	49
Brussels Sprouts	44	6	50
Cabbage	22	7	71
Carrots	10	4	86
Cauliflower	40	6	54
Celery	20	6	74
Corn	11	7	82
Cucumber	24	7	69
Eggplant	18	9	73
Green Beans	21	6	73
Lettuce	30	12	58
Mushrooms	38	8	54
Mustard Greens	31	13	56
Okra	22	8	70
Onions	16	3	81
Parsley	34	12	54
Peas	30	4	66
Potatoes	11	1	88
Radish	10	1	89
Soy Sprouts	43	20	37
Spinach	49	9	42

Summer Squash	20	5	75
Sweet Potatoes	6	3	91
Tomatoes	18	8	74
Turnips	13	7	80
Watercress	40	11	49
Winter Squash	12	3	85

Food Type	**% Protein**	**% Fat**	**% Carbohydrate**
Grains			
Amaranth	16	8	76
Barley	11	3	86
Buckwheat	15	7	78
Corn flour	9	5	86
Millet	12	5	83
Oats	15	8	77
Quinoa	18	9	73
Rice (basmati)	8	2	90
Rice (brown)	8	5	84
Rice (normal white)	6	1	93
Rye	20	7	73
Wheat (Whole)	16	5	79

Food Type	**% Protein**	**% Fat**	**% Carbohydrate**
Beans (Legumes)			
Adzuki	25	4	71
Chick Peas (Garbonzo)	23	12	65
Dal (Red)	28	3	69
Kidney	26	4	70
Lentils	29	3	68
Lima	26	4	70
Mung	28	3	69

Soy	32	37	31
Split Peas	28	3	69
Tofu	40	48	12

Food Type	**% Protein**	**% Fat**	**% Carbo-hydrate**
Nuts & Seeds			
Almonds	12	76	12
Cashews	12	68	20
Filberts	8	81	11
Peanuts	18	68	14
Pine Nuts	8	80	12
Pumpkin Seeds	20	70	10
Sesame Seeds	13	75	12
Sunflower Seeds	17	69	14

Food Type	**% Protein**	**% Fat**	**% Carbo-hydrate**
Dairy Products			
Butter	0	100	0
Buttermilk	40	3	57
Cheese (Cheddar)	25	73	2
Cottage Cheese	52	37	11
Cream	8	90	2
Ice Cream	20	48	32
Milk (whole)	21	49	30
Yogurt	21	49	30

Food Type	% Protein	% Fat	% Carbo-hydrate
Animal Products			
Beef	32	68	0
Chicken (Light meat, w/skin, roasted)	56	44	0
Chicken (Dark meat, w/skin, roasted)	44	56	0
Duck	24	76	0
Eggs	33	65	2
Fish (Bass)	26	56	18
Lamb (chops)	22	78	0
Pork (chops)	23	77	0
Shell Fish (Clams)	68	21	6
Turkey	41	59	0

It is now time to turn back to the traditional Ayurvedic point of view that eating a low protein diet constitutes good health. It is wrongly assumed that all of ancient Indian culture was vegetarian. The truth is that most of the ruling and warrior caste in ancient times where hunters and ate meat. Often the poor would eat anything that was available, as is the case today, whether it is meat or anything else. The Ayurvedic system, as stated in the opening chapters, is not moralistic. There is no good or bad. There is simply the understanding of the effects of eating any substance.

Ayurveda says that meat is a quick way to build tissues, but ultimately of an inferior quality. Ayurveda also considers all animal tissues to be problematic as they promote toxins in the body. By toxin they mean two things – that the substance itself is toxic to the body over long term use, and that during the process of digestion animal flesh breeds toxic bacteria. Additionally, as animal flesh takes from 36 to 48 hours to pass through the digestive system it tends to rot in the intestines before being eliminated.

Traditionally Ayurveda would use meat soups as one method to help a sick patient recover their strength quickly. The use of animal flesh was limited to medical therapies and not considered good for daily consumption. Some meat, particularly beef, was considered to be toxic for human consumption.

The XYZ of Ayurveda

However, the most problematic effect of all animal products – including fish and seafood – is on the mind. Ayurveda says that there are two primary negative effects on the mind. The first is that animal flesh dulls the mind and the second is that it increases violent mental states. While it may seem that we are entering really subjective areas here there is a growing body of scientific data that correlates diet with behavior. As yet, I have not seen any data on the difference between the violent behavior of meat eaters and plant eaters. Perhaps this is just a matter of time before a study is done; but who will fund such a study? The meat and dairy industries?

Certainly there already exists substantial data on the effect of food additives and heavy metals on the social behavior and mental performance of subjects. And there is a general awareness that deficiencies in certain nutrients certainly affect the mind. Hypoglycemia is a simple example of how the mind is affected by the nutritional state of the body. In any case we have the Ayurvedic understanding of meat consumption and its effect on the mind.

If the basic principles that govern nature (VPK) are the ABC of Ayurveda, then it is now time to introduce the XYZ of Ayurveda. In the Ayurvedic system there is an understanding of the mind and another set of principle in which to understand it by. In this book we can call these three principles *Sattva, Rajas, Tamas.* In Ayurveda these three principles are used to refine or further understand anything that occurs in nature – this is a general use that brings a more profound level to the basic ABC methodology. Specifically however, we use the Sattva, Rajas, Tamas to understand mental dispositions in people.[68]

According to Ayurveda each food has one of the three principles dominating in it. Therefore, when you eat a food you take on the dominant quality. This in turn affects your mental state and psychology. This is one of the main reasons why Ayurveda is not fond of eating meat – because all dead animals consist of the Tamas quality or of inertia. At the opposite end of the spectrum are fruits which are comprised of the Sattva quality as they are the lightest food and eating them in no way harms the tree. The qualities of XYZ are as follows:

Sattva – harmony, clarity, intelligence, peace, perception

Rajas – action, movement, agitation, anger, domination, force

Tamas – inertia, dullness, lack of intelligence, perversion, violence

These are classical descriptions of the three principles as applied to the mind in general.

It is interesting to note that Ayurveda considers refined foods, processed foods and chemicals of all kinds (i.e., food additives) to be Tamas dominant. This may sound strange or even crazy, but I think that close observation of our society may support such a conclusion. For example the steady decline in nation wide scholastic scores is just one indication

[68] This is called the Tri-Guna in Ayurveda – Sattva, Rajas and Tamas. They originate in Prakriti and are therefore part of all nature, but for this book we will limit ourselves to the mental relationships.

of the Tamas principle dominating in the common diet. Another aspect of the Tamas principle is violence that has been increasing steadily over the last several generations – along with refined and processed foods.

Recently, due to several tragic events around the country, the government has begun to look at the influence of the media in relation to violent behavior. It will probably take many more tragedies before people become aware that what they eat affects their mind and behavior. There are already a number of studies to support this concept. No doubt the many medical professionals (who swear by the atom / mechanical conception of the universe) will laugh and criticize this kind of approach. What can these people do when their only studies support this view? When the school luncheon diets were changed in New York and in California the scholastic scores improved proportionately. In New York the increase in total school achievement was the largest ever recorded in the United States.

Several other studies exist which show behavioral differences in jails, juvenile retention homes and correction facilities. These studies show that diet alone reduces the number of violent incidents in the facilities. When this kind of information exists it tends to confirm the traditional point of view that fresh, whole foods are the best source for both the body and mind.

One factor that deters many modern vegetarians away from Ayurvedic nutrition is the traditional use of dairy products in that culture. This was discussed in some depth in the section on dairy in chapter 8. Ayurveda considers that dairy is predominant in the Sattva quality – at least traditionally. Suffice to say that the dairy of that era has little or nothing to do with the dairy products of today. Even still some consumption of organic butter and yogurt would be considered good nutrition provided they are not made from low-fat or pasteurized milk. In order for dairy to be considered a nutritious food it has to be whole, fresh and unprocessed – thus comprising the Sattva principle. The making of butter, yogurt and ghee was done from whole milk. While the idea of all that fat may repulse many people, Ayurveda says that the body has a greater ability to digest whole milk than milk prepared in other ways. Pasteurized milk is considered to be poisonous to the body, as there exists no enzyme to digest it.

It is possible that the problem of lactose allergies and intolerance is due more to an inappropriate preparation and processing of milk than of milk itself. According to Ayurveda this is the case. If milk is not prepared in the correct manner the body ceases to be able to digest it. Thus, it turns toxic and poisons the body. According to Ayurveda it is the way that we treat and feed the cows that starts this scenario and then our obsession with eliminating fats and bacteria through processing that render today's milk indigestible. To illustrate this point a press release in July 1998 in Switzerland stated that a link of low fat dairy products to cancer had been found. As already mentioned in Chapter Eight we are still awaiting more information on this finding.

In any case the traditional use of dairy products in Ayurveda is more as a condiment than as a food. People were not living on butter and ghee although these were added to the diet on a daily basis in small amounts.

Really the major problem in today's world with eating any kind of animal product is that of chemical pollutants – which are classified as being dominant in the Tamas quality. All pollutants end up – sooner or later – in the tissues of the animals that we are eating. These chemicals do not leave the human body any more they could leave the animals body. People think that fish are safer than meats but this is far from the truth. Seafood is some of the most polluted sources of food available today and nearly half of all fish sampled by Consumers Union was contaminated with bacterial from human or animal feces.[69] The EPA issued more than 1000 warnings against eating fish from contaminated waters in and around the United States in 1994.[70]

Since 1945 the overall use of pesticides has increased 3,300% and the overall crop loss to insects has also increased by 20%.[71] Unfortunately, meat, poultry and dairy products contain the major source of pesticide residues in the Western diet.[72] Also 95% of human exposure to dioxin comes from eating meat poultry and dairy products.[73] Dioxin is a known potent carcinogen that is also used to bleach women's tampons and panty liners. In this light it is important to recognize that the problem of pesticides stays in the environment for a long time as demonstrated by the findings of this study. Ninety-nine percent of non-vegetarians mothers' milk has significant levels of DDT and only 8% of vegetarian mothers' milk has the same levels.[74]

I think that reasons to continue with a diet based on meat – in relation to health alone – are unfounded by the current data available. It seems that there actually is no good reason to eat a diet based on animal products from a health point of view. It is another thing if you want to eat meats, poultry, seafood or dairy because you like them or want to for other reasons. However, you should be aware that there is actually no need as far as nutritional requirements are concerned. People are always trying to scare would-be vegetarians with stories of vitamin B-12 deficiencies. In fact

---

[69] Rachel's *Environment and Health Weekly,* No. 450, July 13, 1995.

[70] Rachel's *Environment and Health Weekly,* No. 450, July 13, 1995.

[71] Pimental et al., *Handbook of Pest Management in Agriculture,* 1990.

[72] Regenstein, Lewis, *How to survive in America the Poisoned,* 1982

[73] EPA study cited in *USA Today,* September 13, 1994.

[74] *A Brief Review of Selected Environmental Contamination Incidents with a Potential for Health Effects,* prepared by the Library of Congress for the Committee on Environment and Public Works, US Senate (Aug. 1980), pp. 173-74.

there is no known case of B-12 deficiency symptoms. The body needs very little amounts of B-12 which can easily be gained from any fermented product or butter.

All of the old arguments have been proved wrong. Everything from amino acids to B-12 have turned out to be available in plant based diets that are based on whole foods. Of course if you just eliminate meat from your diet and still live on cupcakes, catsup and TV dinners you will end up with some form of malnutrition. But this is a case of poor nutritional choices not of eating or not eating animals. Ultimately the choice is yours. The data is there to show that the less animal products you consume the better your long-term health will be. Remember, it is never too late. Studies have shown that low protein diets have improved everything from bone density to heart conditions even when started late in life. It is never too late to start. Even reducing the amount of animal products consumed will have an enormous impact on your health. An ounce of prevention is worth a pound of treatment, and at today's prices, less expensive too!

10
Poisoned Food

The last chapter has given us an idea about the amounts of petroleum-based insecticides and fertilizers in the food chain. Now this chapter will expand on some of the effects of these chemicals. There is probably no subject closer to human beings than that of intimate sexual relations and the possibility to procreate. The joy of having children is one that is incomparable and is one fulfillment of being human. Likewise, the joy of intimate relations is part of our ability to create.

What happens when we find out that our ability to have children is being reduced daily by our continual consumption of chemicals made from petroleum? This effect may not be limited only to fertility – for both men and women – but, perhaps, even to our ability to have sex.

Unfortunately, this seems to be the situation in the world today. There is more and more information being published on this topic yet the public in general is, as yet, unaware that if the present trend continues having children will be a rarity – not a given right. Although there is huge disagreement between researchers in the biochemical scientific community there is certainly enough information to warrant concern. Several studies published in the medical media in 1992 showed that the developed world sperm counts have dropped in half. In contrast a group of specialists declared in 1996 that there has been no change in the last 20 years.[75]

This is another good example of disagreement in the biochemical world of science. Each group has numerous studies to quote from and each group says that the other group has flaws in their research. A very good book on this subject is *Our Stolen Future* by Dr. Theo Colburn.[76] It presents a very compelling stand for the lowering of the sperm count and other hormonal effects due to environmental factors. I strongly suggest that everyone reads this book! Discriminating readers will have sufficient proof of a major worldwide problem in our food chain and environment.

What is the Ayurvedic point of view? Ayurveda sees both men and women as prone to accumulate toxic substances in the reproductive system. As mentioned in chapter 14 and appendix 1 of this book Ayurveda views the body as a progressive development of tissues each one nourishing the next one. This process begins with food as the source of nutrition and the reproductive system or tissues as the final result of the transmutation of food. According to this view any foreign matter such as petrochemicals would accumulate in the reproductive tissues and cause – among other things – infertility.

Following this line of reasoning Ayurveda would support the school of scientists who say that petrochemicals are affecting the human reproductive system. From the Ayurvedic point of view the long-term consumption of petrochemicals in the food chain would *have to* affect the reproductive system in time. The only question would be when, not if.

Unfortunately, what recent studies are showing is that these effects are often manifesting in the children or

[75] Kolata, Gina, *International Herald Tribune,* March 21, 1996, p. 10.

[76] Colburn, Dr. Theo, 1996.

grandchildren of contaminated adults. The damage to reproductive fluids may be far worse than just infertility. Current studies are showing that genital deformation in second and third generation's offspring is common. This is real news for concern.

I can say from my own professional experience of working with hundreds of people over the last years that it does make an effect. When I follow Ayurvedic methods with my clients I am able to reverse the problems in over 80% of cases. I find that women in general are more susceptible to the immediate effects of these petrochemicals in the food chain. When I have prescribed therapies that counteract the chemical residue in the body women often recover completely.[77] However, men also suffer from these chemicals as frequently, but do not have the advantage of a monthly cycle that alerts them to problems. So when they become impotent or uninterested in sex they wonder why. But a look at how this happens, or has the potential to happen, would make things clearer.

How Environmental Pollutants in Food Affect Hormone Function in Men and Women

Almost all of our synthetic chemicals are based these days on petroleum products and are called petrochemicals. These products are used in the manufacturing of medicines, agrochemicals, canned foods, household cleaning products, plastics, personal hygiene products and even contraceptive creams. It may be hard to believe that the plastic wrap that you use to cover your food with could be adding minute particles of harmful petroleum molecules into your food, but this is probably the case. Many of these products have a hormone like effect on the body and are called "xenobiotics". Chemicals that have a specific estrogen like effect on the body are called "xenoestrogens".

---

[77] See Smith, Atreya, 1999.

To understand this we must look at the function of a cell in the body from the biochemical point of view. According to this view the cell has a porous wall that allows different nutrients to enter into the cell and contribute to the cellular metabolism. The cell also has special doors called receptacles that allow specific nutrients or chemicals into the cell. Hormones have their own doors to enter cells. The problem with petrochemicals is that they have hormone like effects on the cells – this means they block the doors of the normal hormones from entering the cell. This either acts like the hormone or starves the cell of the hormone.

This concept is well understood by the biochemical industry and used to make many hormone-like products for women including birth control pills and HRT. The problem is that the endocrine system (hormone system) is not completely understood by modern science. It also happens to be extremely fine tuned, meaning that a little too much of something can play havoc in other normal hormone functions like digestion or anti-inflammatory responses. As the hormones help control every function in the body we should be far more concerned about the ramifications of playing with this system.

Most petrochemicals tend to have an "estrogenic" effect on the body causing the metabolism to respond to them like they would to estrogen. Estrogen is actually a group of hormones that is present in both men and women. While women have greater amounts of estrogen than men do it still plays an important role in proper metabolic function in men. Women also have testosterones in their body that help balance the action of the estrogens and some petrochemicals also act like testosterone.

Therefore, when a fungicide like Vinclozolin is sprayed on fruits it affects both men and women with its testosterone like effect. Actually, Vinclozolin blocks testosterone from linking up to cells in the first place. Or then there is another fungicide, pyrimidine carbinol, which blocks any sex hormone from being produced at all. Hence, whether one is a man or a woman these chemicals will affect your endocrine system.

Dr. Colburn and associates have identified at least 51 different groups of chemicals in our every day life that have an estrogenic effect. Sometimes these estrogenic chemicals act like estrogen and sometimes they block the reception of estrogen in the cells. Very often the problem is that the estrogenic strength of the chemicals is many times greater than anything normally occurring in the body. Hence the body is bombarded by a huge quantity of a substance that normally occurs in extremely small doses.

One school of science argues that the estrogenic effect of chemicals is too small to make any problem in the body. But, another independent study from Tulane University in New Orleans found that combining different estrogenic like chemicals can produce an effect up to thousand times greater than the individual chemicals.[78] And once more it should be noted that this is a common occurrence in nature due to the extensive use of petrochemicals in agriculture.

Additional studies have shown that even very small amounts of hormones like chemicals – when ingested at the wrong time – can distort the developing fetus in pregnant women. Tiny amounts of these chemicals taken at the wrong time can physically or mentally retard your child's development in the womb. Hence, the argument used that these chemicals exist in too small of quantities to harm people has been proven – tragically – to be very wrong.

Perhaps the most problematic consequence of these chemicals is that the body lacks the ability to recognize them as an invading hormone. The body normally has a self-regulating function that eliminates excess hormones from

---

[78] *Science,* June 7, 1996.

the blood stream. This same function – carried out in the blood stream and orchestrated primarily by the liver – also increases hormones if needed. The result of the body's inability to recognize these estrogenic chemicals as hormones allows them to stay on in body tissues. And as these chemicals do not break down and leave – nor do they stop acting like hormones – their effect is cumulative. Even if you eliminate all sources of these chemicals from your nutritional intake today they will remain on in your body until death unless you take steps to remove them.

Just what exactly are the effects of too much estrogen in the body? Well pick up any brochure on an estrogenic product (like ERT) and read the warnings. The one I have in my file says that these are possible risks:

- Cancer of the Uterus
- Cancer of the Breast
- Gallbladder Disease
- Abnormal Blood clotting

And then there are the side effects:

- Nausea and Vomiting
- Breast tenderness or enlargement
- Enlargement of benign tumors
- Enlargement of fibroids of the uterus
- Retention of excess fluids
- A spotty darkening of the skin, particularly on the face

The physiological effect of estrogen is to promote growth. This means the growth of tumors and cancers. For women this especially means the growth of uterine fibroids. For men it can mean prostrate enlargement.

Many of the current menstrual problems that women have can come from excess estrogen and low progesterone levels in the body. If the estrogen is not directly causing a problem it often inhibits the production of progesterone, the hormone that has the balancing action on estrogen. Some doctors have achieved excellent results in treating women by just increasing the progesterone levels in the body. A pioneer in this field is Dr. John R. Lee who uses natural progesterone to lower the high chemical estrogen levels in the body.[79] While I do not completely agree with Dr. Lee, his work is very innovative and requires support and attention from society. My main disagreement about Dr. Lee's work is his definition of natural progesterone. I have achieved similar results by following the Ayurvedic model that uses no pharmaceutical processing whatsoever.

In addition to the problems cited above on the label of an estrogenic product, excess estrogen is known to cause the fol-lowing problems for women:

- anxiety
- weight gain
- excess bleeding during menstruation
- emotional disorientation
- PMS

For men estrogenic chemicals can cause a lowering of testosterone production which can give men some of the following problems:

- weight gain
- water retention
- enlargement of tumors
- enlargement of prostate
- enlargement of breast fatty tissue
- lower testosterone levels
- possibly lower sperm counts
- increase anxiety

Many doctors have noticed a large increase in high estrogen related problems in recent years. Medical journals

---

[79] Lee, Dr. John R., 1996.

and magazines are filled with stories of many women beginning menopause in their early forties or even beginning premenopause in their late thirties. A large segment of doctors report that these effects are coming from environmental estrogens. The increase of uterine fibroids is now so high – over 40% of women – that it is considered "normal". This is a condition that is a direct result of high estrogen in the blood. It is estimated that between 60 to 80% of women suffer from some kind of premenstrual problem – many of which are caused from high levels of estrogen.

The number of fish that now have large growths and tumors is so great that canneries consider them "normal". A couple of researches found that the level of estrogen coming through the city's water purification system was enormous. They managed to trace this kind of estrogen to the kind used in birth control pills. What sparked their interest was the state of the local fish population – over 80% had tumors from excessive levels of estrogen.

What to do About It ?

It is unlikely that the public is going to demand that the large petrochemical companies stop making or using these products. It is after all a multi–billion dollar industry. Just one best selling pharmaceutical product makes a billion dollars in a year. The extent that we as a culture have become dependant on these chemicals is staggering. Many of these products make life "modern" for people. Agriculture continues to use them even though statistics show that the more pesticides we use the more crops are damaged by insects.[80]

Fortunately there are several things we as individuals can do for our health and the health of our family. The first is to choose food that is grown without chemicals. This is perhaps

---

80. Pimental, et al., *Handbook of Pest Management in Agriculture*, 1990.

the most important step and perhaps the hardest for many people because it greatly limits the places you can eat. Taking the step to buy organic is now relatively easy in many places in the country as consumer awareness grows. If you do not have an organic produce section ask your market to start one, if they do not then start shopping somewhere else. The retailer will have to listen to you if you put your foot down and only buy organic. Also you can demand a fair price. Organic foods used to be very expensive but this is also changing.

One must be aware that the levels of "organic" vary greatly. Recent laws have been passed to make this situation even worse. Remember the large petrochemical companies are not going to give up millions of dollars in profit easily. They are lobbying constantly to be allowed to use lower levels of petrochemicals and still have the label "organic". The larger the food stores the more discerning you need to be. Buying from local people is always best as you can check them out easier and they stand to lose more by losing you as a customer.

If you have the habit to eat out frequently then you will generally have trouble. But here again demand that your favorite restaurant begins to buy organic foods, not only vegetables, but meat also if you eat it. In fact, if you eat meat ONLY eat organic meat as all others are loaded with antibiotics and hormones. Animal products in general are to be avoided for this reason alone. Ayurveda does not consider food that is loaded with antibiotics and hormones to be a good food source. The best diet – if you are concerned by the above information – is one based only on plants.

Once again Mother Nature comes to the rescue. Eating different vegetables can repair or stop the hormone like effect of petrochemicals. These plants include all soy products as well as most dark green leafy vegetables. They also include alfalfa sprouts, whole grains (rye, buckwheat, millet, oats, barley, corn, rice and wheat) and flaxseed oil among many others. Whole grains are good to help remove excess chemical estrogens in the body as they contain lignans, a cellulose material that binds to the chemicals and removes them through a normal bowel movement. Your basic guideline to counteract this trend of chemical hormones is the repeating theme of this book – eat a diet based on whole foods from an organic source.

The advantage of this diet in the context of hormones is that the very mild hormone (called phytosteroid or plant steroid) action of plants often blocks the stronger effects of the chemical variety. The plant hormones block the receptacles and prevent the strong action of the petrochemicals. The plant hormones also have the advantage to leave the body in a short time whereas the chemical variety never leaves on a normal American diet. There are over 300 plants that have phytosteroid or hormone like effects in the body so the key is to eat a varied diet.

If you are a man or woman with a medical problem listed as being related to estrogen (see the above examples) it is strongly suggested that you eat a totally plant based diet with no animal products whatsoever. This should be done at least during the time of treatment and perhaps beyond if you wish to maintain your health.

11
How to Lose Weight Permanently by Increasing Metabolic Function

The real key to losing weight is to have your body functioning at its correct capacity. When a person gains weight it is for two primary reasons – inappropriate food choices and improper metabolic functioning. Both of these factors must be addressed for a person to either lose weight or maintain their present weight. The focus of this chapter is how to correct your metabolic functions in order to have good health.

The Ayurvedic point of view is that weight is lost naturally when the body is functioning normally and a balanced diet of whole foods is consumed. The cases of Jenny, Zelda and Lisa presented earlier in this book are perfect examples of this principle. All of them lost weight simply by restoring correct metabolic functions. There are a number of diseases or problems that can make the metabolism function incorrectly. This would include hormone disruptions, wasting diseases, autoimmune disorders and any serious, life threatening disease. If you are suffering from a serious problem then this chapter will not help you specifically; you will need to see a doctor or practitioner specializing in treating your body, not your disease.

The vast majority of people overweight will benefit from the insights presented in this chapter because, like Jenny,

Zelda and Lisa, their metabolism is probably not functioning up to par. The first step in losing weight is to eat less. The second is to change your diet according to your constitution and begin to use whole foods. Eliminating all refined foods is the most important step in terms of changing your diet. Once the diet has been adjusted or has begun to be adjusted then the second issue of metabolism can be addressed.

In order to change the way your metabolism is currently functioning your lifestyle will also need to be changed. As this is a vast subject it is explained in detail in chapter 12. It is important to stress that changing only one aspect of your life, be it diet, metabolism or lifestyle, will not bring you good health, normal weight and a high quality of life. The Ayurvedic perception is that all aspects of the life must be addressed in order to really bring a state of equilibrium and health to the body and mind. Here we will begin with the body and its physical aspects. In order to know what to change it is important to know what is wrong. Therefore, the place to begin is to understand the problems of poor metabolic functioning.

Explanation of Digestive Problems and Metabolic Malfunctions

Weight gain is one of the most obvious signs of metabolic imbalance. However, there are many other signs – according to Ayurveda – that your body is not functioning at its full potential. The signs vary according to constitution, although any kind of person can experience the following symptoms.

Vata Type Malfunctions:

Gas, constipation, colic pain, gripping, dry stools, bloating abdomen, PMS, dry skin or hair, nervousness, anxiety, insomnia, aversion to cold weather and wind, many food allergies, and irregularity in occurrence of any of these symptoms.

Pitta Type Malfunctions:

Burning in the stomach or abdomen, lose stools, ulcers, inflamed intestines, hemorrhoids, skin inflammation, burning eyes, headaches that are light sensitive, aversion to heat, frequent anger or frustration.

Kapha Type Malfunctions

Nausea, bloating in the stomach, congestion in the lungs or stomach, feeling of heaviness, difficulty to get motivated, desire to eat frequently, aversion to damp and cold, depression, craving for sweets.

These are some of the most common signs that each constitution is out of equilibrium. This indicates that the metabolism is not doing its job correctly, and consequently, some problems are arriving. You do not have to experience all of the symptoms at once. Any symptom, if consistent, will indicate some degree of metabolic disturbance.

The Ayurvedic view of the metabolism is that it strives for equilibrium naturally. The means of understanding the desire of the metabolism to achieve equilibrium is through the three principles that we are calling VPK. Therefore, the Vata type will tend to show the signs of the Vata principle in a state of metabolic disturbance. The Pitta type will tend to show signs of the Pitta principle in a state of disturbance, and likewise for the Kapha type.

When you can identify that there is some disturbance – such as intestinal gas – eliminate the source of the problem or adjust the spices that will antidote the source of the disturbance. If there is no identifiable source it indicates that the Vata principle is playing havoc with your metabolism. In other words, you are experiencing a state that is not optimum for your health. And if left untreated it will – according to Ayurveda – cause a more serious problem in time. If you correct the small disturbances as they arise you can prevent major illnesses from arising.

How to Correct the Metabolism

The best way to correct any metabolic problem is through diet, exercise, lifestyle and by using herbs that promote your constitutional equilibrium or health. Using all of these three together one can achieve a dynamic form of health. This section will focus on the use of herbs as digestive spices to accelerate normal digestive procedures of liquefaction, transformation, assimilation and elimination. When these four stages are functioning normally then your whole metabolism will have the correct support to regain its normal state. Additionally, the classification of foods according to digestive response will be explained.

If you have been living in a state of chronic disturbance then you will need to go through a period of re-educating your metabolism. This is a process that is slow and should not be forced or hurried. In Ayurveda there is an understanding that the body becomes habituated to a substance or habit – changing it quickly can then bring great disruption to the mind and body.[81] Hence, it is necessary to proceed slowly to change long standing habits or problems.

The Ayurvedic understanding of metabolism needs some explanation for this chapter really to make sense. As stated above Ayurveda understands that the body is intelligent and strives to maintain a state of equilibrium. This is a constantly demanding task as the body is adjusting to external temperature, climate, food consumption, clothes (worn or not worn), emotional state, and the general outlook on life of the person concerned.

As each of these factors is always undergoing some fluctuation the body – through the three principles – looks for ways to lower excess and increase deficiencies. In this sense deficiencies is not of nutrients (as is common in biochemical terms), but of the three principles that work in

[81] This is called prakritisatmya in Ayurveda.

conjunction to maintain metabolism. Consequently, the use of diet, lifestyle and herbs can work to move an excess or deficiency of any principle – Vata, Pitta or Kapha.

If one can accelerate the metabolism then the body naturally uses or "burns up" stored fat. This fat accumulation happened because some factor in the mind, diet or lifestyle was not in accordance with the nature of the person concerned. This means that a husband and wife could have the same diet and have very different results because their birth constitutions are different. Therefore, the same food will have different effects on the different metabolisms of the husband and wife. Perhaps one of them will gain weight and the other will not. Perhaps one will feel hungry all the time and the other satisfied.

By finding out what your constitution is and eating and living according to the guidelines for that constitution you will find – in time – that you are losing weight (if you are overweight), gaining weight (if you are underweight) or maintaining weight if you are at the weight right for your body frame. This is good nutrition and health because it will last a lifetime and prevent most illnesses from coming in the first place. *It is never too late to start living right and improving your life!*

The basic idea is the same that was stated in chapter 8 in the section on spices. There are groups of spices that will help each constitutional type digest their food better. These spices will also accelerate (or balance) your metabolism in general. This is the general idea behind the so called "Ayurvedic Teas" that appearing on the market. These teas, called after the three types, bring equilibrium to the type that they correspond to – at least in theory. In practice one needs to ingest six to ten grams of most herbs and spices to change an existing metabolic problem – and this often for a period of some months. However, taking a gram of herbs before or after each meal will slowly correct and maintain proper digestion – especially for the Kapha and Vata types. The Pitta type is generally balanced by eating bland foods or using very mild spices.

The experience of Ayurveda is that the following spices help to increase enzyme function for the different types of people. Mixed or dual types of people use a mix or just one of the spice combinations – depending on how they feel and what side of their constitution is more disrupted. While this cannot be supported by modern science it, nevertheless, works very well. The long tradition of thousands of years tends to give an enormous amount of strength to this particular use of spices. Why else would our ancestors travel for a year to buy nothing more than spices? Gold has always had value, but one should be very careful about discarding, through arrogance or ignorance, the traditional value of spices.

Buy dried spices fresh and grind them up into a powder, in a coffee grinder or by hand. Take half a teaspoon (about one gram) of this powder with a little warm water before or after eating – main meals are the most important.

In addition to taking these spices with meals each person should begin to use the Ayurvedic understanding of how foods are digested in the body. Ayurveda does not use proteins, carbohydrates and fats to distinguish the different kinds of qualities of food. Instead they have an understanding of how the body responds to food in the digestive tract.

This has to do with how long foods take to be digested. Some foods pass through the intestines quickly and others can take several days. Therefore, according to Ayurveda, eating certain kinds of "light" foods (e.g., digests quickly) will promote weight loss and accelerated metabolic function. This is a different system than what we are used to in the Western world, but the logic, and results tend to overcome any doubts about its efficiency.

Below is a list of the different food categories and how fast they pass through the digestive system of a person. Note that the times for people basing their diet on animal products vs. those who are based mostly on plant diets are different. This is because meats are slower to digest than plants and slow down all other products eaten. Remember that faster is not better, the body needs to have some food in it to support proper absorption of nutrients. Liquid based diets will cause long term problems as will "fruit only" diets. (There are exceptions to this rule, but involve aspects that are beyond the scope of this book – if one is doing this kind of diet for a long time it will most likely result in disturbing your digestive capacity unless you are working with a knowledgeable person.)

Classification of Food by Digestion Time

Food Category	**Hours to process** (Diet Based on Animals)	**Hours to process** (Diet Based on Plants)	**Subjective Feeling in The Body**	**Ability to Nourish The Body**
Red Meats	48 to 72	0	Heaviest	Very Great
Fish & Poultry	36 to 48	24 to 36	Heavy	Great
Dairy Products	24 to 36	24	Full	Great
Beans (Legumes)	24 to 30	20 to 24	Full	Great
Nuts & Seeds	24 to 26	20 to 24	Full	Great
Grains	20 to 24	18 to 20	Filling	Very Good
Root Vegetables	20 to 24	18 to 20	Filling	Good
Leafy Vegetables	18 to 22	12 to 18	Light	Valuable
Fruits	12 to 18	6 to 12	Lightest	Some

The idea behind this approach is to eat the "lightest" foods if you are trying to lose weight or correct metabolic problems. A 'lighter' diet will nourish the body less, but an overweight person already has too much "nourishment" according to Ayurveda and so will not become disturbed by this approach.

The primary way that all constitutions can use this chart is to change the order in which they eat foods. Eating "light" foods first will aid the body because it will be able to process them first. Eating "heavy" foods first will cause all other foods that are added in later to ferment and/or putrefy, as their time to digest is much quicker.

Hence, to increase digestive ability one should eat the foods that digest under 24 hours whenever possible. Deep-frying foods adds another six to twelve hours to any food (except dairy which is hard to deep-fry!). The greater the ratio of whole grains and vegetables is to red meats, poultry, fish and dairy the less the time the body will take to digest these foods. The less whole grains, vegetables and fruits that are taken the longer the heavier foods will take to digest.

Thus in order to accelerate digestive and metabolic function (which burns fat naturally) one should eat foods that take the body less time to digest and ingest the spices that help increase enzyme function and promote constitutional equilibrium. If you do this consistently then you will get results naturally, without crash diets or other disturbing methods.

Eliminating Fatigue and Increasing Performance through Food

Increasing nutrient absorption is the best way to increase your performance mentally and physically. It is also the best way to stop feeling fatigued all the time. Here are some general rules for everyone to start feeling better from chronic fatigue.

Eliminate the following from your daily diet:

- All stimulants like coffee, black tea, green tea, and all forms of alcohol
- Eliminate all refined foods from your diet
- Stop using or ingesting white sugar in any form (which means all refined foods).
- Use only cold-pressed oils; stop all refined oils and margarine
- Stop eating any fried foods
- Eat little or no animal products until your energy picks up

Begin to add the following to your daily diet:

- Fresh foods
- Whole foods
- Spices according to your constitution taken with the main meals

There will be a period of reaction to this change; I suggest you follow the advice given in chapter 16 to avoid strong reactions. You should be prepared for some changes in the body and know that they will normally pass in ten days to two weeks. You should not try to do everything at once as this will shock the body. It is better to follow the 21 day plans in chapter 16 to avoid any major problems that can come from stopping coffee or alcohol abruptly. These changes form the basis for the above information to work. If you can do everything together, slowly, over a period of three weeks you will feel like a new person. The effort that you put into any major change will pay you dividends in less that a month – a very good investment!

All of the steps listed in this section above will increase your absorption of all nutrients. As you may remember from earlier discussions in the book, the main principle in Ayurvedic nutrition is increased absorption.

Refined foods impair absorption by coating the intestinal walls. Refined oils have a similar effect and clog arteries and other channels in the body. Stimulants cause the endocrine system to be on a constant rolly-coaster ride through adjusting blood sugars and hormones in the blood – all which leads to adrenal and kidney fatigue (your fatigue). Refined sugar is both a stimulant and a refined food that clogs the channels and over stimulates endocrine function. Fried foods turn oil into free radicals that disturb the integrity of your normal cellular function. The chemical dyes and preservatives in refined processed food affect your moods, mental functions and cellular integrity.

Removing these foods from your diet will have an immediate result of increased energy, mental alertness and a subjective feeling of well being. I suggest following these steps to increase your energy, performance and your desire to be happy and healthy.

12
Lifestyle as Nutritional Support

Ayurveda is based on an integrated vision of the universe. Because of this understanding nutrition is not divided out of the complete lifestyle of the individual. It is the wholeness, or interrelatedness, of the human being with its environment that is important. Extending this point of view further one sees that it is the wholeness or interrelatedness of the human body that must be addressed in the context of its individual environment.

A failure to approach the human being in this manner results in a divisional kind of thinking and approach to reality. This is what Dr. Bohm, the world renowned physicists, calls a "fragmentary" approach. To view nutrition simply as proteins, carbohydrates, vitamins, minerals and the other mico-nutrients is bound to fail in the most important aspect – that of the human body's relationship and interaction with its environment.

At this point the word environment needs to have some clarification. From an Ayurvedic point of view "environment" means everything around you in the physical sense and everything you are engaged in privately and professionally. By extension this means how much stress you are under professionally and privately as well as your subjective feelings of contentment and happiness – or the lack of contentment.

In essence, the word environment according to Ayurveda is your whole life, both internal and external. The many aspects of your life cannot be divided as biochemical elements. The effect of the environment on the human being is a little studied field in modern nutrition and a widely studied and thoroughly documented study in Ayurveda. According to the precepts of Ayurvedic medicine it is absolutely necessary for each person to integrate a lifestyle that is supportive and appropriate for their environment and nutritional intake. Neglect of this precept will most certainly result in the failure of any natural treatment that is undertaken.

Unquestionably, this is of equal importance to any dietary changes an individual may make. Ayurveda gives equal importance to your interaction with your environment (your whole life) as to your dietary choices. While this may seem to be strange or even revolutionary in scope some modern doctors are having excellent results by integrating such an approach into the treatment and prevention of chronic, life threatening diseases. Dr. Dean Ornish is one of these doctors that have become well-known in recent years. The results of the studies conducted by Dr. Ornish are truly amazing.

However, the modern programs of nutrition and lifestyle are still addressing the diseases and symptoms rather than the unique individuality of each person and their special needs. This approach will still be limited in results because there will be certain people for whom the program will be too extreme and others for whom it will not be extreme enough. Therefore, one could greatly increase the results of these kinds of programs by addressing the individuality of people through lifestyle and nutrition. Admittedly, any program that considers lifestyle will work far better than a system that does not.

In all of the cases that I mentioned in this book, Jenny, Zelda, Lisa and Martha, each of them changed their lifestyle.

To the extent that they could change or adjust their lifestyle their nutritional changes were supported and strengthened. This point cannot be stressed enough. I do have clients that are not willing to change their lifestyles and just want to use herbs and food to lose weight – many of them achieve active good results. But in comparison to using a combined approach their cases are less dramatic and they always risk to have the problem reoccur as many times it is our lifestyle that is causing the problem in the first place.

In considering the environment, and the lifestyle that is contained within it, we can, for convenience, consider several categories. These are:

- Climate and Season
- Home
- Profession
- Personal Relationships
- Daily Habits
- Sexual Relations
- Outlook on Life

In the above list one can see that all aspects of the life can fall into one of the categories. Obviously, life is not divided in such a manner and we do so simply to explain the different aspects as all being equally important to our digestion, assimilation and elimination of our nutritional intake.

Climate and Season

There is an unfortunate habit today of eating relatively the same kinds of foods regardless of the climate you live in. An example of this is Miami and Boston. These two cities have very different climates and so, logically, may create a different environment – or receptivity – in people living in both places, to eating any given food. According to nature different foods grow in different climates. There is a reason for this, which, simply enough is that of climatic adaptation.

In other words, the foods that grow in a place are suited for that environment.

Traditionally, this meant that a person would only eat the foods that grew in their own local area. However, we live in an age in which things are not as clearly defined as the more traditional cultures of the past, like in India or Europe. Therefore, we need to closely examine this traditional point and see how we can eat oranges in Boston and apples in Miami – both of which are unnatural food choices according to climatic growing conditions.

First, let us be clear that the best approach is always to eat the foods that are grown in the local of your home as they will be the most adapted to your body's needs in relation to your environment. This is a basic precept that exists in many forms of natural medicine and nutrition – systems that do not view you as a pile of atoms stuck together.

But as we live in a culture that insists to drink orange juice every morning regardless of your individual constitution, the season or your climatic situation we must give some "modern" guidelines. Modern in this sense has little to do with "better" on an "improvement", quite the contrary it is rather a necessary evil of contemporary times.

The basic rule one can follow is to only eat foods when they are "in season". For example, you live in New York and you like to eat oranges. According to the Ayurvedic system you should only eat oranges in the summer months when oranges would be becoming ripe, not in the cold winter months when the cooling, acidic nature of oranges will be disturbing to most people. If you drink orange juice because of the vitamin C then understand that raw tomatoes have more of this vitamin than oranges. Another example of this is eating summer squash in the winter. Or still another is eating kiwis in winter – which are anyway a semi-tropical fruit – hardly the best choice when there are two feet of snow outside.

Modern man has tried to insulate and protect himself totally from the climate and seasons in which he lives. This is obviously a beneficial thing as far as comfort goes, but there is no need to apply it to our nutrition as well. There has been a lot of popular diets in recent years that speak of our genetic food patterns, or how our chromosomes are meant only to digest certain kinds of foods, even that certain types of people are meant to eat certain kinds of foods based on hereditary traits. What none (that I know of) of these system notes is that for as long as humankind has been on the planet he/she has eaten foods that grew in season in their climatic zone. Aside from refined foods, chemical preservatives and the genetic engineering of foods there is probably no greater deviation from our ancestors than eating pineapples in Minneapolis in full winter.

Few people seem to realize that this alone is a major cause of disease today – especially chronic degenerative diseases that are rising in ever increasing numbers. From a biochemical point of view this can be seen as eating a food that cannot be digested due to a lack of the proper enzymes. We have noted earlier in the book that the body can slowly produce enzymes over several generations to digest almost anything. But the last thirty years has seen an enormous increase of food foreign to their place of consumption.

If it is not possible to eat foods from your location – due to social pressures or lifestyle – then at the very least eat the foods in the correct season. This does not mean that you cannot have an orange once a month or even once a week. It means that your daily consumption of foods should be from your local climate and eaten in their normal season.

Obviously, people living in New England and Arizona are going to have very different diets. Most people practicing Ayurveda today are not making adjustments to the climates they live in. People are blindly looking at food lists and seeing that a grapefruit is OK for their type and eating it – without any consideration for the climate or season of the year. This is in conflict to lifestyle as a nutritional support. As much as possible follow this kind of approach and you will avoid creating conflicts between yourself and your environment.

Home

Your living environment is also a support, or detriment, to your ability to use nutrients effectively. This means your actual home – do you live in an apartment, a house? Or do you live in the country, a small town or a large city? Each of these will change how you respond to food and its assimilation. The most important question here is how you feel living where you are. If you like living in an apartment then it will be fine for you.

The question of your home is most important regarding the environment within it. This means how the people living in it feel, what they do when they eat – like watch TV or listen to the radio. This includes the emotional state of the people and their physical activities. A home that is harmonious will help promote the correct use of the food you consume. A home that is disturbed will tend to disturb your assimilation and elimination. While this may seem like a strange concept to you it will make a huge difference if you can correct any disturbing factors in your home environment.

Profession

Your profession is an important consideration in nutrition. The work place has great potential to overstress, or strain, the nervous system. According to modern biochemical research the nervous and endocrine systems control the digestion and assimilation of nutrients. Yet, it is these two systems that suffer the most from stress – most of which comes from the work place. Hence, even using biochemical nutrition we should be able to draw the conclusion that excess levels of stress are damaging to the proper utilization of food.

From an Ayurvedic point of view any stress is too much and should be eliminated.[82] Therefore, stress management is extremely important for nutrition. Bringing work home is a good way to destroy not only your personal relationships, but also your health. Hence, methods need to be taken to neutralize the stress that you do accumulate during the day. Waiting for the weekend is not an effective or efficient way to release stress. Daily methods are far more efficient and effective. Some options will be covered below under the section of habits.

Additionally, any job that has more responsibility is going to be more stressing. Even a simple job like packaging widgets can be stressful if the work environment is stressful – like working in "Uncle Scrooges" Widget Factory. The point is to keep in mind the levels of stress involved. If a CEO and the widget packer are compared in relation to stress the CEO will have, by the nature of his job, to deal with more kinds of stressful situations and in higher levels. Steps should be taken to maintain stress at reasonable levels – at least one needs to eliminate accumulated stress on a daily basis – to maintain correct nutrient absorption.

Personal Relationships

Your personal relationships can be a source of health or illness. It is best to resolve personal problems when they arise and prevent them from accumulating as emotional stress or repressed emotions. It is beyond the scope of this book to address the subject, yet it would be a major flaw not to point out that your personal happiness is, perhaps, the single most important aspect of your health.

Often, for various reasons, we are not able to change a difficult relationship. However, we are always able to change

---

[82] Stress aggravates the Vata Dosha which, in turn, can aggravate the other two Doshas. However, as Vata controls the nervous and much of the endocrine functions it is extremely important to prevent Vata from becoming imbalanced.

how we view the relationship and our response within it. According to Ayurveda suppressed emotions are a major cause of disease and digestive disruptions. This can be seen in the active, achievement orientated macho who suppresses both work stress and person tensions only to die of a heart attack at 45 to 50. We all know people like this (or have known!). It is questionable, from an Ayurvedic point of view whether the diet, the stress, or the repressed emotions did the most damage. Certainly all together create a perfect situation for a serious illness. Hence, it is best to try and resolve any personal situations that may exist and live as peacefully as possible.

Daily Habits

Our lifestyle can be reduced to our daily habits. Thus, this section forms the basis of lifestyle counseling in Ayurveda for all of the major constitutional types. Each type will be listed and explained accordingly. The crux of this information is to provide the kind of life that will support the digestion and elimination of the foods you eat. The rules change for each person and care should be given to follow this advice closely. It is often advised to change this aspect of your life *before changing the actual food* you are eating.

The power of your daily habits is enormous and has the greatest power to help or harm you. The distinction should be made that eating something, or doing something once in a while is OK provided it is not a daily event or action. Ayurveda is not fanatical or reactionary, but rather sees those things that are potentially disruptive for our metabolism and advises us to avoid them when possible. Ayurveda is based on the understanding of the interrelated actions of substances functioning together. It is not moralistic or fanatical, but it provides a practical methodology for health.

In order to better understand the information on our daily habits it is helpful to know which times of the day the three principles predominate in nature. Looking at the list below one can see that the Kapha principle is dominating during the early morning after sunrise. (Note: These figures are averages that should be adjusted to fit your region as they use the peak of the sun's cycle as the middle of the Pitta period, i.e., noon and midnight.) This means that foods that aggravate the Kapha type of person will do their greatest damage during the morning, which is why it is better for the Kapha type not to eat breakfast.

	DAY	**NIGHT**
Type Kapha	7 am to 11 am	7 pm to 11 pm
Type Pitta	11 am to 3 pm	11 pm to 3 am
Type Vata	3 pm to 7 pm	3 am to 7 am

The following tables are related to the table in chapter 5 that gives the quantity of food to eat according to each type's capacity to digest and assimilate. The following tables give the times most appropriate to eat and to perform other activities that are normal during the day or week. The times given are important and should be followed by everyone.

Daily Regime for the Vata Type

The daily regime for the Vata type is basically mild in nature as the Vata person is the most sensitive physically and mentally. They have the least restrictions on food and activities. The primary rule for the Vata type is to bring regularity into the daily schedule. The Vata tends to be a bit irregular in eating, sleeping and most daily activities. Therefore, by bringing regularity into their lives the Vata type can prevent metabolic disturbances that arise from irregular living habits. This is usually a difficult thing for many Vata types.

It should be noted that these represent optimum times, but there are other options. For example I have several artist clients who find it necessary for their work to "live at night". For these kinds of people I encourage them to establish a regular schedule according to their personal situation. If the schedule is regular.then the body can slowly adjust to it. However, if there is no regular eating or sleeping times then the body remains in a perpetual limbo that is not supportive to normal metabolic functions. One should also not apply the rules too strictly – go out late once in a while if you wish.

This type can eat frequently in small amounts. They are also allowed to rest in the afternoon if very fatigued – normally day rest is reserved for the very young, old or sick. However, some Vata types may need more rest. The Vata type needs light kinds of exercise that are not too fatiguing like dance, yoga and thai chi. Massage is very important to maintain the health of the Vata type as is a good amount of sleep each night. By following these suggestions one can prevent the body from becoming sick and aid normal digestion processes.

Meals	7-8.00 a.m.	11.00 a.m.	12-1.00 p.m.	4.00 p.m.	6.30-7.30 p.m.
Breakfast	Mode-rate				
Snack		If needed			
Lunch			Mode-rate		
Snack				Mode-rate	
Dinner					Mode-rate

Activity	6-7 a.m.	8 am - 6 pm	3 - 4 p.m.	8-10 p.m.	10-11 p.m
Wake-up	Sunrise				
Bathing	Hot shower				
Meditation	30 min.				
Exercise		Light			
Work		Creative, avoid stress			
Rest/Nap			If needed		
Massage				Daily on body	
Sex				1-2 times a week	
Bed-time					10-11 pm
Hours of Sleep					8-9 hours

Daily Regime for the Pitta Type

One of the primary things for the Pitta type is not to overwork or overextend themselves in professional or personal activities. The Pitta type is the most goal-oriented of the types and so tends to create challenges of some kind or other. Not pushing oneself to the limit is an important aspect of balancing the Pitta type in daily activities.

The Pitta type needs three good meals in the day, but also needs to avoid overeating or eating too much fried or oily foods as these will cause them to gain extra weight. Taking time alone is very important for them in the morning and some quite activity like meditation, prayer or sitting quietly before the days activities prevents imbalance in the metabolism. Avoiding frustration and fits of anger are an important side of daily maintenance as these strong emotions disturb the Pitta type very quickly. "Cooling down" both mentally and physically (like with a cool shower) is important. Do not allow yourself to over heat emotionally or physically, but rather look for a solution to the problem and resolve it.

Very competitive or strong forms of exercise should be avoided (unless these are part of your profession – in which case you are well suited to your job). Because the pure Pitta type has the potential to overwork or over exercise they should avoid this in their free time or in their hobbies. In fact, hobbies are an important way to balance the Pitta type as they need to be active and kept interested in some pursuit.

Meals	7-8.00 A.M.	11.00 A.M.	12-1.00 P.M.	4.00 P.m.	6.30-7.30 p.m
Breakfast	Large				
Snack		No			
Lunch			Mode-rate		
Snack				No	
Dinner					Large

Activity	6 - 7 A.M.	8 A.M. 6 P.M.	3 - 4 P.M.	8 - 10 P.M.	11A.M. 12 P.M
Wake-up.	6-7 am				
Bathing	Cool shower				
Meditation	30 min.				
Exercise		Mode-rate			
Work		Respo-nsibility, dynamic			
Rest/Nap			No		

Massage				2x week on body	
Sex				2-3 times a week	
Bed-time					11 pm
Hours of Sleep					7-8 hours

Daily Regime for the Kapha Type

The Kapha type needs the strongest forms of techniques in daily activities. Yet, they are usually the ones who are seeking comfort and pleasure the most. A certain amount of discipline and "roughing it" is needed by the Kapha type to maintain balance and weight. These people gain weight the easiest of all types and therefore need to be strict about what they eat and drink. Paying close attention to the times of eating is very important. Skipping breakfast is almost always a good idea as the early morning is not a good time to begin digesting food for the slow Kapha type.

These people need less sleep and more strenuous activities in life. Walking 30 minutes a day is a beginning, but hardly enough for the Kapha type to maintain a healthy metabolism. Strong, active and demanding forms of exercise are needed for this type like jogging, aerobics, competitive sports, tennis, and anything that makes one break a sweat and continue to sweat for sometime.

Meals	7-8.00 a.m.	10-11 a.m.	12-1.00 p.m.	4.00 p.m.	6.30-7.30p.m
Breakfast	No				
Snack		Fruit			
Lunch			Moderate		
Snack				No	
Dinner					Light

Activity	6-7 am	8am-6pm	3-4 pm	8-10 pm 4 pm	11pm-12am
Wake-up	Sunrise				
Bathing	Warm shower				
Meditation	30 min.				
Exercise		Strong			
Work		Manag-ement, with people			
Rest/Nap			No		
Massage				2x month on body	
Sex			2-4 times a week		
Bed-time					11pm-12am
Hours of Sleep					6-7 hours

Daily Regime for the Vata/Pitta Type

The Vata/Pitta type is a mixed type and so needs a little of both the Vata and Pitta in their life. Which one needs more will have to be decided through practice or seeing an Ayurvedic practitioner. Generally speaking a mix of the more mild sides of the Vata and the Pitta will be the most appropriate. Experimenting is the best way to find out what is correct for you. It is interesting to note that if you have a strong aversion to some activity it is probably because you need it!

Meals	7-8.00 A.M.	11.00 A.M.	12-1.00 P.M.	4.00 P.M.	6.30-7.30P.M.
Breakfast	Mode-rate				
Snack		No			
Lunch			Mode-rate		
Snack				If needed	
Dinner					Mode-rate

Activity	6 - 7 A.M.	8 A.M. 6 P.M.	3 - 4 P.M.	8 - 10 P.M.	11 A.M. 12 P.M.
Wake-up	6-7 am				
Bathing	Warm shower				
Meditation	30 min.				
Exercise		Mode-rate			
Work		Respon-sibility, dynamic, creative			
Rest/Nap			No		
Massage				2x Weekly on body	
Sex				2-3 times a week	
Bed-time					11 pm
Hours of Sleep					7-8 hours

Daily Regime for the Vata/Kapha Type

The Vata/Kapha type is a mixed type and so needs a little of both the Vata and Kapha in their life. Which one needs more will have to be decided through practice or seeing an Ayurvedic practitioner. Generally speaking a mix of the strong sides of Vata and the more mild sides of the Kapha will be the most appropriate. Experimenting with the diet is the best way to find out what is correct for you. It is important to note that if you have a strong aversion to some activity it may be because you need it to stay in equilibrium.

Meals	7-8.00 A.M.	11.00 A.M.	12-1.00 P.M.	4.00 P.M.	6.30-7.30 P.M.
Breakfast	Light				
Snack		None			
Lunch			Mode-rate		
Snack				If needed	
Dinner					Mode-rate

Activity	6 - 7 A.M.	8 A.M. -6 P.M.	3 - 4 P.M.	8 - 10 P.M.	11 A.M. 12 P.M.
Wake-up	6-7 am				
Bathing	Warm shower				
Meditation	30 min.				
Exercise		Mode-rate			
Work		Respon-sibility, dynamic, creative			

Rest/Nap			No		
Massage				1x Weekly on body	
Sex				2-3 times a week	
Bed-time					11 pm
Hours of Sleep					7-8 hours

Daily Regime for the Pitta/Kapha Type

The Pitta/Kapha type is a dual type and so needs a little of both the Pitta and Kapha in their life. Which one needs more will have to be decided through practice or seeing an Ayurvedic practitioner. Generally a mix of the stronger sides of the Pitta and the mild sides of the Kapha will be the most appropriate. Experiment with the diet as it is the best way to find out what is correct for you. It is interesting to note that if you have a strong aversion to some activity it is probably because you need it to stay in balance.

Activity	6 - 7 A.M.	8 A.M. 6 P.M.	3 - 4 P.M.	8 - 10 P.M.	11 A.M. 12 P.M.
Breakfast	Light				
Snack		Fruit			
Lunch			Mode-rate		
Snack				No	
Dinner					Mode-rate

Activity	6 - 7 A.M.	8 A.M. 6 P.M.	3 - 4 P.M.	8 - 10 P.M.	11 A.M. 12 P.M.
Wake-up	6 am				
Bathing shower	Warm				
Meditation	30min.				
Exercise		Strong			
Work		Dynamic Manag-ement			
Rest/Nap			No		
Massage				2xmonth on body	
Sex				2-4 times a week	
Bed-time					11pm 12am
Hours of Sleep					6-7 hours

Daily Regime for the Vatta/Pitta/Kapha Type

The Vatta/Pitta/Kapha type is an equal mix and so needs a little of all types in their life. They are considered to be the most strong and least prone to imbalance of all the seven types. Which type needs more attention will have to be decided through practice or seeing an Ayurvedic practitioner. Generally speaking a mix of the more mild sides of the Vata, Pitta and Kapha will be the most appropriate. Experimenting is the best way to find out what is correct for you.

Activity	6 - 7 A.M.	8 A.M. 6 P.M.	3 - 4 P.M.	8 - 10 P.M.	11 A.M. 12 P.M.
Breakfast	Mode-rate				
Snack		No			
Lunch			Mode-rate		
Snack				No	
Dinner					Light

Activity	6 - 7 A.M.	8 A.M. 6 P.M.	3 - 4 P.M.	8 - 10 P.M.	11 A.M. 12 P.M.
Wake-up	6 am				
Bathing	Warm shower				
Meditation	30min.				
Exercise		Mode-rate			
Work		All kinds			
Rest/Nap			No		
Massage				2x month on body	
Sex				2-3 times a week	
Bed-time					11 pm
Hours of Sleep					6-7 hours

Sexual Relations

It is worth noting that in these tables the frequency of sexual relations may be very much less than what is commonly promoted as "healthy" in Western civilization. Ayurveda actually presents a stricter model than that which I have given in this chapter. I made some allowances for culture and psychology. However, note that the information presented here is mainly based on how fast your body (tissue metabolism) can produce sperm and ovum.

According to the seven dhatu concept of Ayurveda the best thing for health, e.g., dhatu metabolism, is sex once every twenty-eight days, or four days for each dhatu to nourish the next in line. This logic means that a strong metabolism will regenerate the sexual fluids completely in twenty-eight days. Unfortunately, if your health is less than perfect this process can take 49 days or longer (7 X 7). Also this metabolic rate slows down with age, and of course is higher in youth.

I have generally suggested that sexual relations vary from one to three times per week as per constitution. This takes into account that dhatu metabolism can nourish the last tissue, shukra, every day provided the diet and lifestyle support that function. This is clearly seen from business persons who have high levels of stress, travel, and irregular diets / lifestyles becoming impotent or disinterested in sex. Ayurveda places the health of sexual function under diet and lifestyle – stress of course being a lifestyle factor.

These tables do not take into account psychological issues, age or specific cultural issues. The main idea to convey is the concept that our ultimate pleasure as humans is also based on diet and lifestyle habits. It is worthy to note that loving sexual relationships are also nourishing on all levels and balance to a great extent the loss of tissue fluids. Thus, in loving sexual relationships the frequency can be increased without loss of health, happiness and psychological fulfillment.

Outlook on Life

Lastly, but not least, our basic attitude towards life provides the means to meet and overcome any kind of health problems that we may encounter. A positive outlook while maintaining a practical approach is a basic ingredient for good health. A positive attitude with poor habits will not generate good health. Or a negative life view with good habits will also tend to not give the best results. A good, common sense (remember when common sense meant something?) approach to life and your lifestyle are foundational for long term health.

According to Ayurveda it is important to avoid extremes on both sides of the spectrum. This is especially true when we begin to change a life time of habits. Sometimes people find they have a health problem, like high blood pressure, and change diet and lifestyle expecting their problem to change in a day or week. The body does not function this way. The high blood pressure is the product of a diet and lifestyle lasting several years or even generations (sixty years) so one cannot logically expect the body to instantly undo a long history of poor habits. However, the human body is a miracle that can repair damage provided you support it. If you follow the advice of Ayurveda you will, over several months, begin to see changes.

It should be remembered that Ayurveda is not about a passing fad, but rather about finding a style of living that supports, maintains and even creates a state of vibrant health. The media is full of studies accounting how Americans are living longer, but in worse health. Many people are contracting degenerative illnesses that modern medicine has no cure for. A large majority of our elderly population take a wide variety of drugs in order to keep living. Is this health? Ayurveda does not consider this way of living to be healthy, attractive, fun or contributing to anything other than the pockets of the pharmaceutical industry. Your health is in your hands and begins with your attitude to life and your daily habits.

13
Dietary Supplements - Myths, Facts and Traditions

There are two main schools today in biochemical nutrition, one that believes in supplementing with vitamins and minerals and one that does not. Within the school that believes in adding supplements to the diet there is a wide variety of dosage and utilization prescribed. Ayurvedic nutrition is basically pro supplementation but in a way different than is understood today.

The problem with consuming any kind of food or dietary supplement lies in our ability to digest and assimilate the product. This is a question central to Ayurvedic thinking and it has been discussed in depth earlier. However, this question becomes critical in the case of supplements as most dietary supplements are extremely difficult to digest. This is due to the fact that they are very concentrated forms of the substance, hence more difficult for the enzymes to process. In fact, it is estimated that most people only benefit from 5 to 25% of any supplement. This can be seen clearly during urination when the other 75 to 95% gives your urine a bright yellow color and strong smell.

Therefore, our first question before taking any kind of dietary supplement should be – what are we able to digest? If there is any kind of digestive disturbance such as gas, bad breath, bloating, constipation, gripping, colic pain, allergies, yeast infections or nausea, food supplements should not be taken. These symptoms indicate that the digestion is not functioning at full power and adding even small doses of supplements will increase the problem. This is often opposite to the current use of supplements to "give a boost" when one is feeling low or tired. In fact, taking a lot of supplements can increase symptoms and fatigue in this situation. The most important signs of low digestive ability is a coating or covering on the tongue and low or variable appetite.

If there is any coating on the surface of the tongue it indicates that food has not been completely digested and is remaining in the intestines. Adding dietary supplements to this situation will only increase the problem. This is easily clarified if you have ever looked at your tongue or the tongue of someone in your family when they have a flu or cold. The flu or colds are indications that the body is filled with undigested matter – especially when a fever is present. In these cases the tongue may be covered with a film. Herbs, spices or other natural products should be taken to clear the undigested food from the system before taking any kind of dietary or nutritional supplement. Your appetite is a good indication of your ability to digest. If your appetite is strong then it can indicate a good power of digestion.

To determine your ability to digest a product is sometimes difficult and it is advisable to visit an Ayurvedic practitioner to have them judge your level of assimilation. If this is not an option then using the indications above should be enough. Very often your subjective feeling of the effect of a product in your body can be a good indication. Many people take supplements that they subjectively feel are not doing anything for them – primarily because they are not. Usually this is because they lack the capacity to digest and assimilate them.

After the question of your capacity to assimilate dietary supplements comes the question of the product itself.

Ayurvedic nutrition views all man made products as toxic and problematic for the enzymes and organs of filtration in the body. The basic difference in viewpoints has already been explained in the beginning of the book and there is no need to repeat the same information. It can be added in the context of food supplements that studies have shown that natural supplements are easier for the body to digest and assimilate.

The main point to make here is that almost anything you buy has gone through some kind of processing to get it in the bottle, powder, capsule or pill that you are taking. Almost everything should be suspect from the Ayurvedic point of view. One guideline could be the same as for food – if it comes in a box, bottle or jar do not buy it. The sole exception to this is a substance that has been ground up – without heat or chemical extraction – and put into a capsule or tablet. This generally means a herb or plant. If this sounds reactionary or unreliable you should consider the following statement made by research scientists at the University of California at Davis:

> "Records of traditional uses of plants as medicines provide a better chance of identifying sources of effective therapeutic compounds than random screening alone. For example, records for original folkloric uses of 119 plant-derived drugs currently in use in the world showed that about 74% of these purified compounds are being sold commercially as medicines for the same or related uses that they were put to in traditional systems."[83]

This means that by today's biochemical standards ancient medical systems like Ayurveda are still 74% accurate in their use of therapeutic substances – like herbal dietary supplements. If a different standard of comparison than the biochemical system was used that rate could have been closer to 100% instead of 74%. This should be coupled with the

[83] Unander, David W. et al., *Journal of Ethnopharmacology*, No. 30, 1990, pp. 233-64; also Farnsworth et al. 1985; and Farnsworth, 1988.

fact that plants have no damaging side effects when used properly. This cannot be said for the current use of vitamins and mineral compounds.

The current popular trend of mega doses of supplements is frightening to many researchers and doctors because the long-term effects are not known. Nor are they likely to be known any time soon, but the above point is clear. By following the traditional utilization of plants and herbs as supplements you have a 75% chance to be healthy. There is no percentage available for the current practice of using large daily doses of manufactured supplements. The fact is that the long-term use of mega doses is not known. The question is more of being a guinea pig than of good health practices. A guinea pig can die or live longer, one just does not know.

Another point is that even taking a water-soluble vitamin like vitamin C on daily basis puts extra strain on your organs of filtration – the liver and kidneys. Any man made supplement will have a negative effect over time on the kidneys and liver. Yes, even the so-called 100% natural vitamins that you have in the cupboard. Additionally, tests have been around since the late forties that show that the body assimilates and uses natural forms of vitamin C much better than synthetic forms.[84] Why then should one choose to take a manmade product that stresses the filtration system of the body and has questionable effects over the long term?

Still another point to understand is that the repeated use of any vitamin or mineral for long periods tends to create a deficiency of the very item being taken. This is because the body begins to lose the ability to produce and synthesize the vitamin or mineral you are taking on a regular daily basis. It has been thought for years that the body could not manufacture, synthesis or produce certain vitamins or "essential" nutrients from food. With this theory it becomes

[84] *The Wealth of India,* vol. III, 1952, p. 169.

necessary to "supplement" nutrients in the diet. This is the foundation of the dietary supplement industry and most nutritional systems in the world. This school of thought is still in the majority as far as biochemical nutrition is concerned.

The problem is that biochemical studies have existed for over thirty years that prove this stance inaccurate and faulty. The human body has been shown to produce vitamin C, something thought to be impossible. The study was done by measuring the total intake of vitamin C and comparing them to the waste amounts of vitamin C excreted.[85] Several studies have consistently repeated these results demonstrating that the body can do what it is not supposed to be able to do.

The Ayurvedic point of view is that the body is not separate from the mind or even the environment in which it lives. This point of view accounts for the possibility that the body – through its organic consciousness – creates whatever is needed provided it is given the right raw materials. The right raw material is food, plants and herbs, not manufactured pills or vitamins. This potential of the body is explained beautifully by Dr. Ballentine in his classic book of more than twenty years ago –

> "That the unconscious as well as the conscious mind may tune the metabolic machinery to change vitamin requirements, or even to create certain vitamins or, more amazingly yet, to transmute one element into another, is understood only by a handful of biophysicists and is, so far at least, beyond the capacity of even the most sincerely motivated practitioners of medicine or nutrition to comprehend."[86]

One must then question the basic assumption of the biochemical nutritional theory that the body is unable to manufacture what it needs. It appears from biochemical

---

[85] Ballentine, Dr. Rudolph, 978, p. 533.

[86] Ballentine, Dr. Rudolph, 1978, p. 573.

studies that the body *is* capable of producing everything that it needs provided a basic diet of whole natural foods is followed along with a healthy and happy attitude towards life. These studies destroy the concept of "deficiencies" and the need to supplement them.

Myths of Marketing Supplements

If we have decided to take a supplement we are then faced with an almost impossible task to decide *which* one to take. Just walking into a health food store is enough to kill you with choice. A drug store is little better. The overwhelming amount of products is, in itself, a problem. After this primary problem (for which there seems to be no cure) one is left with reading labels. Again one choice could be not to buy it if it has a label.

All manufacturers would like you to buy their product, but the problem with dietary supplements is that they can, from the Ayurvedic point of view, harm your health over time. Some of the worst offenders are the ones that claim to be 100% natural. At least with synthetic supplements your choice is clear – you know what you are taking and you made your choice accordingly.

It is one of the greatest myths in marketing to call a product natural. If it were 100% natural it would still be hanging on the tree, bush or ground (or as often is the case in Traditional Chinese medicine, crawling around somewhere). There are practically no "natural" methods of product preparation. The products that are clearly natural are ground up herbs and plants. Even these are often mixed up with other unknown products to produce a "synergetic effect". What these other products are and what the synergetic effects are is usually unknown. Traditional formulas do have time proven, documented synergetic effects and generally can be trusted. Your basic guideline in this matter should be that if you want a 100% natural supplement, eat organic broccoli.

Any kind of vitamin or mineral product, by necessity, has gone through a process of refinement. Therefore, it cannot be 100% natural. Every time a product goes through a refining process it becomes a little harder to digest and slightly less alive, making it that much more difficult for the enzymes to break down. All processing reduces the potential life of the product. One super hyped product to "block" fat in the body is supposes to be all natural – derived from a seashell. While no one argues that a seashell is 100% natural, doctors promoting the product are quick to point out that eating ground up seashells will not have the same effect. Ah ha! So eating the source does not have the same effect? What then, pray tell me, is the 100% natural process that changes the 100% product into a different 100% natural product?

This is also clear in women's products based on the Wild Yam family. Everyone tells you that their products are completely natural, derived from the Wild Yam, but they say, eating a Wild Yam will not help your hormone balance. Manufacturers and certain doctors who promote these products say that simple laboratory procedure "enhances" the effects of the raw material. Another good one is that the procedure just "tweaks the cellular structure" to "make it better". Tweaking cellular structure is probably one reason why we have so much cancer in our society. It is these same pharmaceutical companies that claim, in a court of law, that the complete removal of a woman's reproductive organs improves their lives.[87] Obviously, they know better than nature or God. In the meantime they are happy to "tweak" your cells, your food's cells and any other cells they can get their hands on.

The bottom line is that supplements are a huge business and large pharmaceutical companies are producing the majority of the products. I have come across various reports

---

[87] Robbins, John, 1996, p. 119.

– which I cannot substantiate – that say between 75 to 90% of all dietary supplements sold in the United States are made by three major manufactures. All the labeling comes from smaller companies or drug store chains that package the products for the retail market. Once more it has to be stressed that these companies are concerned with profit, not your health.

Many of today's nutritionists are adamant that people need supplements. On one hand there is ample information to support their assertions; provided you accept the faulty theory that the body is not intelligent and cannot adjust or synthesize what it needs. And, on another hand, which kind of product should you choose and which one will you actually be able to assimilate? There is no sense in taking a supplement if 75% of it is going down the toilet. Would you knowingly throw 75 cents of every dollar you spend on supplements down the toilet?

The dietary supplement industry sells over a billion dollars of products every year. And it would seem that a majority of these products are simply putting additional stress on your organs of assimilation and filtration as they find their way to the sewer and the water ecosystem.

Who Needs Supplements?

According to the latest information accumulated over the last three decades it appears that everyone needs supplementation in their diets. Ayurveda has the same stance, but means something different and uses different products. I usually give all of my clients' herbal formulas and supplements (actually I work with various pharmacies that prepare the herbs according to my diagnosis of each client – I do not use ready made supplements). Once more it is important to understand that each case history recounted in this book included herbal digestive supplements to increase metabolic function. This has been a key factor in the recovery of each of my patients.

As mentioned above studies have shown that the body is capable to produce things that it normally does not. The problem for the biochemical model is that they do not recognize the body as being intelligent or as an extension of the conscious mind. This then confines them to a "yes or no" situation – either the body makes nutrients or it does not. So when information is collected in studies that are not either "yes or no" they have to choose.

Ayurveda does not have this conflict because it sees the body as an extension of the mind and its greater environment, the conscious universe. Therefore a choice is not necessary. Rather the whole context of a situation is studied and then a conclusion can be reached based on the facts available. Let us look at today's social and cultural climate in the Western world from the Ayurvedic point of view.

Ayurveda always begins with the most subtle first, which is the mind. Hence, our first questions should be concerned with the state of happiness and contentment of Western society. Ayurveda views a happy person as a healthy person and one whose body is better able to respond to changing needs of nutrition, stress or immune response.

Are we happy and contented as a culture? While there are many happy individuals it would seem to most people that Western culture is generally not contented or very happy. This then will impair the intelligent body and unconscious mind's ability to manufacture or synthesis what nutrients it may need. The happier and more fulfilled in life you are the greater your capacity will be for your body to produce needed nutrients.

Another factor of our cultural psychology is our ability to cope with stress. The common figure quoted in the media these days is that 80% of all diseases stem from stress. In fact it is not so much the stress as it is how we deal with it. Many studies have been done that indicate a suppression of immunity results from poor stress management.[88] In Ayurveda our capacity to synthesis nutrients is related to both immunity and hormone function – both of which are impaired by prolonged exposure to stress.

The second factor would be the basic nutritional intake. Unfortunately, the average American consumes 40% of their daily calories from refined white sugar.[89] Sugar consumption inhibits the immune system of the body, but how much sugar and for how long? The suppressive effects of all forms of sugar begin 30 minutes after consumption and last more than five hours. One hundred grams of sugar reduces the ability of the Neutrophis (white blood cells) to destroy harmful bacteria in the body. The average American consumes over 150 grams of sucrose (white sugar) per day, effectively suppressing the immune systems ability to respond for at least one third of the day or half of your waking day.[90] However, if the total amount of sugars, including glucose and fructose, is consumed then the total time of immune suppression is closer to the whole waking day. The Neutrophis comprise roughly two thirds of your total white blood cells, suppressing them is hardly a good idea.

Aside from these bright facts the use of highly processed foods by Western society reduces not only nutrient intake but also many other unknown components in food. These unknown components are now being studied in conjunction to cancer treatment and prevention. So far the results are extremely positive. It is very likely that the main cancer prevention treatment of the future will be a whole food diet. Articles and books are already beginning to appear that propose this view. Of course, this is also the Ayurvedic point of view as well.

---

[88] A good book on this subject is, *Who Gets Sick*, by Blair Justice, Ph. D., Tarcher.

[89] Robbins, John, 1996 pp. 5.

[90] Pizzorno, Lara, MA, October 1995, pp. 24.

It is possible to have malnutrition in the United States and eat all day long; in fact this is the case with many overweight children and adults. The primary cause of this is processed foods. It is estimated that 60% of the population in the United States suffer from a deficiency of two or more nutrients. Some medical researchers are of the opinion that the majority of dieters are malnourished. As 1/3 of the United States population is dieting at any given moment that could potentially mean a huge number of people.

Therefore it appears that unless you are already eating a diet based primarily on whole foods, i.e., non-refined – you are probably deficient or malnourished to some extent. The chance of this increases dramatically if you only eat prepared foods or restaurant foods.

Additional factors come from the environment. This includes a broad array of chemicals that are in our environment from agricultural products and other petrochemical based products like household cleaners. Any petrochemical product – be it a medication like a birth control pill or a fertilizer – puts a strain on the liver and kidneys. The liver is the largest gland in the body and has the primary role in digestive enzyme production and maintenance. The use of, or exposure to, any petrochemical slowly, over time, impairs the liver's normal enzyme functions. The liver also plays a key role in the immune and hormone systems. These functions also become impaired over time.

The tragic result for Western culture in general is a wide variety of untreatable or un-diagnosable illnesses; many of which are the common degenerative diseases. These are accompanied by increases in cancer, heart disease, infertility and impotency. It is naive not to acknowledge the role of environmental chemicals, hormones in meat and widespread use of antibiotics as a direct cause of these and many other problems. The liver and kidneys play a major role in all of these problems according to Ayurveda and herbal supplements or medicines can directly help in rejuvenating both liver and kidney tissues. *Perhaps what we need to supplement the body with is not more manmade nutrients, but organic substances that help promote normal metabolic function.* As there is little or no research in this field we are once more left with the traditional medical wisdom of Ayurveda.

In conclusion it should be noted that almost everyone needs some kind of supplement because all of us are exposed to at least one of the above problems; most of us two or three. The only question now is which kind of dietary supplement should we use?

Supplements That Your Body Can Actually Assimilate

Ayurveda has used herbs for many thousands of years successfully. Herbs have been used medically for the full duration of this time. Yet, they have also been used to maintain health or as supplements. Historically these substances were normally call rejuvenators[91] in Ayurveda.

It would require several books to effectively explain and present this branch of Ayurveda.[92] However, in relation to the main subjects of this chapter herbs have a definite advantage over any other kind of dietary supplement. Unfortunately, they are scoffed at and down-played by the modern doctor and nutritionist. This is primarily due to ignorance of the present medical and nutritional profession rather than any inherent fault of the plant kingdom.

Herbs can be considered as concentrated foods. They are complex in composition, which makes them difficult to study in a biochemical lab. However, because of this they tend to have a mild, even therapeutic action on the human body. This makes them less desirable for medications, but

---

[91] This is called "Rasayana" in Sanskrit, and form one of the eight branches of traditional Ayurvedic medicine.

[92] See the author's textbook, Smith, Atreya, 2009.

more desirable for dietary supplements. Herbs have many minerals and vitamins as well as carbohydrates, fats and proteins. In essence they are a very balanced food.

They are easy for the body to digest and assimilate if taken in the right doses by the right person, at the right time. They are not only easy for the digestive enzymes to break down; many herbs even have the ability to increase enzyme production in the liver or small intestine. In fact they are a major support to the digestion of other foods. The appropriate use of herbs with a meal helps the body to digest food more completely. Additionally, the herbs please the sense of taste and increase our pleasure of eating and consuming food. Hence, the mind is also pleased.

In Ayurveda it is said that one should take herbs and spices daily to keep the digestive enzymes functioning correctly.[93] Failure to do this usually begins the disease process through the poor processing and assimilation of nutrients and food mass.

Another major area of interest for large pharmaceutical companies is the detoxifying mechanism that many herbs show. Some of these herbs are even able to eliminate heavy metals from deeper body tissues and glands.[94] Yet one can achieve a more balanced result from the use of the herb itself and also benefit from the nutrient content which is lost with any biochemical processing procedure.

Traditionally there are classic digestive formulas (Dipana) for each type of person:

- Hingashtak Churna (Vata)
- Trisugandhi Churna (Pitta)
- Trikatu Churna (Kapha)

---

[93] In other words to keep Agni in a balanced state.

[94] Particularly Amlaki or Amla.

These consist of three or more herbs and spices that promote proper digestion and assimilation of nutrients for each major type of person. These formulas can be used in a variety of ways. For example many Ayurvedic teas are beginning to appear in the markets and health food store. Inevitably these teas are based on the following classic formulas. Hence one can take them as teas, cook with them or actually take a teaspoon of them in a powdered form after eating.

Use each ingredient in equal amounts. These are basic ingredients that are available in the United States and are easy to take as a tea or powder. According to your digestive needs one can add any other herb or spice to this bias. An example would be to add Turmeric powder to enhance liver and blood cleansing properties while still increasing enzyme function.

I have achieved very good results with my clients by having them simply buy the digestive spices; grind them up in a coffee grinder, and take half a teaspoon before or after eating to promote digestive function. Drinking a tea is weaker in therapeutic effect and harder to gage the dosage. This is a maintenance practice of the digestive system and does not constitute a therapeutic treatment. If you are sick see a medical practitioner.

The utilization of herbs is a science and should not be done in a haphazard manner or without guidance. One should not "play" with herbs and more than you would consider "playing" with a cabinet full of biochemical medicines. While herbs are safe when used properly, they can, nevertheless, make one ill when used incorrectly.[95]

Another point to keep in mind is that all spices are irradiated when they are imported into the United States.

[95] Refer to the following book for more guidance on the Ayurvedic use of herbs and spices- Frawley, Dr. David & Lad, Dr. Vasant, 1986.

Buying your favorite spice in the supermarket and using it as a digestive aid will have limited therapeutic value and perhaps cause problems because of the radiation treatments. It is a better choice to buy local (e.g., from your country) spices and herbs whenever possible. Also organic spices are a major plus in this regard as well.

Herbs are a perfect source for dietary supplementation in today's world for a number of reasons. The fact that they are complex in nature adds to their balanced and even effect on the digestive metabolism. The enzyme promoting properties of Cumin, Fennel, Fenugreek, Turmeric, and Black pepper have been well known for centuries. People now forget that the major reason for the ancient trade routes to be opened to the East were to buy spices. These spices were valued because of their medical, digestive and pleasure giving qualities.

Additionally, many herbs have antioxidant effects that are extremely helpful in today's polluted environments. There is one classic formula worth mentioning in this regard alone called "Triphala" or "three fruits". This formula is balanced for all constitutional types and improves digestive capacity for everyone over time. It is also a rejuvenator of the digestive system, specifically the colon. Long term use increases all vitamin absorption especially vitamin C, and the B complex. The triphala formula also has strong anti viral and bacterial effects. I suggest taking one 500mg tablet after every meal each day for six to twelve months. Then stop for a month and begin a cycle of taking triphala daily for two months and stopping the third month. One can repeat this throughout the life to promote good assimilation. Be aware that in excess (2 to 6 grams at a time) this formula can cause lose stools for the Vata and Pitta types. The Kapha type is seldom affected in this way. Also most meat-eating people will not find it to have a laxative effect. In the dose given above no one will have this effect – but remember – more is not always better!

While the high-tech society in which we live has many advantages we should not ignore the many benefits that nature gives us freely. Herbs and spices are not only life giving they make eating a more pleasurable experience and they have no negative long-term side effects. They do, however, have the side effect to increase your health. It is reasonable to be skeptical, the only way to know is to try it and feel the difference.

14
Increasing Immunity Through Diet

The concept of immunity, or a principle that prevents and responds to disease, is central to the Ayurvedic system. In the Ayurvedic view food is the source or factor that increases or decreases our basic vitality and resistance to illness. However, the whole process of building immunity from food is a little different than how we think today, so this chapter will give a brief explanation.

Before approaching the subject of immunity as an outcome of diet it is important to understand that Ayurveda recognizes that people are born with different levels of resistance and strength. Not everyone is created the same in their ability to resist disease or in basic stamina. Ayurveda recognizes that each person is born with a basic strength that cannot be changed. So diet and immunity can only be increased to this natural, or natal level, not beyond. Hence, it is unrealistic to imagine that one can increase immunity beyond what is genetically possible for your body. However, one can bring the resistance to disease up to its maximum potential through right dietary habits according to Ayurveda.

Ayurveda states that the capacity to respond to stress factors, physical and mental, are related to the inherent strength of the individual. This concept in Ayurveda is represented by the term *Bala*. There are two kinds of Bala, inherent and developed. This idea of inherent strength is modified by lifestyle and the aging process.

Another primary idea in Ayurvedic thought is that of a primordial essence that supports the inherent strength of the person. This concept, Ojas, is a form of refined cellular nutrient extract that is created by the correct metabolism of food and its resulting refinement through various systems and enzyme actions, mainly on a cellular level. It is indicated that Ojas is also of two kinds, inherent and developed. This theory is worthy of note as Ojas is said to support the primary strength, Bala, as well as primary structures of the organism through supporting cellular growth and function. There is no direct relationship to an equivalent concept in modern anatomy and physiology. The Ojas is in a subtle distilled state that has not as yet been identified by modern science. The refined cellular nutrient extract can be modified by lifestyle and the aging process.

A third factor in immunity is the global concept of enzyme activity, or Agni, as a primary defense. Ayurveda states that there are thirteen different groups of enzymes (Agni) that represent different activities. The primary group of enzymes is in the lower stomach and duodenum area. This theory proposes that any pathogen entering the body in the form of liquid or solid matter must first pass this enzyme barrier to reach nutrient assimilation and the bloodstream. A secondary area of five enzyme groups resides primarily in the liver and prevents pathogens from respiratory or digestive systems from entering the bloodstream. A third area of seven enzyme groups exists on a cellular level and aids in the tissue specific functions, differentiated by functional activity rather than by location. The enzyme activity can be modified by lifestyle and the aging process.

Thus, according to Ayurveda, immunity is the result of both inherent strength (Bala), proper metabolism that creates an active distilled cellular nutrient extract (Ojas) that supports all organic functions and enzyme activity (Agni). Immunity represents both the totality and interrelationship of these three Ayurvedic concepts. At the same time immunity is also dependant on homeostasis as both Bala and Ojas are dependant on correct dosha function to form their developed aspect versus their inherent aspect. Enzyme activity is also directly dependant on homeostasis and will either become variable, hyperactive or hypoactive according to doshic disruption. Additionally, the presence of non-digested food (Ama) accelerates the incorrect or compromised functions of homeostasis. Thus, the presence of non-digested matter is also an important cause of reduced or compromised immune response usually directly related to enzyme activity.

From the Ayurvedic point of view immune response is dependent on twenty-one factors; three doshas, two forms of Bala, two forms of Ojas, thirteen groups of Agni and Ama. From this we can surmise that the possible number of interactions for these 21 factors is very large. Thus, immunity in Ayurveda is a complex response of the organism involving a number of systems and functions supported by inherent factors and developing factors.

Homeostasis is responsible for the correct development and function of Bala, Ojas and Agni. Once these two elements, Bala and Ojas, are compromised the immune response will suffer according to Ayurveda. Once enzyme function is compromised there is an increase of non-digested substances that also causes an effect on the immunity. Both of these factors interact and are interrelated resulting in delayed immune response, inhibited immune response, or incorrect immune response depending on a number of factors.

The Ayurvedic vision is that the body is composed of different layers. This is a functional point of view as the layers do not mean layers like an onion – peal one off and there is another underneath. On the contrary, the concept of the different layers is of tissue metabolism and development.[96] In other words, each layer is classified according to its function in utilizing nutrients abstracted from food not from physical locations. It is interesting to note that each of these layers or tissues can also be nourished from non-material sources such as feelings and thoughts.

According to this view each tissue is nourished from the previous one and in consequence nourishes the tissue following it. Whether we use the word "tissue" or "layer" any word falls short of the original Sanskrit word which is multidimensional in meaning and scope. One meaning of the word *Dhatu* is "to support"; another is to "maintain"; another is to "nourish". Thus we see that the word "tissue" gives a partial or limited idea of the Ayurvedic term. It is the food we eat that begins this process of nourishment and support of the body.

The seven tissues are – plasma and lymph; red blood cells and veins; muscle and ligaments; fat (adipose tissue) and connective tissues; bones; bone marrow and nerve tissue; and, reproductive tissue (sperm and ovum). The final outcome of metabolizing food is Ojas or one of the principles of immunity. The final substance, Ojas, is not only created from the proper nourishment of all of the previous tissues, but it also forms a closed loop to nourish each of the previous tissues when it is developed. Therefore, when the principle Ojas is low or deficient it is unable to nourish the previous tissues, which means that they in turn will not be creating sufficient or good quality Ojas to support themselves.

Note that when Ojas is strong it supports Baala as well as the seven tissues. Hence, the concept of Ojas in Ayurveda is actually a form of metabolized *Prana*, or vital energy. This same stored, metabolized Prana is the origin of Vata dosha. Thus, we see that a poor diet will affect immunity by

[96] These are the seven Dhatus in Ayurvedic thought.

reducing the outcome of tissue metabolism, Ojas, which in turn affects Baala, Dhatu and Dosha.

Dietary Support to Immunity

To increase our immunity we need to increase our ability to digest and assimilate what we eat. We also need to eat things that we can digest and assimilate. This is the basic starting point.

What we eat first becomes fluid which is absorbed into the blood and then into the plasma. The plasma transports the mico-nutrients around the body through a complex series of channels that have no pumping mechanism (i.e., heart). Instead the plasma and lymphatic system require the "normal" activities of the muscles to pump or move nutrients throughout the plasma. Consequently, if there is little or no exercise then the body will become under-nourished because the plasma cannot carry the nutrients all over the body. This causes congestion and stagnantation. Interestingly enough it also causes increased appetite, as the body is not receiving the nutrients that it needs and so asks for more food.

Therefore, in order for the basic "juice" or nutrients[97] of the body to be absorbed exercise is mandatory. A failure to get this basic nourishment results in the mal-formation of all the tissue levels of the body. This will quickly result in lower immunity. Note that the first response to any pathogen in the body happens from the white blood cells that live in the lymph tissues. Lack of exercise causes congestion and stagnantation in the lymphatic tissues, which prevents the proper immune response. Hence, the bottom line is that you need daily exercise.

When the plasma is nourished it divides the nutrients into three parts. One part it keeps as nourishment, one part

[97] The juice or nutrients of the food are called Rasa collectively in Ayurveda.

is rejected as waste, and one part is used to nourish the next level - blood. The blood re-absorbs nutrients from the plasma and again divides them in three parts. The part that is rejected as waste combines with the rejected matter of all other tissues to be cleaned and excreted by the liver (via the gall bladder) and kidneys. Obviously, people who have gall bladder problems are taxing their systems ability to excrete waste products produced in normal metabolism function. Gall bladder problems can also come from foods that have excess acidity which the body then must eliminate in the above described manner – both of which strain normal function and cause congestion or calcification in the bile ducts. In general all toxins (or non-digested substances) from the digestion end up in the liver first and are then transported throughout the body.[98]

In fact the waste product from any of the tissues can become toxic and pollute the body if retained. Consequently, Ayurveda gives great importance to proper evacuation of waste materials (*Mala*). It should be noted here that a "correct" stool is one that is in one piece, neither too hard nor too soft, neither too dark, nor too light, not overly smelly, and one that floats just under the surface of the water. A stool that sinks, according to Ayurveda, shows a poor digestion with too many of the solid nutrients passing through undigested. A stool that floats on the surface like a boat shows better digestion, but shows an over retention of the solid matter in the colon. Additionally, a stool that is in many or several pieces shows malabsorption in the intestines. If your stool is not "correct" change your diet until it becomes correct. This is true, generally, for all constitutions.

The blood then goes on to nourish the muscle tissues. The muscle then nourishes the fat level. Problems of the fat and muscles indicate that the plasma and blood metabolism

[98] Ama (non-digested food) is absorbed in the digestive tract and then moves throughout the Srotas into the Dhatus. During this process it mixes with the doshas according to function and location.

of nutrients is not working properly. The fat tissue should not be addressed directly, the preceding tissues must be balanced until they are digesting and assimilating the nutrients that they receive correctly. Trying to work on muscle or fat tissue directly without addressing the plasma and blood tissues is faulty and will result in a failure of any diet that is concentrating on weight loss.

When the metabolism of muscle and fat is functioning normally then the bones are nourished well. Ayurveda says that the bones receive direct nourishment from the assimilation of micronutrients from the colon as well. In Ayurveda the health of the colon determines the health of the bones as the elements needed to form bones are absorbed at this stage. The use of nutrients from the fat levels and the colon form good, strong bones. The consumption of hard to digest foods that coat the walls of the colon contribute directly to osteoporosis. These are foods like white refined flour and red meats.

When the bone tissues are functioning normally (and the colon) then the bone marrow and nerve tissue are nourished. In order for the nervous system to be stable and strong the whole nutritional metabolism must be functioning well. The more disturbed the metabolism of the tissues is the more likely a person is to have nervous disorders. The biochemical view is that much of our immunity is produced in the bone marrow. According to Ayurveda the bone marrow and nerve tissues are supported by all of the rest of the body. Generally when this level of the body becomes weakened or diseased then serious problems manifest and are difficult to heal. Thus, when disease hits this level it is of a serious nature and it affects the health of the whole body.

When the bone marrow tissue is working correctly then it nourishes the reproductive system. The reproductive system is atomic according to Ayurveda because it is the most potent product of the body. One sperm and one ovum are enough to create an explosive reaction that results in the impossible (for modern science) feat of creating life. Hence, the view of Ayurveda is that this is the strongest physical element of the body. The reproductive system shows the overall health of a person to a great extent. Unfortunately, due to the vast numbers of xenobiotic chemicals, or hormone mimicking chemicals, this level of the body is often affected out of the traditional sequence given above. The petrochemicals that have xenobiotic effects can go directly to the last tissue level, bypassing the normal process of digestive refinement that protects the reproductive system.

This is one reason why I have put so much emphasis on avoiding animal products that are contaminated with these chemicals (this means *all* animal products that are not grown organically). Normal pharmaceutical drugs that your doctor gives you also have the potential – depending on what they are – to directly enter the reproductive tissues. This is why so many of modern drugs have the unwanted side effect of impotency and infertility.

Any kind of sexual debility indicates a failure in previous tissue formation and metabolism – unless you are taking pharmaceutical drugs. In the case of using prescription or non-prescription drugs the results can be sexual impairment through bypassing the body's normal steps of metabolizing nutrients. Please note that this can mean pre-menstruation problems or pre menopausal disturbances (although menstruation is a by-product of the plasma tissue normally). It can also indicate problems of the prostate or erection in men.

If the reproductive system is working well then the immunity will be strong. This is because the reproductive system divides the nutrients it receives into three parts as all of the previous tissues do. The part that is passed on becomes the principle Ojas which in Ayurveda is the vitality and preventive force from disease. Ojas then goes on to nourish all seven of the tissues from plasma to reproductive tissues as well as Bala and, indirectly, Dosha.

Ayurveda recognizes many foods and herbs that nourish the last tissue level. By extension these same foods and herbs are known to increase the Ojas principle or immunity. In Ayurveda these substances are called aphrodisiacs because they strengthen and nourish the reproductive system. They are not aphrodisiacs in the sense of increasing excitement. There is a whole class of foods and herbs that, if eaten regularly, increase reproductive potential and immunity.

By using this same logic one can see that an over-indulgence of sexual intercourse will deplete the seventh tissue and so affect the immunity. For a person who is weak, ill or has chronic low immunity sexual abstinence becomes an important part of recovering health and strength according to Ayurveda. At least one should abstain from orgasm in this situation (for men and women) although if sick all sexual relations should be suspended until better health is regained. This works both ways — if a person (man or woman) is uninterested in sexual relations it can indicate a weakness of the seventh tissue level of the body and the immunity. Thus, a way to treat this situation (rather than as a psychological or emotional problem) is to increase nourishment to the reproductive tissues.

Foods and herbs that increase immunity also increase fat in the Kapha type or Kapha mixes. This is because the Kapha type normally has the strongest immunity and is the most physically strong of the seven types. Thus, care is needed when a Kapha type or a Kapha mixed type is using these foods or herbs. Below is a list of the major foods that are considered to increase immunity. REMEMBER that this only works if you can digest the foods and herbs listed below. Also, taking large amounts of these foods is a good way to congest the body and *cause* disease. *Small amounts taken over long periods of time are the best way to increase health, strength, fertility, virility and immunity.*

Note that foods that correspond to the reproductive parts of plants or animals are considered to be the strongest in power to build the immunity. However, Ayurveda does not use animals parts like other forms of traditional medicine as they not only kill the animal but effect the mind (Tamas guna) in a negative manner.

Foods:

-Fresh nuts soaked in water and pealed

-Warm boiled raw milk

-Honey

-Ghee

-All fresh whole grains

-Fruits to some extent

Before using herbal substances it is advised to consult a practitioner to have them adjusted to your constitution and personal power of digestion and assimilation.

Herbs:

Latin name	**Indian name**	**English name**
Asparagus adscendens	Safed Mushali	none
Asparagus racemosus	Shatavari	none
Commiphora mukul	Guggulu	none
Emblica officinalis	Amalaki	Indian Gooseberry
Glycyrrhiza glabra	Yaṣṭīmadhu	Licorice
Mucuna pruriens	Kapikacchū	Cowhage
Sida cordifolia	Bala	Country Mallow
Terminalia chebula	Haritaki	none
Tinispora cordifolia	Guduchi	none
Withania somnifera	Ashwagandha	Winter Cherry

It should be noted in closing that Ayurveda recognizes that immunity can be strengthened by the correct use of the mind and senses. According to Ayurveda the sense organs are the doors of the mind to the material, physical world. The right use of both mind (unconscious, intellect, emotions and intelligence) and senses increases immunity because it establishes a state of equilibrium. Today we call a disturbance in this relationship being psychotic or in mild cases neurotic.

The primary method of using the mind to increase immunity is to "withdraw" the mental attention from the physical world and bring the five sense organs to a state of rest. This is called "withdrawing the senses" or "withdrawal from distraction" and implies turning the attention inwards rather than outward for a brief time each day. This requires a conscious effort as opposed to sleep, which is an unconscious action. The result of doing this on a daily basis is mental equilibrium and increased immunity.

15

Descriptions of Foods by Constitution

This chapter largely consists of food charts that provide more specific advice for each constitutional type and supplements the information given in chapter 8. These charts should be used in the context of that information for the best results.

An effort has been made to distinguish between very aggravating and mildly aggravating foods as per constitution. This also applies to the opposite situation of very beneficial and mildly beneficial foods. In both cases an attempt has been made to show the variegated qualities of food in relation to an individual. The headings, Best, Medium, Mixed, Sometimes, Rarely and Worst have been chosen to give an indication of food actions on any given constitutional type. For the mathematical minded I have also included a percentage indication to show the percentage of use that is beneficial for any given type. This would mean that a food in the "Best" column could be used 100% of the time by the person corresponding to the chart. By the same token a person choosing a food in the "Rarely" column would use the food only 20% percent of the time.

The following chart will clarify the percentage idea. However, I have adjusted the number of times per week to correspond to the amount needed to aggravate a person.

Hence, 20% is 1-2 times per week instead of four as eating a lemon four times a week is enough to aggravate a Pitta type, but not 1 or 2 times. The following chart can give you an idea as to the amount needed to disturb you. Note that almost no food is listed as 100% because it is possible to overeat or consume any food to the point of aggravation. Also note that almost no food is listed as "Worst" or 0% because in most cases eating a food once per week will not aggravate your constitution. Therefore, we see that the majority of foods fall into a general use area for all of the constitutions.

100%	21	times in the week
80%	16-18	times in the week
60%	8-10	times in the week
40%	3-4	times in the week
20%	1-2	times in the week
0%	0	times in the week

It should be pointed out that a variety of foods need to be eaten in a week's time. If you eat a certain kind of food every day, day in and day out, it will have greater power to disturb you and cause disruption in your metabolism. It is far better to eat a variety of foods during the week. An example could be that you are a Vata type and eat a grapefruit each morning. After some time this could create a problem, so it would be better to eat the grapefruit three or four mornings a week and have oranges the other mornings. This will prevent you from becoming oversensitive to any one food and give you a broader array of nutrients that different foods have.

Eating a broad selection of foods is the best way to achieve a broad spectrum of nutrients. Eating the same foods all the time creates a narrower spectrum of nutrients and so sets up a possible situation of malnutrition. Additionally, it is more pleasing to the taste to have a variety of foods than just one kind of food over and over again. Please refer back to chapter

12 on lifestyle to check on how you should eat during the day to optimize your health and performance.

One should also strive to foods that are fresh and in season. When this is not possible eat foods that are primarily from your geographical and climatic area. It is OK to eat foods from other places and seasons provided they form not more than twenty percent of your weekly food consumption (see chart above).

Effect of Individual Foods on Different Constitutional Types
Food Lists for the Vata Type of Person

Vata Type / Fruits

Type of Food	Effect of food on constitution					
	Best 100%	Med-ium 80%	Mix-ed 60%	Some Time 40%	Rarely 20%	Worst 0%
Cherries		X				
Dates		X				
Figs		X				
Grapefruit		X				
Grapes		X				
Lemons		X				
Limes		X				
Mango		X				
Papayas		X				
Pineapples		X				
Prunes		X				
Rasp-berries		X				
Straw-berries		X				
Apples (Cooked)			X			

Apricots			X			
Bananas			X			
Oranges			X			
Peaches			X			
Pears			X			
Persim-mons			X			
Plums			X			
Pome-granates			X			
Apples (Raw)				X		
Cran-berries					X	
Melons (all)					X	
Dried Fruits						X

Vata Type / Vegetables

Type of Food	**Effect of food on constitution**					
	Best 100%	Med-ium 80%	Mix-ed 60%	Some Time 40%	Rarely 20%	Worst 0%
Cooked Onions	X					
Avocado		X				
Beets		X				
Carrots		X				
Chilies		X				
Cilantro		X				
Parsley		X				
Radish		X				
Seaweeds		X				
Sweet Potatoes		X				
Artichoke			X			
Bell Peppers			X			
Corn			X			

Eggplant			X			
Green Beans			X			
Mustard Greens			X			
Okra			X			
Peas			X			
Potatoes			X			
Summer Squash			X			
Tomatoes			X			
Turnips			X			
Watercress			X			
Winter Squash			X			
Asparagus				X		
Cauliflower				X		
Celery				X		
Chard				X		
Cucumber				X		
Spinach				X		
Sprouts				X		
Broccoli					X	
Brussels Sprouts					X	
Cabbage					X	
Lettuce					X	
Mushrooms					X	
Onions (raw)					X	
Raw Vegetables					X	

Vata Type / Grains

Type of Food	Effect of food on constitution					
	Best 100%	Med-ium 80%	Mix-ed 60%	Some Time 40%	Rarely 20%	Worst 0%
Wheat	X					
Couscous		X				
Oats		X				
Rice (basmati)		X				
Rice (brown)		X				
Amaranth			X			
Quinoa			X			
Barley				X		
Buckwheat				X		
Corn				X		
Millet				X		
Rye				X		
Granola					X	
Rice (normal white)					X	
Uncooked grains					X	

Vata Type / Beans (Legumes)

Type of Food	Effect of food on constitution					
	Best 100%	Med-ium 80%	Mix-ed 60%	Some Time 40%	Rarely 20%	Worst 0%
Mung		X				
Tofu			X			
Adzuki				X		
Chick Peas					X	

Kidney					X	
Lima					X	
Dal					X	
Lentils					X	
Pinto					X	
Soy						X
Split Peas						X

Vata Type / Nuts & Seeds

Type of Food	Effect of food on constitution					
	Best 100%	Med-ium 80%	Mix-ed 60%	Some Time 40%	Rarely 20%	Worst 0%
Almonds (pealed)		X				
Pecans		X				
Pine		X				
Walnuts		X				
Brazil			X			
Cashews			X			
Filberts			X			
Macadamia			X			
Sesame			X			
Coconut				X		
Pumpkin				X		
Sunflower				X		

Vata Type / Dairy

Type of Food	Effect of food on constitution					
	Best 100%	Med- ium 80%	Mix- ed 60%	Some Time 40%	Rarely 20%	Worst 0%
Buttermilk	X					
Ghee	X					
Butter		X				
Cottage Cheese		X				
Cream		X				
Kefir		X				
Milk (whole)		X				
Sour Cream		X				
Yogurt		X				
Cheese			X			
Ice Cream					X	

Vata Type / Animal Products

Type of Food	Effect of food on constitution					
	Best 100%	Med- ium 80%	Mix- ed 60%	Some Time 40%	Rarely 20%	Worst 0%
Eggs	X					
Fish (all)	X					
Chicken		X				
Duck		X				
Turkey		X				
Shell Fish			X			
Beef				X		
Lamb				X		
Pork						X

Vata Type / Oils

Type of Food	Effect of food on constitution					
	Best 100%	Medium 80%	Mixed 60%	Some Time 40%	Rarely 20%	Worst 0%
Ghee	X					
Sesame	X					
Almond		X				
Avocado		X				
Butter		X				
Olive		X				
Coconut			X			
Mustard			X			
Peanut			X			
Sunflower			X			
Corn				X		
Safflower				X		
Soy				X		
Canola					X	
Margarine						X

Vata Type / Sweeteners

Type of Food	Effect of food on constitution					
	Best 100%	Medium 80%	Mixed 60%	Some Time 40%	Rarely 20%	Worst 0%
Jaggery	X					
Maple Syrup		X				
Molasses		X				
Non Refined Sugar		X				
Fruit Sugar			X			
Honey			X			

Brown Sugar					X	
White Sugar						X
Artificial Sweeteners						X

Vata Type / Spices

Type of Food	Effect of food on constitution					
	Best 100%	Med-ium 80%	Mix-ed 60%	Some Time 40%	Rarely 20%	Worst 0%
Cardamom	X					
Fennel	X					
Nutmeg	X					
Asafoetida		X				
Basil		X				
Cinnamon		X				
Cloves		X				
Coriander		X				
Cumin		X				
Fenugreek		X				
Ginger		X				
Salt (rock)		X				
Turmeric		X				
Black Pepper			X			
Cayenne			X			
Garlic			X			
Horseradish			X			
Mint			X			
Mustard			X			
Salt (sea)			X			

Vata Type / Beverages

Type of Food	Effect of food on constitution					
	Best 100%	Med-ium 80%	Mix-ed 60%	Some Time 40%	Rarely 20%	Worst 0%
Milk	X					
Sour Fruit Juices		X				
Herbal Teas (spice or tonic)		X				
Sweet Fruit Juices			X			
Water			X			
Beer				X		
Wine				X		
Tea (black or green)				X		
Coffee						X
Hard Alcohol						X
Ice Cold Drinks						X
Soft Drinks						X

Vata Type / Vitamins & Minerals

Type of Food	Effect of food on constitution					
	Best 100%	Med-ium 80%	Mix-ed 60%	Some Time 40%	Rarely 20%	Worst 0%
Vitamin C	X					
Vitamin A		X				
Vitamin D		X				
Vitamin E		X				
Calcium			X			
Zinc			X			

B Complex					X	
Vitamin K					X	
Iron						X

Summery of Vata Type Food Groups

Type of Food	Effect of food on constitution					
	Best 100%	Med-ium 80%	Mix-ed 60%	Some Time 40%	Rarely 20%	Worst 0%
Fruits			X			
Vegetables			X			
Grains		X				
Beans					X	
Nuts & Seeds		X				
Dairy		X				
Oils		X				
Animal Products			X			
Sweeteners			X			
Spices		X				
Beverages		X				
Vitamins & Minerals				X		

Food Lists for the Pitta Type of Person

Pitta Type / Fruits

Type of Food	Effect of food on constitution					
	Best 100%	Med-ium 80%	Mix-ed 60%	Some Time 40%	Rarely 20%	Worst 0%
Apples	X					
Pome-granates	X					
Cran-berries		X				
Dates		X				
Figs		X				
Grapes		X				
Melons		X				
Pears		X				
Persim-mons		X				
Pineap-ples		X				
Prunes		X				
Mango			X			
Oranges			X			
Plums			X			
Rasp-berries			X			
Apricots				X		
Bananas				X		
Cherries				X		
Papayas				X		
Peaches				X		
Straw berries				X		
Grape-fruit					X	
Lemons					X	
Limes					X	

Pitta Type / Vegetables

Type of Food	Effect of food on constitution					
	Best 100%	Med- ium 80%	Mix- ed 60%	Some Time 40%	Rarely 20%	Worst 0%
Cauli-flower	X					
Cilantro	X					
Sunflower Sprouts	X					
Alfalfa Sprouts	X					
Celery	X					
Asparagus		X				
Broccoli		X				
Brussels Sprouts		X				
Cabbage		X				
Cucumber		X				
Green Beans		X				
Lettuce		X				
Mush-rooms		X				
Okra		X				
Peas		X				
Bell Peppers			X			
Corn			X			
Parsley			X			
Potatoes			X			
Raw Vegetables			X			
Summer Squash			X			
Winter Squash			X			
Beets				X		
Carrots				X		
Chard				X		
Cooked Onions				X		

Eggplant				X		
Mustard Greens				X		
Radish				X		
Seaweeds				X		
Spinach				X		
Sweet Potatoes				X		
Turnips				X		
Watercress				X		
Avocado					X	
Tomatoes					X	
Chilies						X
Onions (raw)					X	

Pitta Type / Grains

Type of Food	**Effect of food on constitution**					
	Best 100%	Med- ium 80%	Mix- ed 60%	Some Time 40%	Rarely 20%	Worst 0%
Wheat	X					
Barley		X				
Granola		X				
Couscous		X				
Oats		X				
Rice (basmati)		X				
Blue Corn			X			
Millet			X			
Rice (brown, long)				X		
Amaranth				X		
Buckwheat				X		
Corn				X		

Rice (brown, short)					X	
Quinoa				X		
Rye				X		
Rice (white)					X	

Pitta Type / Beans

Type of Food	Effect of food on constitution					
	Best 100%	Med- ium 80%	Mix- ed 60%	Some Time 40%	Rarely 20%	Worst 0%
Adzuki	X					
Mung	X					
Lima		X				
Tofu		X				
Chick Peas			X			
Kidney			X			
Pinto			X			
Soy			X			
Split Peas			X			
Dal				X		
Lentils				X		

Pitta Type / Nuts & Seeds

Type of Food	Effect of food on constitution					
	Best 100%	Med- ium 80%	Mix- ed 60%	Some Time 40%	Rarely 20%	Worst 0%
Coconut		X				
Sunflower		X				
Pine Nuts				X		
Pumpkin				X		

Sesame				X		
Almonds (pealed)					X	
Cashews					X	
Filberts					X	
Pecans					X	
Walnuts					X	
Brazil						X
Macadamia					X	

Pitta Type / Dairy

Type of Food	Effect of food on constitution					
	Best 100%	Med-ium 80%	Mix-ed 60%	Some Time 40%	Rarely 20%	Worst 0%
Cream	X					
Ghee	X					
Milk (whole)	X					
Butter (unsalted)		X				
Cheese (unsalted)		X				
Cottage Cheese		X				
Cheese (salted)				X		
Kefir				X		
Buttermilk					X	
Ice Cream					X	
Sour Cream					X	
Yogurt					X	

Pitta Type / Animal Products

Type of Food	Effect of food on constitution					
	Best 100%	Med-ium 80%	Mix-ed 60%	Some Time 40%	Rarely 20%	Worst 0%
Chicken (light meat)			X			
Turkey (light meat)			X			
Eggs				X		
Fish (fresh water)			X			
Chicken (dark meat)				X		
Duck					X	
Fish (salt water)					X	
Turkey (dark meat)				X		
Beef						X
Lamb						X
Pork						X
Shell Fish						X

Pitta Type / Oils

Type of Food	Effect of food on constitution					
	Best 100%	Med-ium 80%	Mix-ed 60%	Some Time 40%	Rarely 20%	Worst 0%
Ghee	X					
Butter		X				
Coconut		X				
Olive			X			
Soy			X			

Sunflower			X			
Corn				X		
Safflower				X		
Sesame				X		
Almond					X	
Avocado					X	
Peanut					X	
Canola						X
Margarine						X
Mustard						X

Pitta Type / Sweeteners

Type of Food	**Effect of food on constitution**					
	Best 100%	Med-ium 80%	Mix-ed 60%	Some Time 40%	Rarely 20%	Worst 0%
Jaggery	X					
Fruit Sugar		X				
Honey (fresh)		X				
Maple Sugar		X				
Maple Syrup		X				
Non Refined Sugar		X				
Brown Sugar				X		
Honey (old)				X		
Molasses				X		
Artificial Sweeteners				X		
White Sugar					X	

Pitta Type / Spice

Type of Food	Effect of food on constitution					
	Best 100%	Med-ium 80%	Mix-ed 60%	Some Time 40%	Rarely 20%	Worst 0%
Coriander	X					
Cilantro		X				
Fennel		X				
Cardamom			X			
Cumin			X			
Mint			X			
Turmeric			X			
Basil				X		
Cinnamon				X		
Nutmeg				X		
Salt (rock)				X		
Asafoetida					X	
Cloves					X	
Fenugreek					X	
Ginger					X	
Salt (sea)					X	
Black Pepper					X	
Cayenne						X
Garlic (raw)					X	
Horseradish					X	
Mustard						X

Pitta Type / Beverages

Type of Food	Effect of food on constitution					
	Best 100%	Med- ium 80%	Mix- ed 60%	Some Time 40%	Rarely 20%	Worst 0%
Water	X					
Sweet Fruit Juices		X				
Herbal Teas (fruit or astringent)			X			
Milk (whole)			X			
Tea (green)			X			
Beer				X		
Coffee					X	
Ice Cold Drinks					X	
Sour Fruit Juices					X	
Spicy Herbal Teas					X	
Tea (black)					X	
Wine (red)					X	
Hard Alcohol					X	
Soft Drinks (colas)				X		
Wine (white)					X	

Pitta Type / Vitamin & Minerals

Type of Food	Effect of food on constitution					
	Best 100%	Med- ium 80%	Mix- ed 60%	Some Time 40%	Rarely 20%	Worst 0%
B Complex		X				
Vitamin K		X				
Calcium			X			

Iron			X			
Zinc			X			
Vitamin A					X	
Vitamin D					X	
Vitamin E					X	
Vitamin C					X	

Summery of Pitta Type Food Groups

Type of Food	Effect of food on constitution					
	Best 100%	Med- ium 80%	Mix- ed 60%	Some Time 40%	Rarely 20%	Worst 0%
Fruits		X				
Vegetables		X				
Grains		X				
Beans			X			
Nuts & Seeds				X		
Dairy			X			
Oils					X	
Animal Products					X	
Sweeteners			X			
Spices					X	
Beverages		X				
Vitamins & Minerals				X		

Food List for the Kapha Type of Person
Kapha Type / Fruit

Type of Food	Effect of food on constitution					
	Best 100%	Med-ium 80%	Mix-ed 60%	Some Time 40%	Rarely 20%	Worst 0%
Apples		X				
Cran-berries		X				
Dried Fruit		X				
Pome-granates			X			
Apricots				X		
Grape-fruit				X		
Lemons				X		
Limes				X		
Papaya				X		
Prunes				X		
Cherries					X	
Figs					X	
Grapes					X	
Mango					X	
Melons					X	
Oranges					X	
Peaches					X	
Pears					X	
Persim-mons					X	
Pineap-ples					X	
Plums					X	
Rasp-berries					X	
Straw-berries					X	
Bananas						X
Dates						X

Kapha Type / Vegetables

Type of Food	Effect of food on constitution					
	Best 100%	Med-ium 80%	Mix-ed 60%	Some Time 40%	Rarely 20%	Worst 0%
Broccoli	X					
Cabbage	X					
Celery	X					
Alfalfa Sprouts		X				
Asparagus		X				
Beets		X				
Brussels Sprouts		X				
Carrots		X				
Chard		X				
Chilies		X				
Cilantro		X				
Green Beans		X				
Lettuce		X				
Mushrooms		X				
Mustard Greens		X				
Onions		X				
Peas		X				
Radish		X				
Sunflower Sprouts		X				
Turnips		X				
Watercress		X				
Bell Peppers			X			
Cauliflower			X			
Parsley			X			
Potatoes			X			
Spinach			X			

Corn				X		
Eggplant				X		
Okra				X		
Seaweeds				X		
Summer Squash				X		
Tomatoes				X		
Winter Squash				X		
Avocado					X	
Cucumber					X	
Raw Vegetables					X	
Sweet Potatoes				X		

Kapha Type / Grains

Type of Food	**Effect of food on constitution**					
	Best 100%	Med-ium 80%	Mix-ed 60%	Some Time 40%	Rarely 20%	Worst 0%
Barley		X				
Granola		X				
Rye		X				
Amaranth			X			
Buckwheat			X			
Corn			X			
Millet			X			
Quinoa			X			
Rice (basmati)				X		
Couscous					X	
Oats					X	
Rice (brown)					X	
Wheat					X	
Rice (normal white)				X		

Kapha Type / Beans

Type of Food	Effect of food on constitution					
	Best 100%	Med-ium 80%	Mix-ed 60%	Some Time 40%	Rarely 20%	Worst 0%
Adzuki	X					
Dal		X				
Lentils		X				
Lima		X				
Soy		X				
Kidney			X			
Mung			X			
Pinto			X			
Split Peas			X			
Tofu			X			
Chick Peas				X		

Kapha Type / Nets & Seeds

Type of Food	Effect of food on constitution					
	Best 100%	Med-ium 80%	Mix-ed 60%	Some Time 40%	Rarely 20%	Worst 0%
Pumpkin			X			
Sunflower			X			
Coconut				X		
Sesame				X		
Almonds (pealed)				X		
Cashews					X	
Filberts					X	
Pecans					X	
Pine Nuts					X	

Walnuts					X	
Brazil Nuts						X
Macadamia					X	

Kapha Type / Dairy

Type of Food	Effect of food on constitution					
	Best 100%	Medium 80%	Mixed 60%	Some Time 40%	Rarely 20%	Worst 0%
Buttermilk		X				
Soy Milk		X				
Goats Milk			X			
Ghee				X		
Kefir				X		
Butter					X	
Cottage Cheese					X	
Milk (whole)					X	
Sour Cream					X	
Yogurt					X	
Cheese						X
Cream						X
Ice Cream						X

Kapha Type / Animal Products

Type of Food	Effect of food on constitution					
	Best 100%	Medium 80%	Mixed 60%	Some Time 40%	Rarely 20%	Worst 0%
Chicken			X			
Turkey			X			
Duck					X	
Eggs					X	

Fish (all)					X	
Shell Fish					X	
Beef						X
Lamb						X
Pork						X

Kapha Type / Oils

Type of Food	**Effect of food on constitution**					
	Best 100%	Med-ium 80%	Mix-ed 60%	Some Time 40%	Rarely 20%	Worst 0%
Mustard		X				
Safflower		X				
Sunflower		X				
Corn			X			
Ghee				X		
Peanut				X		
Sesame				X		
Soy				X		
Almond					X	
Avocado					X	
Butter					X	
Canola					X	
Coconut					X	
Olive					X	
Margarine						X

Kapha Type / Sweeteners

Type of Food	Effect of food on constitution					
	Best 100%	Med- ium 80%	Mix- ed 60%	Some Time 40%	Rarely 20%	Worst 0%
Honey			X			
Jaggery				X		
Fruit Sugar					X	
Molasses					X	
Non Refined Sugar				X		
Artificial Sweeteners				X		
Brown Sugar					X	
Maple Syrup					X	
White Sugar					X	

Kapha Type / Spice

Type of Food	Effect of food on constitution					
	Best 100%	Med- ium 80%	Mix- ed 60%	Some Time 40%	Rarely 20%	Worst 0%
Black Pepper	X					
Cardamom	X					
Cayenne	X					
Cloves	X					
Garlic	X					
Ginger	X					
Horseradish	X					
Mustard	X					
Turmeric	X					
Asafoetida		X				

Basil		X				
Cilantro		X				
Cinnamon		X				
Coriander		X				
Cumin		X				
Fenugreek		X				
Parsley		X				
Fennel			X			
Mint			X			
Nutmeg			X			
Salt (rock)					X	
Salt (sea)						X

Kapha Type / Beverages

Type of Food	Effect of food on constitution					
	Best 100%	Med- ium 80%	Mix- ed 60%	Some Time 40%	Rarely 20%	Worst 0%
Herbal Teas (spice)		X				
Tea (black or green)			X			
Warm Water			X			
Coffee				X		
Sour Fruit Juices				X		
Wine (white)				X		
Wine (red)					X	
Beer						X
Cold Water					X	
Hard Alcohol					X	
Ice Cold Drinks					X	
Milk (all kinds)					X	

Soft Drinks					X	
Sweet Fruit Juices					X	

Kapha Type / Vitamins & Minerals

Type of Food	**Effect of food on constitution**					
	Best 100%	Medium 80%	Mixed 60%	Some Time 40%	Rarely 20%	Worst 0%
B Complex			X			
Vitamin C				X		
Vitamin K				X		
Calcium					X	
Iron					X	
Vitamin A					X	
Vitamin D					X	
Vitamin E					X	
Zinc					X	

Summery of Kapha Type Food Groups

Type of Food	**Effect of food on constitution**					
	Best 100%	Medium 80%	Mixed 60%	Some Time 40%	Rarely 20%	Worst 0%
Fruits			X			
Vegetables		X				
Grains			X			
Beans		X				
Nuts & Seeds				X		
Dairy					X	
Oils					X	
Animal Products					X	

Sweeteners					X	
Spices	X					
Beverages				X		
Vitamins & Minerals				X		

16

The 21 Days Plan to Feel Better

This chapter is actually a supplement to the book and many people will not find it necessary to review or use this material. However, for those of you who like to have clear instructions on how to avoid problems that often occur through dietary changes this chapter will be of value. Additionally, people who suffer from chronic problems of obesity and / or eating disorders this chapter will provide safe instructions for you to begin to change. Remember that there is no substitute for professional guidance and the support of other people when you are beginning to change your nutritional habits.

These plans should serve as a basis. For best results you should adjust things to fit your individuality. Using this plan for 21 days will give you a good idea where to make adjustments. Without the advice of a professional Ayurvedic doctor or trained practitioner I would advise you to follow the guidelines for the plan best suited for you for the 21 days, after which you can begin to make adjustments. These are general guidelines.

Another note worthy point is that I am beginning with people who may be eating a "Standard American Diet" (SAD). Thus, the plan includes information on reducing canned, frozen and processed foods from the diet. If you already eat a whole food diet, but find that you are unsatisfied with it, look closer at the times to eat (see chapter 12) and which foods are the best for you from the lists in chapter 15. This will usually make sufficient enough changes to help you become healthier. Please note that there is a certain amount of humor in these plans to lighten the changes!

COOKING – to find good recipes for actually cooking, I strongly recommend the following book from Amadea Morningstar that uses "normal North American food": *Ayurvedic Cooking for Westerners*, Twin Lakes, WI; Lotus Press, 1994. This book is simple and easy to use and follow. Ms Morningstar has an MA in biochemical nutrition and has studied for many years Ayurvedic nutrition with some of the best Ayurvedic doctors in India and the USA. Moreover her recipes actually taste good!

Plan for the Vata People

Day 1- Begin by deciding to do the most difficult thing - eat regular meals at regular times! Figure out which times you can eat three meals and a snack or four light meals in the day. Once you have done this stick to it at all costs. This may be the single most important factor in stabilizing your metabolism and nutrient absolution.

Day 2- How hungry are you? Decide if your appetite is strong and constant; constant but slow; or changing most of the time. A pure Vata type will normally have somewhat of a variable appetite and digestion. You need to increase your power to assimilate the nutrients in your food and stabilize your appetite to a more even level. Buy the digestive spices listed in chapter Thirteen, grind them up and begin to take them before meals (two times per day is enough). Eat cooked food! Eat less raw foods.

Day 3- Go by "cold-pressed", organic sesame seed oil. It should be clear and it will cost more than you are used to, do not worry; a bottle lasts a long time. Throw out the following things – all other oils and margarine. As of today begin to rub a few drops of sesame oil on your temples each night, if your sleep is disturbed rub it on the bottom of your feet also. Begin to use sesame oil to cook – you can buy and use sunflower or olive oil (also cold-pressed) for non-cooking dishes like salads. Today you can also go and buy some grains, fresh nuts and anything else that you may want from the same store that sells organic oils.

Day 4- Drink two large glasses of warm water right when you wake up – between 6 to 8 am. Begin to eat when you eat, instead of doing a thousand other things at the same time (like reading this). Reduce by 1/3 the amount of cigarettes you smoke (if you smoke).

Day 5- Reduce coffee or tea intake to a maximum of two cups per day, preferably drink them after you eat something. Avoid drinking coffee or tea before meals. Sell your microwave oven.

Day 6- Stop drinking soft drinks (colas, etc.). Eat nuts when you want, but do not mix them with fruits or other foods. If you have a fall of energy in the day eat fruit or buy a good quality of honey and mix ´teaspoon of it in warm water to pick you up.

Day 7- Stop drinking anything ice cold or cool with meals. Drink warm water with food if you need liquids.

Day 8- Stop buying canned food (keep a can of tomato sauce for that emergency pasta dish), frozen food and food in boxes. Go to the store or farmers market and buy real vegetables. Take them home and look at them – yes, you are actually going to have to cook them! Cook some grains (the ones that you bought last week and have been looking at all week) and vegetables and eat them!

Day 9- Do not beat yourself for not taking your digestive spices and missing meals last week – *just do it now.* Get serious about living better and enjoy life.

Day 10- Look for cookbooks that say something like – "1001 Ways to Cook Rice". When you find there are not any stop mixing weird stuff together like nuts and salad, fruits and lettuce, begin NOT to mix things together unless they are cooked (more that two or three things is still not advised even when cooked). Mixing too many foods together is hard to digest.

Day 11- Stop all raw foods for now. Eat green salads with oil and vinegar or other oily kinds of sauces to antidote the raw leaves – no raw carrots or other foods besides lettuce for the moment. Fruit is still OK.

Day 12- Reduce your coffee or tea intake to one cup per day – after meals. Cut the cigarettes again by 1/3 (if you smoke and do not want to stop, do not worry, you will not have to reduce more than this!).

Day 13- Cut out dried foods like cookies and chips (sweet or salty does not matter, it is the dryness). Begin to cook apples or pears or other fruits and eat them for snacks or desserts.

Day 14- Eat one meal per day of grains and vegetables that you cook yourself – you don't need to spend more than 20-30 minuets to prepare a meal.

Day 15- Congratulate yourself! You made two weeks already! Go out to eat and have a good time! (Remember to take your digestive spices before you go and not to drink the ice water!)

Day 16- If you are still eating in fast food places for lunch, stop. Eat a sandwich and have a soup, but avoid fast food like the plague. Keep nuts or fruits for snacks.

Day 17- Reduce eating meat (if you eat meat) to not more than three times per week. Dinner–time is fine to eat meat when you do, buy organic and prepare it yourself – avoid restaurant meat dishes.

Day 18- Throw away any white sugar you have laying around and buy non-refined sugar. Its time to empty your cupboard of those hidden cookies and potato chips. Do not buy any more. Cooked apples with raisins and cinnamon taste much better anyway.

Day 19- Empty your freezer, but this time give the contents to your neighbor; keep the frozen pizza for emergency rations – save the ice cream for your Pitta type friends who are not interested in their health. Do not eat any yourself!

Day 20- Invite a vegetarian friend over or invite yourself over to their house and have them cook you a meal. Feel their skin, look into their eyes to see if they are healthy – if they can do it so can you! Give them your coffee machine when they or you leave. If you go over to a friend be careful not to buy anything – like insurance or stock – as it may disrupt your digestion to think about business.

Day 21- Eat two meals of cooked grains and vegetables each day that you make yourself. You are on your way! Avoid dry, cold, raw and processed foods 85% to 90% of the time and you will be in good health. Remember to drink two large glasses of warm water each morning and take the digestive spices at least twice a day before meals. Stimulants (coffee, tea, wine, beer, alcohol, refined sugar, and cigarettes) are especially aggravating for Vata types and should be avoided as much as possible.

Menu Suggestions for the Vata type

Breakfast	**Cooked cereals – oats or rice porridge / sour juices / milk or soy milk**
Snack	Fruit
Lunch	Whole grains or wholegrain pasta / vegetables / animal products (optional) / salad with dressing or oil
Snack	Sweet Fruit or fresh nuts
Dinner	Whole grains or wholegrain pasta / vegetables / salad with dressing or oil

Plan for the Pitta People

Day 1- Decide in advance not to try and fit all 21 days into this afternoon's schedule. The best thing you can do now is to stop eating all fried food – especially in fast food (or any) restaurants. Even at home, just do not do it. Fired foods also mean donuts or anything that is deep-fried.

Day 2- Stop drinking orange juice every morning. Feed yourself three good meals in a day, breakfast is *not* the most important meal of the day, they *all* are. Check your digestive power-hungry every three to four hours on the hour? Normally the pure Pitta type will have a strong appetite and digestion – keep giving it food. Hungry between meals? Eat fruit or raw vegetables (carrots, celery, etc.). Try and remember where you buy real food.

Day 3- Throw away all oils and your margarine. Toss the low-fat products and go buy organic butter. Make ghee, see chapter 8 on how to do it. This is a major step as oils are not good for you generally, but ghee will balance your appetite without clogging your arteries. Cold-pressed olive oil can be used on salads and pasta – do not cook with it though. Skip the butter on toast altogether if you can, but it is still better than margarine as it will not turn to plastic in your veins.

Day 4- Cut in half all of the fermented foods you eat – wine, beer, yogurt, cheese, miso, soy sauce, tempeh, yeast, yeast breads (bread can be taken every other day), etc. Now that you remembered where to buy whole foods you can go there and buy some – grains, vegetables and beans are a good start (remember those things?).

Day 5- Cut in half all of the acidic foods you eat – bananas, citrus fruits, coffee, pickles, and sauerkraut, etc. This especially means soft drinks like colas as they are very acidic and leech all the minerals from your body (aside from overtaxing your liver and pancreas).

Day 6- Begin to love bland food – remember the heartburn from the last Mexican meal? Greatly reduce all spices; regular use should be limited to those listed in chapter 15 under spices. Now is a good time to stop all very spicy foods and the spices themselves.

Day 7- Stop buying canned foods. Throw away the tomato sauce as it will cause major acidic problems – use fresh tomatoes to cook with when you must have them. Throw out all the sugar in your house – buy some non-refined sugar for now.

Day 8- Celebrate the new week by having a garage sale to sell your microwave oven, deep fryer and coffee maker. As long as you are at it, sell the foods you used to cook in those things too! (If you have not thrown them out already!)

Day 9- Today is a good day to find your kitchen again. Once you have found it convince yourself that it has other purposes besides making coffee (anyway, you sold the coffee machine yesterday). When you have convinced yourself that your health is a worthwhile investment cook a meal consisting of whole grains, vegetables and a salad. (This is assuming you haven't done it already on day four!)

Day 10- Stop all white wine and vinegar - you may as well stop coffee at this point since the coffee machine is gone.

Tea is OK for you if you feel too dejected. If you smoke reduce the amount you consume in half.

Day 11- Reduce your intake of meat (i.e., fat) in half – no more than four meals per week. Understand that you will feel lighter – do not mistake this for being empty.

Day 12- Buy some of those tasteless white cubes called tofu and soak them in tamari. Tamari looks like soy sauce but is not fermented, you can recognize it by the price, it is twice the cost of soy sauce. Tamari will make the tofu taste like something – soaking it for thirty minutes is the minimum time – overnight makes a good meat substitute.

Day 13- Now is a good time to clear out the freezer. Keep Aunt Sally's home made jam, the ice cream and throw the rest. Reconfirm that bland food is delicious!

Day 14- Two weeks already! Open your last bottle of champagne to celebrate (now you can only have it at marriages and weight-watcher meetings) – champagne is far too acidic to consume on any kind of regular basis. Learn about older red wines as they will disturb you less. Water, sweet fruit juices and flower based herbal teas are the best beverages for you – begin to drink them!

Day 15- Stop all of the fermented foods you eat – bread is OK if you do not have any kind of food allergies – if you do stop it as well.

Day 16- Stop all of the acidic foods you eat – bananas, citrus fruits, pickles, etc.

Day 17- Start cooking two meals a day (no, toasting bread does not count!). Breakfast, lunch or dinner, whatever fits into your schedule. Use a lot of whole foods (no, these do not come in a can).

Day 18- Now that you are cooking two meals a day you can clear out the cupboards of all those boxes of stuff. Feed them to the dog. Go buy sacks of grains if you need something to clutter up your cupboards.

Day 19- Eat aunt Sally's jam over the ice cream – you may as well go for it because ice cream will be limited to leap years from now on. No need to fill your freezer up again unless you freeze your own cooking.

Day 20- Invite a Vata type over and cook them a meal – they are often lousy cooks and you can show off your new tofu dish. Do not accept their coffee machine if they happen to offer you one. Perhaps you can sell them some stock or insurance after dinner just so you do not feel like you have totally wasted your time.

Day 21- Admit to yourself that it was better to take 21 days instead of an afternoon to do this (or review what happens to your body when you shock it if this *is* the first afternoon!). Avoid acidic, sour, spicy and fried foods – other than these you can eat what you like. Be aware not to overeat, but eat good meals three times per day.

Menu Suggestions for the Pitta type

Breakfast	**Eggs (x2 week as an option) or granola – toast and juices**
Snack	None or fruit
Lunch	Whole grains or wholegrain pasta / vegetables / beans / animal products (optional) / salad or raw foods
Snack	None or sweet fruit
Dinner	Whole grains or wholegrain pasta / vegetables / beans / salad

Plan for the Kapha People

Day 1- The first thing to do is to convince yourself that there is life after dinner (or breakfast, or lunch). This is not so difficult because when you are not eating you can be thinking about what to buy, how to cook it, then you can actually cook it, and then, you can eat it. Actually, this is what you may be doing now. Avoid this kind of scenario. Take the time to plan your meals carefully and cook tasteful, enjoyable food. But do not live around food and eating. If you can manage this you have made the primary step. Skip breakfast, you do not need it anyway. If you are hungry at 10am or 11am eat some fruit (it grows on trees).

Day 2- How are you feeling today? Sluggish? Tired? Begin by getting your digestion going so you can stop the tendency of tissue accumulation. Look in chapter 13 for the digestive spices that suite your constitutions. Buy them and grind them up into a powder. Take them twice a day after your main meals. Also go buy some fresh ginger root and see if you can eat four to eight slices of fresh, pealed ginger root before lunch and dinner. Add a little salt on them. The purpose of this is to increase your digestive capacity. If you cannot eat (or find) the ginger root use the powdered spices alone.

Day 3- Stop drinking all soft drinks like colas. Remember what the clear liquid is called? (Water?) Drink it instead. Anything cold or ice cold should be treated as if it was radioactive (it probably is anyway). Avoid all ice-cold beverages as if your life depends on it (it does). Drink warm water with meals or not at all. Drink coffee only in the morning. Remember morning? It is the time that you normally drink a liter of that black stuff to get out of bed.

Day 4- Go through your cupboard and give all of your oil back to Texas, it will kill you quicker than anything else. Buy some "cold-pressed" sunflower oil for emergencies or visitors. Basic rule – you do not need any, do not use it. If you have margarine or shortening throw them out immediately before they jump into your arteries and turn to plastic.

Day 5- Go through your cupboard (the other one) and throw out all of the cake, brownie and pudding mixes. Also throw out the three bags of white sugar. Buy fruits and honey. During the next few weeks if you feel like having sweets take a half of teaspoon of honey in warm water. Send your stash of chocolate to Siberia – they need it up there. While you are in the cupboard throw out the canned and boxed food also. Eat less!

Day 6- Once these nutritional sins are eliminated we can start on changing the *food*! Beans, beans, the magical food! If you never thought much about beans it is because you never knew all things that you could make from them. Look for cook books that have titles like: "How to Make Four Million Bean Dishes in an Afternoon". These kind of books will help you to realize that beans are a versatile food. But today start by going and buying whole grains, vegetables, fruits and a few beans. Cook some and see what happens.

Day 7- Start eating vegetable soups (that you make) in the evening with salads. Avoid meat or fish in the evening. It is better for you to eat heavy foods (animal products) at lunchtime.

Day 8- It is best to become friends with a cow – cows are better friends than many people – anyway if you eat any dairy at all you will end up looking like a cow. Cut your dairy consumption in half today. Do not use any low fat dairy products, buy full fat and dilute with water if you need to have dairy. Stop eating cheese altogether.

Day 9- Look closely at what kinds of grains you can eat. Wheat is very fattening and should be avoided. Bread is problematic because of the wheat and yeast inside. Better grains are those that are diuretic like barley, rye, corn, quinoa and buckwheat. Start avoiding all breads and pastries other than rye breads (non-yeasted is best). Wholegrain pastas are OK.

Day 10- Stop taking all forms of sugar – in any form, no candy bars, etc. This means that you cannot buy any kind of refined or processed food as they all have sugar in them. You can still take the honey water when needed or use small amounts of honey on other things. (Please note that once you have gotten off sugar and broken the addiction you will not only have more energy, lose weight easily, but you will find your sense of humor returning. Perhaps in a few months you can have some sugary stuff, but for the time being avoid like the plague – it is just as deadly.)

Day 11- Stop being depressed about not having sugar – it is just a withdrawal symptom! Get into cooking some very tasty vegetarian dishes. Variety in food is what will help the most. If you are trying to lose weight do not mix too many foods together in one dish. Simple preparations are simple to digest. Now is the day to get serious about how much coffee you are drinking. However much it is it's too much. Coffee is like sugar and you will have far more energy when you get off of it completely. Reduce what you drink in half today.

Day 12- Now is the time to really eat less. Cut your amount of food by 1/3 in quality. Be strict about this as it will take time for your stomach to shrink a bit. Do not be extreme in any direction! Remember desserts *do* count and you need to avoid them completely for the time being. Begin to use more spices in cooking, they will help everything from sugar withdrawals to digestion.

Day 13- By now you have realized that eating too many beans in a meal is as bad as having no dessert (only different). Plan your meals with a little of everything. You can keep food for two days in the fridge (Traditional Ayurveda says do not eat food that is not fresh, but we have to start someplace!). Another possibility is to cook four or five portions of a dish and freeze the other portions. This is a way to have a variety of food on your plate without cooking for two hours at each meal. This helps psychologically – do it.

Day 14- Congratulations! You are still alive! Check yourself out and make sure you are still alive (pinching works well). Jog around the refrigerator twenty times to show it who the boss is. Cook something Italian to boost your psychology and to please your stomach.

Day 15- Time to use that last box of brownie mix that you had hidden in the back of the cupboard, after all, you are starting the third week already! But really, this is the *last* dessert for a while!

Day 16- Limit all dairy use to once or twice a month. Cut your coffee consumption in half again. Remember coffee is like a credit card – the bill still arrives – only later. Beat yourself for not taking your digestive spices religiously – *do it now.*

Day 17- Buy stock in a spice company – use the spices liberally to support your investment. They taste better than technology anyway. Keep the level of spices moderate but consistent in your cooking – the idea is not to burn your mouth, but to stimulate digestion. If you have gas, burning or other signs of indigestion you may be using too many spices at once or too much of any one. Spicing food is an art! Take your time to learn it.

Day 18- Reduce once more the amount of food you eat – stop once and for all the second helpings. Keep your plate not more than ¾th full at any meal.

Day 19- Limit your consumption of meat and fish (if you eat them) to twice a week in the middle of the day. Never mix dairy and meat or fish together – at any time.

Day 20- Invite a Vata and Pitta type over for dinner because they are both generally lousy cooks. They are really missing a good five-course meal. Make them a vegetarian extravaganza and stun them – they will never forget you. Be aware not to accept the coffee machine or to buy stock after the meal.

Day 21- Heavy oily foods and animal products are best avoided as they congest and clog your system. Keep your digestive capacity high with spices and by eating less food. Eating two meals a day is enough for you, eat fruit if you need more energy between meals. By following these simple steps you will maintain your health.

Menu Suggestions for the Kapha type

Breakfast	**None**
Snack	Sour fruit
Lunch	Whole grains or whole grain pasta / beans / vegetables / animal products (optional) / salad
Snack	None
Dinner	Vegetable soups / vegetables / some grains / salad

Plan for the Dual Type People

All of the dual types can benefit from reading the above advice for each of the pure types. As about half of all people are mixed or dual types this section is very important.

The reason that no day-by-day plan is listed for the dual type is that there is an infinite number of possible combinations for a person. The traditional way Ayurveda advised dual types was to change the diet according to the seasons. This will be highlighted below. The idea behind this is that each principle, Vata, Pitta, or Kapha will tend to increase the most during a particular season of the year. Therefore, by eating a diet that tends to reduce the dominant principle in nature one avoids health problems.

An example of this is clearly seen in the fall when many people find that they are more stressed or agitated than in other times of the year. According to Ayurveda the Vata principle is dominant at this time and tends to cause nervous sensitivities or disorders. Therefore, eating a Vata type diet when Vata is part of your constitution will help to prevent or reduce nervous tensions or aggravations.

Another example of this is that the Kapha principle increases during the winter and early spring. A failure to keep the Kapha principle from increasing would cause the metabolism to become slower or sluggish causing weight gain in water or fat accumulation. Hence, eating a diet that reduces Kapha – as outlined above in the *Plan for the Kapha People* – one can stop or even reduce extra fat.

Here are the general times of the year to eat a diet associated with each type for North America. If your climate or location is different then these guidelines will change a little. Also there is quite a difference between Texas and Minnesota. So be aware that you may need to do some adjusting in this table.

Season	**Vata/ Pitta type**	**Pitta/ Kapha type**	**Vata/ Kapha type**
January	Vata	Kapha	Vata
February	Vata	Kapha	Kapha
March	Pitta	Kapha	Kapha
April	Pitta	Kapha	Kapha
May	Pitta	Pitta	Kapha
June	Pitta	Pitta	Kapha
July	Pitta	Pitta	Kapha
August	Pitta	Pitta	Vata
September	Vata	Pitta	Vata
October	Vata	Pitta	Vata
November	Vata	Kapha	Vata
December	Vata	Kapha	Vata

As one can see by looking at the above chart each principle is given six months out of a year. Looking at when to change your diet and do so at the right time of year. A failure to do this will often result in some kind of illness like a cold, flu, fever or other problem.

Therefore, in conclusion, the main points are to go slowly, eat whole foods, reduce processed foods, and eliminate refined sugars and stimulants like alcohol and coffee. By going slowly your body has time to adjust without severe withdrawal symptoms. Depending on your level of consumption of refined foods you will most certainly experience some kind of withdrawal symptoms from sugar and food additives. Common signs are headaches, depression, fatigue and nervousness. These signs will normally pass in seven to ten days. As always it is advised that you seek professional help in this matter if problems arise.

17
Improve the Quality and Length of Your Life

Ayurvedic nutrition is actually the freest and most open system of eating in the world. In fact you can eat anything you wish – you will, of course, either benefit or not from your choice. However, if you learn which foods are the best for you, you will also be able to eat foods that are that less beneficial for you occasionally. While an effort has been made in this book to make you aware of the effects of certain foods and processing procedures, one does not necessarily have to never enjoy an ice cream again (even though it has the potential to disrupt all types).

After reviewing the information in this book some people will choose to follow a diet that is best for their constitution and others will follow a looser form using foods that are less beneficial for their constitution. Ayurveda is an open system so any approach is valid. *One does not have to eat organic foods or become a vegetarian even though the long-term health benefits of this approach are clearly presented.* Ayurveda and constitutional nutrition is about finding the foods that benefit your personal metabolism. It is not about being rigid or fanatical.

Trust your own experience of food, eating and how your body responds to digesting what you have eaten. This is the primary point. Constitutional nutrition is about adjusting dietary intake to the individual based on metabolic differences as observed by thousands of Ayurvedic doctors over a period of several thousand years. However, the point is to follow your individual needs, not to superimpose another system or set of values on yourself.

It is unlikely that most people will be eating all the foods that benefit them in a manner that is beneficial. This is the main thrust of the book – to refine and direct general groups of people to diets that match their basic individual needs. One must apply effort to change food habits or addictions. Just because one of the general plans does not fit your tastes do not throw it away. Follow it for 21 days and see if you do not indeed feel much better. Obviously, eliminating refined foods, stimulants and other destructive foods will make anyone feel better. This reflects a basic truth of Ayurveda – start with the obvious.

Sufficient time should be taken to change nutritional habits (or begin them!). Ayurvedic nutrition is about a life long nutritional plan. It is not a fashion or passing fad. Individual orientated diets are the obvious nutritional choice for many people already and the trend is growing at a surprising rate. However, it is only the Ayurvedic system that offers us a time tested, practical and logical individualized nutritional system. We know from our present experience and the experience of thousands of doctors that this system works. It is not the idea or theory of any one person or group, but it simply follows the laws of nature. Whether one believes them or not does not change the function of nature and the fact that they work. Crying that the earth is flat will not change the nature of the earth. So too, "modern" nutritionists discarding the Ayurvedic system are simply ignoring the obvious workings of nature and the system that reflects its actions.

While some effort has been made to enlighten people as to certain effects of the modern lifestyle and chemicals in the food chain an attitude of fatalism is certainly counter productive. Instead there is much each individual can do for themselves and their families health. The first and most important step is to demand organically grown products from your market – whether plant or animal origin. This is the most important factor in preserving long term health for future generations. The additional elimination or reduction of animal products from the diet would increase any benefits several thousand or even million times due to the concentration of deadly chemicals in animal fat and tissues.

Nevertheless, it is not that we should lose sight of the most important factor – our health lies in our hands. What we pick up and put in our mouths either has a beneficial or detrimental effect on the assimilation of nutrients and formation of bodily tissues. This encompasses the metabolism of cells as well as the metabolism of the digestive tract. *Therefore, our desire to feel better and take control of our lives is probably the most fundamental step anyone can make to improve their health.*

The real purpose of Ayurvedic nutrition is to empower you with choice and ultimately peace of mind. Following the Ayurvedic guidelines is meant to provide the freedom to choose healthy foods and not respond to market manipulations. Each individual should be very clear that name brand foods are no longer a guide to good health or sound nutrition. All food companies are motivated by profit and market shares. In order to get you to buy their product they are using any conceivable method to influence your mind and choice. There is nothing wrong in this with most products. Unfortunately, food is our basic fuel and all modern processing methods – without exception – lessen the nutritional value of your food.

As we have seen just adding vitamins and other supplements is not sufficient to replace everything that has been refined out – simply because no one knows everything that has been removed in the process. The basic perspective of modern nutrition is based on a fragmentary vision of the body and the material universe that it inhabits. During the last ninety years there have been huge changes in the perception of this material universe and in the manner in which it functions. Yet, little effort has been made by the biochemical industry to apply these newfound observations to medicine or nutrition.

This is the primary reason why modern nutrition (and to a great extent modern medicine) is failing. However, as is usual with large companies or governments, it will be the people that will decide – or demand – a fundamentally different way of approaching health and nutrition due to the cost involved.

It is my experience and the experience of many other professional health care practitioners that Ayurveda will provide the foundation for a new world medical and nutritional system. The fundamental approach of Ayurveda is to treat the person not the disease. More than 80% of the major illnesses of our time are directly related to diet and/or lifestyle. The almost complete failure of modern nutrition to correct or prevent these kinds of diseases is apparent. The unwillingness of the medical community to admit that all chemical treatments of food and all refining processes affect food far beyond nutrient content is another major problem.

While people are contracting cancers at an alarming rate and more and more children are born with birth defects and genital deformations the medical and food industries stand by and say that our food and nutritional systems are safe and sound. They often say that no proof exists as they twist and manipulate studies to condone the view of the funding company and new "wonder drug" as it races to the drug store shelf. This whole trend can be stopped.

Each person can simply choose to buy real whole food. Each person can simply refuse to eat chemical food additives and the thousands of pesticides, fungicides, and preservatives that are put on all our food. Each person can simply refuse to eat hormone laced meat that is pumped up with antibiotics – medicines that may have saved your life if you had not ingested them on a regular basis through food. Each person can become aware of marketing and how it causes each of us to buy the foods we do. The smiling face on the label hides chemical poisons that alter metabolic functions in your body – it is indeed a strange world we live in today.

In short, Ayurvedic nutrition is about eating real, "normal" food in a manner that is more human and relaxed. It is about enjoying life, having a good time and putting things in their proper place. Food is an important part of our lives yet it tends to either be too important or not important at all. One attitude brings indulgence and the other brings indifference. Both lead to poor food choices that eventually cause the metabolism to function in less than an optimum manner. According to Ayurveda this is the primary cause of disease.

Therefore, by consciously choosing the kind of food that will benefit your body you take control of your life, your health and your happiness. It is true that happiness is not dependent on health, but health is certainly dependent on happiness. Ayurveda can help you towards both of these goals by helping you become aware of your nature and how you respond to your environment and food. Ayurvedic nutrition is about understanding the unity and interrelated functioning of the universe – and our irrefutable presence in this interrelationship.

Appendix : The Difference Between Biochemical and Ayurvedic Nutrition

This is a supplement section to the main part of the book. Initially this section was a primary part of the book. However, I feared that it might be too dense for the average reader. Nvertheless, I personally feel that this section is critical to a complete understanding of Ayurvedic nutrition and so it has been posted on my website at various times over the last ten years. It is difficult on several levels. This section involves not only two different medical and nutritional systems, but also a lifetime of social conditioning. Our social conditioning may present the most difficult aspect in comparing the systems. In this section we will look at both systems and understand their different approaches.

As stated in the introduction, modern science is a belief system. As a system it has socially replaced the traditional role of religion as the ordainer of health and happiness. The dilemma today is that modern medicine is failing to reward many people with the "promised land" of health and happiness. Over the last decade dissatisfaction with the current medical approach has caused an enormous increase in more natural and traditional forms of health care. For some curious reason the traditional forms of medicine are called "alternative" forms of health care. This raises the questions whether a diet based of whole foods is an alternative. It is indeed an alternative to eating higher processed junk food.

In addition to modern medicine losing the interest and faith of the majority of people it also has numerous internal factions. In the scientific field itself there is little agreement on collected data. What data is collected is usually interpreted differently by different people. Most subjects have at least two different points of view and very often, many more. Unfortunately, the common person is not aware of the different points of view as the scientific community usually bands together to present a public point of view while they argue amongst themselves the merits or demerits of either standpoint.

The benefits of modern medicine are many. Yet, the dangers are numerous. Modern nutrition is an outcome of modern medicine (allopathy). Hence, what applies for modern medicine also applies to modern nutrition. The purpose of this book is not to criticize or condemn anything, anyone or any system. But rather to really look at some of our fundamental beliefs of nutritional science and see if they are true and if they actually work. One basic truth needs to be understood – modern medicine and nutrition do not fully understand the complete functioning of the body. This point must be stressed in the beginning.

Science is based on presumptions and theories that we often mistake for reality. Professor Bohm explains this beautifully:

> "What will be emphasized, first of all in scientific research and later in a more general context, is that fragmentation is continually being brought about by an almost universal habit of taking the content of our thought for 'a description of the world as it is'. Or we could say that, in this habit, our thought is regarded as in direct correspondence with objective reality....us, in scientific research, a great deal of our thinking in terms of theories. The root 'theory' derives from the Greek

'theoria', which has the same root as 'theater', in a word meaning to 'view' or 'to make a spectacle'. Thus, it might be said that a theory is primarily a form of insight, i.e., a way of looking at the world, and not a form of knowledge of how the world is."[99]

Having clarified that modern nutrition is operating with different theories and not on any real direct knowledge of reality, outside of numerous fragmented laboratory studies, we can begin to look at the various sub-divisions of biochemical nutrition.

We can roughly divide the present nutritional models into two groups – biochemical and natural. These two categories do not work well, however. The main reason is that the term "biochemical" is used to describe modern medicine – to look at things as a sum total of its parts, or chemicals. Or as some physicists call it the "atomic building blocks" as it is based on the concept of the atom as being the fundamental unit of matter (or as was later found out the components of the atom). This belief system has a mechanical way of looking at and understanding the functioning of the universe.

The problem is that "natural" nutrition and "natural" medicine are also using the same mechanical model to understand the universe and the human body. An attempt to change this approach in the last decade with "mind / body" systems or "holistic" approaches has helped somewhat. Unfortunately, they are usually practiced or applied through a mechanical model of the universe. We are actually left with one mechanical system and two approaches – a "biochemical materialistic" and a "natural materialistic".

There is a third option that actually contains both the biochemical and the natural approaches, yet it goes beyond both in scope. It is Ayurveda. This system has a totally

[99] Bohm, David, 1980, pp. 3-4.

different point of view and does not use the mechanical model at all – yet it understands it well. It just finds it very limited in scope. Remember that we are still using surgical techniques developed by the ancient Ayurvedic physicians. They had a very good understanding of the mechanical structure and form of the body and universe. It is by the recognition of the mechanical approach – its pros and cons – that Ayurveda can include it. And as all of its methods, medicines and therapies are "natural" it also includes the naturalistic forms of medicine. However, Ayurveda is based on a vision of wholeness and unity that is supported by a conscious intelligence that goes beyond the purely mechanical view.

To understand the differences between the systems we need to look at each one of them, then we can compare.

Biochemical View Follows a Mechanical Model

The modern view of medicine and nutrition is that the totality is made up of the individual parts. If we understand the parts individually then we understand the whole. Currently nutrition and medicine are based on the Newtonian model of physics or of mechanics. As the world of physics is changing and many scientists have been moving away from mechanical physics to "new physics" over this last century, we may wonder if mechanical nutrition has the same validity as we once thought.

This approach tries to reduce everything in the physical universe to a form of matter and then understand its function. Various means are created and used to measure the components under study. However, these measurements are subjective concepts and are imposed on the material universe by the human mind. This is extremely interesting in physics and the study of all physical matter. Nonetheless, the human being is composed of more than just physical matter

To date this approach has not understood the meaning of life or the beginning of creation. Yes, there are numerous theories, but these are just theories, which tend to change as time passes. This mechanical approach also tries to reduce the mental and emotional functions to physical components.

Scientific studies are based on subjective measurements along with another subjective standard that is related to it by some, hopefully, logical means. Something is then observed according to these two subjective classifications and compared. Usually the purpose is to prove or disprove something so the measurement and the standard have to fit the initial concept or theory of the creator of the study. *But neither the standard nor the unit of measurement has any context outside of its use for the study.* This is important to understand, as applying these kinds of studies to the human body is fraught with problems as we will see later.

It is also interesting to note that science acknowledges and integrates information to the extent that it is able to use it and fit it into an existing model. If something does not make sense – which means it does not fit into a current view – then it is discarded. Generally things are used that fit into and support a logical growth and progression of thinking in any specific area. Once more it must be noted that much of the data discovered in research is not used, as it does not fit into any currently known model.

Biochemical approaches are invasive to the body and mainly use man made substances to induce physical responses. The relation to the mind is only considered in relation to the chemical function and does not account for things like how you feel. These methods require that the person is passive and accepts an outside authority in the form of a medication or person, or both. One needs to give up personal responsibility to the trained professional. This method relies heavily on machines and instruments to measure and judge what is normal or not. The patient is reduced to the purely physical aspects and again is not considered subjectively. For example people are not questioned if a therapy or test that zaps their body with unseen radiation is disturbing or frightening for them.

In nutritional science the mechanical approach tries to reduce the body into a factory and the food into a form of fuel that feeds the factory. It tries to understand the physiological functions and needs of the body and see how these relate to the fuel source. It sounds pretty simple and clear until we look at the size and complexity of the factory.

The body has about a trillion cells (a trillion = 1,000,000,000,000,000,000). Each of them functions according to its role in the body. A liver cell functions like a liver cell and a tissue cell functions like a tissue cell. We do not know why they do this or how they "know" their correct function in the body. Genes, RNA and DNA are used to explain this action, but this has not completely resolved the issue. Modern medicine in general does not acknowledge an inherent principle of intelligence in each cell or a principle of life that integrates these cells. Currently it is in fashion to blame many social problems and diseases on genetics. While genetics must play an important role, the unity of the body's intelligence as a whole is not addressed (similarly, a universal intelligence or consciousness is not addressed either).

In fact, the mechanical model of understanding the cell is decidedly limited. The cell itself is made up of numerous different kinds of molecules that are in constant interaction with other molecules. Each of these relationships affects the overall functioning of the cell. Yet, to study a cell without understanding or accounting for the subtle actions of the molecules that make it up is very limited, if not down right wrong. Many innovative research scientists are projecting the model of quantum physics into the cell itself. This view perceives the interaction of the molecules as an energetic relationship that goes far beyond the idea of a bunch of molecules floating around in saline fluid relating only in a mechanical manner to external stimulus.

The function of any cell in the body is complex. Moreover, the body has some form of intelligence that governs the cells as a whole and individually. When cells do not behave in the right way they are destroyed and eliminated by a maintenance network in the body – the immune system. Biochemical nutrition does not understand the complete picture of this factory – it's just too big and too complicated.

The vastness is one problem. Another is the interrelationship between systems. This is the hardest for us to understand, as we have never been told about this concept. Here we come back to the study model that needs to create a subjective unit to measure things, and another standard that needs to be created to judge it against – fragmentation. Statistics can now be gathered and defined according to these two subjective factors. But this approach leaves out the fact that not one system, cell or organ in the body functions alone.

The real problem at this point is that it is physically impossible to study all the possible relationships between a trillion cells – not to mention the relationships going on within each individual cell. Even if we reduce the cells down to their organ, gland, system or function the possibilities are still infinite. How then can we structure our study – which begins with a concept and two subjective factors – with so many possibilities? We must decide what is more important to the issue under study. But how can we do this if we do not understand the total relationship of the body? We cannot.

Another example of the difficulty inherent in this approach is the organisms that live in the body itself. The large intestine is the primary site of a major colony of guests that live in the human body. One researcher has been so bold as to state that the colon supports a whole ecoculture that is impossible to presently comprehend. This is a pretty bold statement, one that becomes clear with the following information. The colon supports between 400 to 500 bacteria that help to digest and process food and nutrients. The colon also supports another 100 to 200 fungi that contribute to the digestive process. Additionally, there are about 100 different kinds of virus living with the bacteria and fungi.

Imagine a room with 700 dogs, cats and rats. The bacteria, fungi and viruses are not of the same species, they are very different in composition, action and effect. First try to understand all of the possible relationships between the individuals in any one group. Then add the relations between the three different groups. We now have a very complex ecosystem that – if disturbed – would result in chaos for one or all of the various groups. In the human body this ecosystem is normally kept in balance by a healthy diet and lifestyle. It is thrown into turmoil by the use of drugs, poor diet, artificial foods, and some medications like antibiotics.

There is an additional factor. Each person has a different set of inhabitants. This means that our dogs, cats and rats are different from person to person, culture to culture and continent to continent. This makes a very real challenge for the biochemical researcher – how to find a common or average set of digestive flora in the human body? In fact, all human bodies present these kinds of challenges and what is truly amazing is the progress and understanding that does exist. Biochemical medicine has made truly remarkable progress in understanding certain functions of the body. It is due to the brilliance of doctors, chemists and biologists over the last several hundreds years that many diseases have been largely eliminated from humanity.

The task is truly monumental. Especially when we add an additional factor – the complexity of food itself. Natural food - not processed or refined – is filled with many things besides vitamins, minerals, proteins, carbohydrates, and such. There are, as yet, many unidentified components in food as a whole. Even with all the known items that comprise food the interrelationship between them all is extremely complex and not well understood. What is known is then based on a subjective energy unit. What is the mainstay of the biochemical nutritional model? The calorie. What exactly is a calorie? It is a measurement of heat. Nutritionally one calorie is the amount of energy needed to raise the temperature of a liter of water 1° centigrade. This is a subjective way of measurement, which is used to determine the energy source of fuel or food.

Clearly understand that this way of measuring energy consumption is subjective as described above and may have little or no bearing on nourishing the body. This is clearly seen in that one can easily gain 2000 calories by eating cakes, jams, and candies yet gain absolutely no nutritional value for the function of the metabolism. This is in fact the exact situation in the United States today.

Using the methodology of the calorie we cannot understand the total relationship within the digestive system much less the relationship between the nervous and hormonal systems which control all metabolic function including the digestion of food and ultimately the assimilation of nutrients. The complete function of nervous or hormone systems are not fully understood within themselves so how can the interrelationships with processing nutrients be understood? Do two partial pieces of information make a complete understanding? The calorie works well in the laboratory, but in fact has little value in human nutrition.

In this light we can begin to question whether or not a calorie has any meaning outside of the physics lab. First question yourself – do you watch your calories? If no, it obviously has not prevented you from living. If yes, did the watching of your calorie intake work for you? Roughly one-third of you will say yes and the other two-thirds no. Studies have shown that most people following diets have tried more than one diet – the average number for dieters is five. Modern diets are using the subjective calorie measurement as a means to judge food intake. Why then do dieters statistically fail over 80% of the time?

Once more we are faced with the answer that there is a number of issues involved – a faulty unit of measurement may be one. Certainly the whole psychological state of the dieter must be considered. How can we do that with a mechanical model – with the biochemical model? Tell the person that they have no will power? Tell them that their problem is psychosomatic? Tell them to see a counselor? Certainly all these factors are important. It is problematic to view the psychological state as a mechanical function. How do we find our way through this mess when we look solely at the mechanical level?

Another problem with the biochemical model is that it changes with time. As the functions and relationships in the body are understood better then the previous ideas, concepts and theories are revised, changed or discarded. This is a healthy process of learning and change. The problem is that this confirms the partial knowledge we have of the body and yet we continue to develop treatments only based on fractional knowledge. This does not make good sense. We are not going to build a rocket when we only understand 60% percent of the procedure. If we do try to build the rocket we will get a 65% finished product. Because, let's assume, we learned 5% during the process of manufacturing. The problem is that this 60-65% knowledge is being applied to our health – it may cure us or kill us – we just do not know.

Large companies and people in the health industry do not actually question the fundamental approaches behind the current therapies. They also do not mention that they only have partial knowledge of the human body. The public in general has been conditioned to think that modern science does understand the majority of the functions of the body and the complexity of fuel intake through food consumption. This is simply not true.

To digest any given item we need to consider a number of subsystems in the body and a mind boggling array of minerals, vitamins and other nutrients. This complexity is compounded by hundreds of bacteria, fungi and viruses that assist and contribute to process of converting nutrients. This all facilitated by enzymes – something that we still know very little about. Plus, nothing can function in the body without the nervous system and the hormones that serve as the body's messenger service. As already mentioned these two systems are not completely understood. When we add in all the enzymes that are needed to carry out the actions of the messages of the nervous and hormone systems we increase the complexity. When we then add the raw materials that all three components need to function we get a very complex interrelationship. Finally, add the raw material that hormones are made of – cholesterol – and we indeed have a confusing situation.

What if we give the body too much or too little of a raw material? Yes, imbalance or even chaos results. In fact, no one knows what happens. There has been no study that examines the long-term use of mega doses of nutrients, or completely eliminating an element like cholesterol. Heart disease on one hand can certainly be viewed as too much of raw material as can type II diabetes or obesity. Certainly, we know the result of too little of many nutrients in the form of degenerating diseases or malnutrition.

Additionally, biochemical nutrition does not consider the source of the raw materials to be important beyond their chemical structure, e.g., sugar is sugar, refined white or unrefined. This is strange, as studies have existed from as early as 1936 showing that the effect of refined white sugar is very different than raw sugar in sugar cane. It is well known that sugar causes tooth decay, yet a study of South Africans who chew four stalks of sugar cane a day have better than average teeth and a low percentage of cavities.[100]

This finding was repeatedly supported in laboratory studies. The same correlation was found with diabetes, sugar consumption, and sugar cane workers in Central America. Once more, these results were supported by laboratory studies and found to be true. The fact is that refined sugar has a very different effect on the body than raw, non-refined sugar. Yet, the biochemical nutritional community continues to state that the molecular structure is the same, so all sugars function in the same way in the body. This is in direct conflict with their own information and simply not true. This also extends to all foods, not just sugar, as we have seen in this book.

On a more specific level, biochemical systems do not talk about the physical residue that is left in the body from man made chemicals or highly refined foods. They are aware of these residues and consider them to be negligible. The question of residue and what constitutes a problematic amount is completely prone to subjective measurement. Who decides what amount of waste is acceptable in the body and by what means?

This is a major difference in the two mechanical schools – the natural and biochemical. The biochemical says a molecule is a molecule regardless of where it comes from. They do not explain that the effect on the body's ability to

[100] Ballentine, Dr. Rudolph, *Diet and Nutrition: a Holistic Approach*, 1978, pp. 58.

eliminate an organic (from an alive source) and inorganic (from a dead or manufactured source) is different. Things produced in a factory or laboratory pose problems for the body's enzymes, as the material is not inherent in nature. Hence, some part of the material is always left unprocessed. Biochemists shrug off this fact. They assume that the liver and kidneys – the organs of filtration and processors of toxins – will manage, hopefully, to get rid of the residue.

The school of natural medicine knows that the source is very important. This understanding is filtering into the biochemical community and many books now tell you to add a lot of fresh vegetables and grains in your diet. The last ten years has seen an enormous increase of books and diet plans listing the importance of fresh food sources. If the molecule structure is the only important factor then why is there this revival in biochemical nutrition for fresh food? Well, it is because scientific studies have been showing this difference for the last 25 years.

Old habits die hard. Especially when there is a strong economic implication on change. So now you find every new book on nutrition telling you to eat more fresh things, but not going into qualitative differences. This includes items like chemical additives and preservatives, synthetic vitamins, refined foods, and generally huge economic industries.

We can summarize the mechanical systems as qualitative. They are primarily looking at the quantity of things and trying to understand the relationship of things in that context. Things can be measured, compared and studied accordingly. However, can we judge life through quantity alone? I personally know happy people with average or low incomes and very unhappy people with large incomes. Can we then only use a quantity – a subjective concept of measurement – to judge any aspect of life? Dietary or otherwise?

This is the fundamental question we need to ask ourselves. Are we only worth the car we drive, the brand of cloths we wear, or the coffee brand we drink? Can we as an individual be reduced to a measurable object? Our joys, hobbies, passions, our feelings and ideas; are all these measurable objects? If this is not true, if we are more than a product consumer, more than a food factory, how far is quantitative nutrition valid?

The primary response for all of us should be to look around and see if this model of viewing the world is working. What is your personal experience? Do you really want to be seen as an amount of anything? I think not. I believe that each of us wants to live and enjoy life fully with a healthy body and mind. Being reduced to a statistic, average or number is not part of my understanding of health or happiness. To use this same understanding for nutrition is extremely limited perhaps even dangerous. My own experience is that biochemical nutrition just does not work consistently.

Ayurvedic View Follows a Mind / Body Model

Ayurveda views life as a complex interrelationship of forces – some chemical, some physical and some subtle, like mental functioning. It says that you have to try to understand life through understanding the totality. Trying to go through individual parts will not help you to understand the totality of life because it is not limited to the parts. Each part cannot be seen outside of the totality to which it belongs and supports.

This view recognizes that each part has an individual quality, action and function. This is not questionable and is not in conflict with the mechanical model of understanding the universe. However, this is only the beginning point and not the end point that the biochemical approach wishes it to be. From this point on the differences begin.

Ayurveda takes the stance that due to the interrelationship of all matter one cannot understand it outside of its numerous relationships. For example, each form of matter is dependent on another. The four main states of matter, solid, liquid, transformative, and gaseous all exist in a field or space. They are in constant interaction with each other and form the universe through this continuous interaction.

Ayurveda also is of the view that if something works outside of the human body the same must be applicable – on some level – within the human body and vice versa. This is very much like some of the modern physicists applying "new physics" to cellular function instead of the old Newtonian model. If quantum physics is working in time or space, according to Ayurveda, it must also be applicable to some level of the body. We as humans are totally interrelated to our environment through food production and consumption.

There is another major difference between the two systems. The Ayurvedic system understands and respects a quality of intelligence in life. Their view is that one cannot separate the two.[101] Moreover, they extend this concept of intelligence from a cosmic level down to a cellular level. From their standpoint it is the same conscious intelligence manifesting on different levels throughout the many spheres of life.

While this is a philosophy that one may reject or accept it is, nevertheless, very useful in understanding the functions of the human body. This view poses many problems for modern science – primarily because there is no way to measure this intelligence. One is limited to experiencing it on some level as it is existential.

However, when the concept of an intelligent principle is used to understanding the human body many things are

---

[101] In Ayurveda this is the concept of Purusha and Prakriti, consciousness and latent matter.

simplified in practical application. One major difference is in approach. Instead of viewing the body as a battlefield in which we need to destroy or fight something we suddenly have the option of promoting a cohesive intelligence response from the body. This is a huge shift from the biochemical point of view. Even when the modern doctor or nutritionist is not fighting something they are replacing or supplementing some "deficiency". *The real deficiency may be a lack of cohesive intelligence.*

Modern nutrition says that the human body cannot produce certain nutrients alone and that they need to be consumed through dietary intake. These are referred to as "essential" nutrients. Interestingly enough some modern studies have proved this to be untrue. In one study, pregnant women were found to urinating out more of an "essential" nutrient than they had consumed through diet. Leading the researchers to the conclusion that, somehow, the body must be producing it – something that was thought to be impossible.[102] But as this does not fit into the currently held belief system, and there is no current model to fit it into, it is basically disregarded.

However, if we use the Ayurvedic point of view that the body is intelligent and that this intelligence is a cohesive force that is connected to our mental and psychological functions it becomes explainable. The body, when given the proper environment, nutrients and mental support can produce anything that is needed. There are many examples of this. One is the study cited above. Another is the classic story of how vitamin C became known to prevent scurvy in the English navy.

We know that a diet missing fresh foods and fruit caused scurvy on the old sailing ships and the addition of these foods eliminated the disease. Or do we? What has never been satisfactorily explained is why between one-fourth to one-

---

[102] Ballentine, Dr. Rudolph, 1978, p. 533.

third of most crews were not getting scurvy. Why did a certain number of sailors not come down with the disease? The answer has never been explained satisfactorily, but when we apply the concept of an intelligent body we see – for some reason – certain sailor's bodies could produce enough vitamin C to prevent getting scurvy on the same diet as the others that did contract the disease. Ayurveda has a way to explain this through constitutional or metabolic differences.

Another example that could be used are the many modern cases of spontaneous remission from life-threatening disease. There are many well-documented cases of people recovering from cancer and other deadly diseases. These cases present problems for the scientific community, as there is no current model to classify them into. The usual response is that "it's impossible". Occasionally, someone will grudgingly admit that it is a "miracle". Once again Ayurveda sees this as a cohesive effort on the human, not just the body or the mind, but the whole being, to get well.

Numerous cases exist that explain how people have simply decided not to die – they make changes in their life – and they live. These are not isolated events. Unfortunately, no one understands why certain people can do it and others cannot. There is a significant and interesting explanation of this in Ayurveda. It is beyond the scope of a book on nutrition to fully address this issue however.[103]

The Ayurvedic concept of intelligence extends beyond the body and into nature in all respects – even into food. In

---

[103] The concept of life in Ayurveda is called "Prana" which means "before breath". The tradition states that the Prana (life) binds the soul to the body, when this link is weakened then life begins to leave the body as in the cases of degenerative diseases like cancer. The remedies revolve around awakening the life (Prana) and intelligence in the body and mind which will then naturally strengthen the link to the soul.

[104] See above note no. 5 – the Prana is missing from the food and so weakens the link to the body.

fact, according to Ayurveda, one of the primary reasons for the increase of degenerative diseases today is due to a major decrease in the "life" of our food.[104] Much of our food is refined and preserved to a point that it is "dead" for Ayurveda.

The Ayurvedic point of view is that life is intelligent and intelligence is life. Hence, if one of these is lacking then so is the other. At this point it is good to understand the logic behind preserving and refining foods. The more "alive" a food is the quicker it deteriorates. The more refined it is the longer it lasts, sometimes almost indefinitely – like white sugar. If we apply Ayurvedic logic here the questions would arise how much life is left in something that does not deteriorate, and if the amount of life is reduced so must the amount of intelligence in the food. The main purpose of preserving foods is to extend the shelf life, it has nothing to do with nutritional value. It is a question of economics – if food spoils fast more of it will go to waste and someone will loose more money. The longer it lasts the less money that will be lost. Your diet is determined by profit, not nutritional value.

Just to give an example of the link between life and intelligence we can use vitamin C again. Each cell in the body has receptors for nutrients and vital substances, like vitamins and hormones. If you eat an orange the fruit is alive and the vitamin C in the orange (along with the many other nutrients) will go to the correct receptors on the appropriate cells. Not only will the vitamin C be able to find the right cells to go to it will also be able to find the right receptors on the cells. This signifies intelligence. However, if you take a synthetic vitamin C tablet (like what you buy 90% of the time in the store) it does not know which cells to go to nor does it know which receptors to go to on any given cell. The synthetic vitamin C, the one made in a factory, has the same molecular structure as the vitamin C in the orange. But one major factor is missing – the orange is alive and so has intelligence and the tablet of vitamin C is dead and therefore has no intelligence.

The basis of biochemical nutrition in this respect is to bombard every cell with a vitamin or nutrient in the theory that some deficiency will be eliminated. As the man made vitamin C floods all the cells it can reach before it is excreted by the body it has a warrior like attitude and effect on the body. When the vitamin is in the process of flooding the body it effectively blocks the cells from receiving any other nutrients or even hormones. To the extent that the synthetic substance stays in the body, that is the extent that other functions will be blocked. In the case of vitamin C this process is rather quick and relatively harmless – unless the process is repeated daily for prolonged periods of time. Then the usual result is that the body's intelligence is disturbed and it stops to produce and or synthesize the nutrient being consumed.

The above process is the foundation of biochemical medicine and nutrition. It relies on the body being flooded with something (either medication or nutrients) in order to have a *consistent measurable* response. This allows the scientist to know if a substance is taken what kind of response they can expect. The more a product floods the body, or systems of the body, the more reliable it is from the biochemical point of view. This means that if you take an aspirin 90% of the time it will stop your headache.

The problem with this scenario is that it slowly destroys the cohesive intelligence in your body as mentioned above. Interestingly enough, natural occurring vitamin C that you get in herbs or foods has been shown to be more effective than synthetic vitamin C in laboratory studies.[105] This leads one to question the effectiveness of any synthetic nutrient. The Ayurvedic point of view is that all the nutrients added to your foods – all the ones that have been taken out to

---

[105] *The Wealth of India*, vol. 3, 1952, p. 169.

prevent it from deterioration and economic loss – are not only of limited value, but are causing the body to lose its natural intelligent cohesiveness.

None of this can be proved beyond a doubt in a laboratory as intelligence is not a measurable substance (although it is obvious if it is absent!). The things that can be proved are largely ignored like the example of natural occurring vitamin C working better in the body than synthetic forms or the ability of the body to produce vitamin C (see footnote 5). There is another way to test things though and this is a vital part of Ayurveda. For every effect there must be a cause. This is the basis of Ayurvedic methodology – the law of cause and effect.[106]

The importance of this cannot be overstated and exemplifies one of the main differences between the biochemical approach and Ayurveda. The prime concern in Ayurveda is not the effect – the symptom – but the reason why it is there in the first place – what is the cause. Modern biochemical sciences are primarily concerned with stopping the symptoms – the effects. In some cases the cause is looked for but as biochemical systems lack the understanding of cohesive intelligence in the body they generally fail to understand the cause. Cancer is a case in point. After billions of dollars of research and study the cause is still unknown – much of the process is known, but not why it starts.[107]

Consequently, Ayurveda will look very differently at obesity than modern nutrition. The first thing that an Ayurvedic practitioner will look for is the reason why a person is obese. The problem could have a number of reasons – for instance

---

[106] This is the law of Karma or action, which provides the basis for all therapeutic treatments.

[107] See above note no. 5 as it gives the basic Ayurvedic explanation for cancer although there is much more to the subject. Some of Dr. Deepak Chopra's books provide very interesting information on this subject. See the bibliography for references.

a thyroid problem, other hormone imbalances, impaired liver function, diabetes, poor nutrition, poor eating habits, and psychological factors or simply over indulgence in food. Treating the effect, obesity, without understanding the cause is foolhardy according to Ayurveda. Why would a person go on a strict diet when the problem is due to liver malfunction? Or why go on a strict diet which could provoke the psychological insecurities that cause the person to overeat in the first place?

Hence, the failure to address the cause of any effect or symptom will inevitably lead to failure according to Ayurveda. Modern biochemical people laugh at this and proudly hold up the score card of success in stopping the symptoms of numinous diseases. The difference is actually on the definition of heath. Lacking symptoms is not health according to Ayurveda. Health is a dynamic state that also includes happiness of mind and the non-reliance on medication – natural or synthetic. The sad truth is that suppressing a symptom will only delay its reoccurrence in another, perhaps more difficult to treat, illness.

The importance of cause and effect also extends to logic. Logic is the other method that was mentioned above that can be used instead of, or when, a laboratory is not suitable. The logic of biochemistry is often laughable. An example of this kind of logic was stated quite wonderfully by Dr. Lee in his book on natural progesterone when he speaks about how the "deficiency" model has dominated modern medicine for the last century. He says that if one applies "deficiency" to most "disorders" one then finds the need to supplement the "deficiency". An example of this is menopause; a natural change of hormone levels in the body suddenly became a "deficiency disease" with the need to "supplement" the body with medications. Dr. Lee humorously points out that this is like saying that a headache is a "deficiency disease" that one

[108] Lee, John R., 1996.

needs to supplement the body with aspirin. But why stop here? Why not prevent headaches by "supplementing" the "deficiency" with aspirin on a daily basis?[108]

In contrast to this the logic of Ayurveda is excellent. If my dog is pregnant I know she will have puppies. She will not have kittens. I also know that some other dog was involved. I therefore know the cause, the present symptom, and the eventual effect or outcome. Frequently scientists twist this scenario to the extreme. The present day situation is quite serious – sometimes we are told that what we feel in our body is not true, or that we are not sick. In actual fact this is a failure of logic on the part of the professional. If we are sensing or feeling something then there must be a cause for the symptom. Usually the case is that the symptoms are not "serious" enough for biochemical therapies – in other words, it does not warrant starting a war. The example of the dog is simple, but how can we apply this logic in nutrition or problems relating to nutrition?

Obviously, we need some kind of working model to understand the differences in people, their different situations, different climates and psychological states. A haphazard-fragmented logic will not suffice. We need a consistent logical system that will work in both the mico level of the body and the macro, or cosmic, level of the universe. In Ayurveda this is achieved by understanding the different manifestations of life itself. A system of three principles is recognized as controlling the primary states of matter in our universe.

These three principles are also a subjective creation of man to some extent. However, the primary difference is that we can observe their function on all levels of nature, including our bodies. It is through the use of these three principles that Ayurveda understands the different constitutional types of people. This concept is not foreign to the modern scientific world.

In the 1950's scientists already understood that each person had a different metabolism. One important work in this field was published by Roger Williams in which he cited study after study that proved the individual nutritional requirements of people varied enormously.[109] This was also proven to be true with laboratory animals. While this is understood and accepted as factual even today no mechanical model exists for the professional nutritionist to adapt the accepted average requirements to the needs of an individual.

Consequently, what Ayurveda has to offer us is a system with an individual approach. Each of us is different so how on earth can one diet or nutritional plan work for everyone? Remember that this is scientific fact, no one has the same nutritional needs. Unfortunately, biochemical nutrition cannot offer us any method to work with individuals even though it knows this to be true. Not only are we at a loss for an individual nutritional model we are also lacking a method to understand the universe as it is interrelated to the human being.

Conclusion

This then is an attempt to compare two different points of view on nutrition. By the very complexity of the subject there is bound to be flaws in my presentation of both sides. This is meant as an introduction and is purposefully presented in a manner to provoke you to think about both systems. The present world functions on marketing principals – no one has your best interest in mind – everyone is going to try to sell you something. Therefore, now more than ever, it is important that you find out for yourself what is true, what is questionable, what is probable and what is false. Your life and the life of your children may depend on your choices.

---

[109] Williams, Roger, 1956.

It is my own experience, first in my own life, and second in my professional practice, that Ayurvedic nutrition brings a quality of life that goes far beyond feeling good. It eliminates many problems that are considered incurable by modern nutritionists and doctors. Losing weight becomes a real possibility – not just a dream. Abundant energy and much more are available to those who are willing to follow the system. The real question is – what are you willing to do?

Ayurveda is not a system of magic pills or of fads. It is a real system that has been continuously used for thousands of years; it could not have continued to exist for this long if it did not work. But it is a system that you have to do yourself. You have to take control of your own life and not buy into anyone else's belief system. You have to make the effort for your own health – no, you do not have to run 10 miles every day or be a super model that starves herself to death. You do need to take responsibility for yourself and what you put into your mouth. If you are willing to try, and to proceed slowly and patiently, the system will work for you, an individual, as it has worked for millions of others over thousands and thousands of years.

Bibliography

"A Brief Review of Selected Environmental Contamination Incidents with a Potential for Health Effects," *Library of Congress for the Committee on Environment and Public Works,* US Senate (Aug. 1980), pp. 173-74.

Acres. USA, PO Box 8800, Metairie, Louisiana, 70011, April 1994.

Appleton, Nancy. *Lick the Sugar Habit,* Garden Park City, NY: Avery Publishing, 1996.

Astanga Hridayam, vols. I-III., Tr., Murthy, Prof. K.R. Srikantha, Varanasi, India: Krishnadas Academy, 3rd edn. 1996.

Ballentine, Dr. Rudolph. *Diet and Nutrition: A Holistic Approach,* Honesdale, Pa: Himalayan International Institute, 1978.

Bohm, David. *Wholeness and the Implicate Order,* London, UK: Routledge & Kegan Paul Ltd., 1980.

British Medical Journal, 1994; 308:283-84

Brody, Jane E. "Dr. Spock's Disputed 'Vegan' Legacy", *International Herald Tribune,* June 22, 1998, p. 3.

"Cancer & Diet", *Newsweek*, November 30, 1998.

Caraka Saṁhita, vols. I-III, Tr., Dash, Dr. Bhagwan Sharma, Dr. R.K., Varanasi, India: Chowkhamba Series Office, 1992.

Chen, J., Campbell, T. C., et al. *Diet, Lifestyle, and Mortality in China: A Study of theCharacteristics of 65 Countries*, Oxford University Press, Cornell University Press, and the China People's Medical Publishing House, 1990.

Colborn, Theo, et al. *Our Stolen Future*, New York: Penguin Books, 1996.

EarthSave International, Box 68, Santa Cruz, CA 95062 or http://www.earthsave.org.

Egger, et al, "Controlled Trail of Oligoantigenic Treatment in the Hyperkinetic Syndrome", *Lancet*, 1985, p. 16.

"Food Choices and the Planet." *EarthSave report.*

Frawley, Dr. David. *Ayurvedic Healing: A Comprehensive Guide*, Salt Lake City, UT: Passage Press, 1989.

____. *Ayurveda and the Mind; The Healing of Consciousness*, Twin Lakes, WI; Lotus Press, 1997.

____. *Gods, Sages and Kings; Vedic Secrets of Ancient Civilization*, Salt Lake City, UT; Passage Press, 1991.

____. and Dr. Vasant Lad, *The Yoga of Herbs*, Twin Lakes, WI: Lotus Press, 1986.

____."Growing Pains: Why Hopes for Global Biotech Treaty Withered", *International Herald Tribune, 25 February 1999.*

Heyn, Birgit. *Ayurvedic Medicine: The Gentle Strength of Indian Healing*, New Delhi, India: Indus-Harper Collins India, 1992.

James, Barry. "Trade War Looms Over Hormone Beef Ban as EU Reiterates Health Fears," *International Herald Tribune,* May 13, 1999.

Joshi, Dr. Sunil V. *Ayurveda and Panchakarma,* Twin Lakes, WI: Lotus Press, 1996

Lee, Dr. John R. *What Your Doctor May Not Tell You About Menopause.* New York, NY: Warner Books, 1996.

Mctaggart, Lynne. *What Doctors Don't Tell You,* London, Throsons, 1996, p. 12.

Morningstar, Amadea. *Ayurvedic Cooking for Westerners,* Twin Lakes, WI: Lotus Press, 1994.

____. *The Ayurvedic Cookbook,* Twin Lakes, WI: Lotus Press, 1990.

Murray, Micheal T. *The Healing Power of Foods,* Rocklin, CA; Prima Publishing, 1993.

Pimental, et al. *Handbook of Pest Management in Agriculture,* 2nd edn., Boca Raton, Fl: CRC Press, 1990.

Pitchford, Paul. *Healing with Whole Foods,* Berkeley, CA: North Atlantic Books, 1993.

Positive News, No. 18, Winter 1998.

Quan, Richard, M.D. "Effects of Microwave Radiation on Anti-infective Factors in Human Milk", *Pediatrics,* vol., 89, No. 4, April 1992.

Quillin, P. *Safe Eating,* New York: Evans, 1990.

Rachel's Environment and Health Weekly, No. 450, July 13, 1995.

Rapp, Dori. *Is this your Child?,* New York: William Morris, 1991.

Robbins, John. *Diet for a New World,* New York: Avon Books, 1992.

_____. *Diet for a New America*, Walpole, NH: Stillpoint Publishing, 1987.

——. *Reclaiming Our Health*, Tiburon, CA: HJ Kramer Inc, 1996.

Roche, F. *The Complete Book of Natural Foods*, Boulder, CO; Shambala Publications, 1983 pp 258-59.

Sharma, Dr. Priya Vrat. *Sodasangahrdayam: Essentials of Ayurveda*, Delhi, India: Motilal Banarsidass Publishers, 1993.

Smith, Vaidya Atreya, *Ayurvedic Healing for Women*, York Beach, Me: Samuel Weiser, Inc. 1999.

_____. *Practical Ayurveda: Secrets of Physical, Sexual & Spiritual Health*, York Beach, Me: Samuel Weiser, Inc. 1998.

_____. *Prana: The Secret of Yogic Healing*, York Beach, Me: Samuel Weiser, Inc. 1996.

_____. *The Secrets of Ayurvedic Massage*, Twin Lakes, WI: Lotus Press, 1999.

Svoboda, Dr. Robert. *Prakruti: Your Ayurvedic Constitution*, Albuquerque, NM: Geocom Ltd.,. 1989.

____. *Ayurveda: Life, Health and Longevity*, New Delhi, India: Penguin Books India, 1993.

____. *Dravyaguna for Westerness*, Sauve, France, Editors Turiya, 2009.

Weil, Andrew. *Health and Healing*, New York, NY: Houghton Mifflin Co. 1983.

INDEX

A

Acidic Foods 10, 102, 106, 107, 285, 286

Adzuki Beans 125

Alcohol 29, 31, 59, 144, 154, 195, 196, 257, 267, 276, 283, 294

Alfalfa Sprouts 186, 260, 270

Algae 143

Allergies 11, 14, 15, 28, 33, 49, 58, 105, 115, 123, 124, 135, 164, 165, 173, 188, 189, 219, 286

Almonds 126, 139, 168, 253, 255, 263, 272

Aluminium 79

Amaranth 167, 252, 261, 271

Anabolic 60

Animal Products 122, 130, 131, 141, 142, 159, 160, 161, 164, 169, 170, 174, 175, 185, 186, 187, 193, 195, 242, 254, 258, 264, 268, 273, 277, 284, 287, 289, 292, 297

Antibiotics 129, 130, 131, 141, 186, 229, 299, 308

Appetite 16, 35, 57, 105, 149, 152, 220, 239, 280, 284

Apples 116, 147, 148, 165, 200, 249, 250, 259, 269, 282, 283

Apricots 165, 250, 259, 269

Artificial Sweeteners 145, 146

Asparagus 166, 244, 251, 260, 270

Assimilation 6, 30, 46, 47, 49, 50, 51, 64, 65, 76, 85, 86, 96, 132, 138, 190

Astringent Food 56

Avocado 139, 166, 250, 255, 261, 265, 271, 274

Ayurveda 1, 3, 5, 6, 7, 8, 9, 10, 21, 23, 24, 25, 26, 36, 40, 45, 47, 48, 49, 50, 51, 53, 54, 55, 59, 61, 64, 65, 66, 67, 69, 73, 74, 75, 76, 77, 83, 84, 85, 86, 88, 91, 92, 93, 96, 97, 98, 99, 103, 104, 105, 109, 111, 112, 113, 115, 120, 121, 125, 128, 132, 133, 134, 135, 137, 138, 141, 142, 143, 145, 146, 147, 148, 149, 150, 151, 153, 154, 155, 156, 169, 170, 171, 172, 173, 178, 185, 186, 188, 189, 190, 192, 193, 194, 197, 198, 201, 204, 211, 215, 216, 217, 221, 226, 227, 228, 229, 230, 231, 235, 236, 237, 238, 240, 241, 242, 243, 244, 245, 290, 292, 295, 296, 298, 299, 303, 304, 314, 315, 317, 318, 320, 321, 322, 323, 324, 326, 327, 328

Ayurvedic Nutrition 24, 25, 27, 43, 47, 48, 61, 82, 85, 92, 146, 172, 173, 195, 196, 219, 221, 280, 295, 296, 297, 299, 301, 324

B

Balance 20, 36, 59, 60, 65, 75, 83, 89, 93, 104, 106, 118, 119, 125, 126, 137, 144, 147, 163, 181, 187, 192, 208, 209, 211, 213, 216, 225, 231, 233, 241, 284, 308

Bananas 59, 165, 250, 259, 269, 285, 286

Barley 167, 186, 252, 261, 271, 289

Basil 256, 266, 276

Bass 169

Beans 15, 80, 106, 107, 109, 124, 125, 126, 153, 161, 162, 166, 167, 168, 193, 251, 252, 258, 260, 262, 268, 270, 272, 277, 285, 287, 289, 290, 292

Beef 129, 130, 169, 170, 254, 264, 274, 327

Beer 154, 257, 267, 276, 283, 285

Beets 166, 250, 260, 270

Bell Peppers 118, 121, 166, 250, 260, 270

Beverages 54, 106, 107, 109, 113, 114, 149, 150, 154, 257, 258, 267, 268, 276, 278, 286, 288

Black Pepper 115, 126, 147, 148, 149, 233, 256, 266, 275

Blood 6, 15, 28, 29, 30, 35, 56, 57, 58, 78, 79, 93, 97, 98, 99, 106, 107, 121, 122, 123, 133, 144, 150, 162, 182, 184, 196, 217, 228, 232, 236, 238, 239, 240, 241

Body Frame 12, 191

Body Odor 15

Breast 49, 130, 142, 152, 184, 182

Brazil Nuts 273

Broccoli 118, 119, 166, 224, 251, 260, 270

Brussels Sprouts 118, 119, 166, 251, 260, 270

Buckwheat 167, 186, 252, 261, 271, 289

Building 2, 67, 123, 125, 135, 136

Butter 127, 132, 133, 134, 138, 140, 141, 147, 168, 172, 173, 175, 254, 255, 263, 264, 273, 274, 284

Buttermilk 254, 263, 273

C

Cabbage 15, 118, 119, 120, 166, 251, 260, 270

Caffeine 153

Calcium 90, 91, 144, 163, 164, 257, 267, 277

Canola Oil 140

Carbohydrate 43, 56, 59, 60, 82, 95, 99, 108, 163, 193, 197, 231, 309

Cardamom 117, 132, 148, 149, 256, 266, 275

Carrots 166, 250, 260, 270, 282, 284

Cashews 168, 253, 263, 272

Catabolic 60, 61

Cauliflower 118, 119, 166, 251, 270

Cayenne 59, 126, 256, 266, 275

Celery 166, 251, 260, 270, 284

Chard 251, 260, 270

Cheese 82, 132, 147, 148, 168, 254, 263, 273, 285, 289

Chemical Additives 313

Cherries 165, 249, 259, 269

Chewing 84

Chick Peas 167, 252, 262, 272

Chicken 169, 254, 264, 273

Chilies 250, 261, 270

Cilantro 250, 260, 266, 270, 276

Cinnamon 59, 117, 132, 147, 148, 256, 266, 276, 283

Clams 169

Climate 23, 66, 67, 74, 88, 111, 116, 154, 155, 190, 191, 199, 201, 202, 227, 293, 322

Cloves 256, 266, 275

Coconut 139, 253, 255, 262, 264, 272, 274

Coffee 102, 149, 151, 152, 153, 192, 195, 196, 232, 257, 267, 276, 281, 282, 283, 285, 287, 288, 290, 291, 294, 313, 314

Colon 85, 113, 116, 122, 147, 233, 240, 241, 307, 308

Constitutional 5, 10, 21, 25, 26, 40, 41, 43, 44, 45, 46, 51, 52, 53, 54, 55, 61, 69, 98, 103, 104, 113, 115, 117, 119, 140, 204, 233, 247, 249, 295, 317, 322

Cooked Food 110, 112, 113, 114, 280

Cooking 64, 74, 75, 76, 77, 78, 79, 110, 112, 113, 114, 117, 120, 126, 127, 133, 134, 138, 139, 140, 145, 146, 148, 280, 281, 286, 287, 290, 291, 327

Coriander 149, 256, 266, 276

Corn 69, 122, 139, 166, 167, 186, 250, 252, 255, 260, 261, 265, 271, 274, 289

Cottage Cheese 168, 169, 254, 263, 273

Cranberries 59, 165

Couscous 252, 261, 271

Cream 14, 60, 93, 132, 168, 169, 179, 180, 254, 263, 273, 283, 286, 287, 295

Cucumbers 82

Cumin 126, 148, 149, 233, 256, 266, 276

D

Dairy 15, 80, 82, 106, 107, 108, 109, 112, 123, 128, 129, 130, 131, 132, 133, 135, 136, 141, 159, 168, 170, 172, 173, 174, 175, 193, 194, 254, 258, 263, 268, 273, 277, 289, 291

Dairy Products 80, 108, 112, 128, 129, 131, 132, 135, 136, 159, 168, 172, 173, 174

Dal 125, 167, 168, 253, 262, 272

Dates 7, 165, 249, 259, 269

Deed 7, 122, 132, 140, 149, 154, 171

Decaffeinated 153,

Dessert 87, 282, 290, 291

Diet 1, 5, 6, 7, 10, 20, 21, 24, 44, 45, 47, 51, 58, 66, 69, 71, 72, 75, 80, 81, 83, 84, 86, 89, 90, 91, 92, 93, 95, 96, 97, 98, 99, 102, 103, 108, 113, 114, 116, 117, 119, 120, 121, 122, 135, 136, 137, 142, 145, 146, 151, 155, 156, 157, 159, 160, 161, 162, 163, 164, 165, 169, 170, 172, 173, 174, 175, 177, 185, 186, 187, 188, 190, 191, 193, 194, 195, 196, 201, 204, 212, 213, 216, 217, 219, 223, 224, 226, 228, 229, 235, 238, 240, 241, 279, 292, 293, 295, 296, 297, 298, 301, 308, 310, 313, 316, 317, 318, 321, 323, 325, 326, 327, 328

Digestive 1, 10, 14, 21, 27, 30, 34, 45, 46, 47, 48, 49, 51, 53, 61, 64, 65, 67, 68, 69, 80, 81, 83, 85, 89, 90, 96, 99, 102, 105, 106, 108, 110, 111, 113, 114, 125, 126, 135, 147, 148, 151, 154, 156, 170, 190, 193, 194

Digestive Enzymes 46, 47, 48, 49, 61, 74, 81, 112, 132, 231

Digestive Formulas 231

Digestive Problems 26, 69, 76, 80, 86, 151, 188

Digestive Process 46, 47, 64, 65, 81, 84, 90, 152, 308

Digestive Strength 14

Disease 5, 10, 16, 17, 20, 24, 26, 30, 31, 32, 36, 49, 50, 51, 56, 57, 61, 67, 73, 75, 86, 91, 95, 97, 101, 103, 105, 118, 120, 122, 127, 128, 131, 133, 136, 137, 138, 139, 140, 144, 146, 155, 156, 157, 161, 162, 182, 188

Disorders 17, 34, 58, 71, 72, 73, 97, 103, 187, 188, 241, 279, 292, 321

Drugs 44, 71, 72, 101, 131, 160, 217, 221, 242, 308

Dry 12, 13, 28, 32, 110, 116, 136, 147, 152, 155, 189, 283

Duck 169, 254, 264, 273

E

Earth 54, 159, 296, 323, 326

Eating 8, 14, 17, 30, 34, 35, 56, 60, 63, 64, 65, 66, 67, 68, 70, 73, 74, 76, 77, 78, 81, 82, 83, 84, 85, 86, 87, 88, 90, 96, 97, 111, 112, 116, 118, 119, 120, 122, 123, 128, 141, 142, 145, 147, 148, 149, 156, 159, 160, 163, 164, 165, 169, 170, 171, 173, 174, 175, 185, 186, 191, 192, 193, 194, 195, 199, 200, 201, 202, 204, 205, 206, 207, 209, 225, 229, 231, 232, 233, 234, 248, 279, 282, 284, 287, 288, 289, 290, 292, 293, 295, 296, 299, 302, 309, 321, 327

Eating Habits 14, 8, 35, 123

Eggplant 82, 118, 121, 166, 251, 261, 271

Eggs 82, 124, 126, 169, 254, 264, 273, 287

Elements 28, 156, 198, 237, 241

Emotional 6, 37, 52, 53, 56, 67, 71, 73, 76, 183, 191, 202, 203, 208, 243, 305

Emotional Response 17

Emotional Tendencies 18

Endurance 16, 30, 31

Environment 1, 16, 66, 67, 68, 70, 71, 73, 98, 103, 116, 117, 120, 132, 141, 142, 143, 148, 157, 159, 160, 174, 178, 179, 184, 197, 198, 199, 200, 202, 203, 223, 227, 229, 233, 299, 315, 316, 325, 327

Enzyme Function 47, 48, 49, 51, 59, 60, 87, 91, 96, 97, 105, 108, 113, 116, 124, 133, 144, 146, 147, 148, 150, 151, 192, 194, 195, 229, 232, 237

Enzymes 46, 47, 48, 49, 53, 60, 61, 74, 81, 82, 112, 123, 132, 144, 146, 147, 201, 219, 221, 225, 231, 236, 311, 313

Exercise 34, 65, 68, 85, 114, 155, 190, 206, 207, 208, 209, 210, 211, 212, 214, 215

F

Face Shape 13

Fat 21, 28, 30, 31, 36, 40, 56, 60, 86, 95, 98, 124, 127, 132, 135, 136, 137, 138, 140, 141, 147, 162, 163, 165, 166, 167, 168, 169, 173, 191, 193, 194, 225, 231, 238, 240, 241, 243, 284, 286, 289, 293, 297

Fat Content 122, 132, 142

Fat Tissue 98, 99, 240, 241

Fatigue 50, 195, 196

Fennel 148, 149, 233, 256, 266, 276

Fenugreek 149, 233, 256, 266, 276

Figs 165, 249, 259, 269

Filberts 168, 253, 263, 272

Fire 77, 143, 284

Fish 80, 82, 135, 142, 143, 159, 169, 170, 173, 174, 184, 193, 194, 254, 264, 274, 289, 291

Flour 122, 124, 167, 241

Fluid 31, 56, 57, 58, 149, 154, 179, 183, 216, 239, 307

Food Classifications 103

Food Cravings 14, 146

Food Group 81, 82, 90, 104, 105, 106, 107, 108, 109, 115, 116, 118, 258, 268, 277

Food portion 82

Food Sensitivities 15, 121

Fresh Foods 127, 195, 316

Fried Foods 15, 29, 36, 140, 195, 196, 287

Fruit Juices 96, 113, 150, 257, 267, 276, 286

Fruit Sugar 255, 265, 275

Fruits 29, 81, 82, 83, 96, 106, 107, 109, 110, 113, 115, 116, 117, 118, 161, 164, 165, 171, 180, 181, 193, 194, 233, 244, 249, 250, 258, 259, 268, 277, 281, 282, 285, 286, 289

G

Garlic 121, 256, 266, 275

Gas 14, 15, 28, 32, 50, 57, 77, 96, 105, 115, 116, 120, 126, 147, 151, 188, 189, 190, 219, 291

Genetic Makeup 51

Ghee 82, 119, 133, 134, 135, 138, 139, 140, 141, 173, 244, 254, 255, 263, 264, 273, 274, 284

Ginger 117, 147, 148, 149, 256, 266, 275, 288

Grains 59, 80, 81, 82, 106, 107, 109, 116, 119, 121, 122, 123, 124, 125, 135, 137, 164, 165, 167, 186, 193, 194, 244, 252, 258, 261, 268, 271, 277, 281, 282, 283, 284, 285, 287, 289, 292, 313

Granola 252, 261, 271, 287

Grapefruit 165, 201, 248, 249

Grapes 165, 249, 259, 269

Green Beans 166, 251, 260, 270

Green Vegetables 118, 119

Gums 13

H

Habit 8, 14, 17, 31, 35, 36, 40, 63, 81, 87, 91, 123, 124, 129, 140, 146, 185, 190, 199, 203, 204, 205, 216, 217, 235, 279, 296, 302, 313, 321, 325

Hair Quality 12

Hands 13, 15, 16, 28, 29, 50, 217, 225, 297

Herbal 89, 146, 221, 226, 230, 244

Herbal Tea 83, 150, 154, 257, 267, 276, 286

Herbs 1, 47, 51, 54, 61, 102, 146, 148, 190, 191, 192, 199, 220, 222, 223, 224, 226, 230, 231, 232, 233, 234, 243, 244, 319, 326

Holistic 3, 23, 69, 303, 325

Honey 82, 112, 144, 145, 244, 255, 265, 275, 281, 289, 290

Hormone 89, 129, 130, 136, 141, 142, 150, 179, 180, 181, 182, 183, 186, 187, 188, 196, 225, 228, 229, 242, 299, 309, 311, 318, 319, 321, 327

Horseradish 256, 266, 275

Hot 10, 14, 17, 29, 32, 35, 38, 60, 81, 82, 106, 121, 140, 148, 150, 152, 155, 207

Hydrogenated Oils 136

I

Ice Cream 60, 93, 168, 169, 254, 263, 273, 283, 286, 287, 295

Immune 16, 17, 28, 30, 31, 49, 51, 97, 128, 131, 138, 143, 150, 163, 227, 228, 229, 237, 239, 307

Immunity 50, 56, 58, 72, 73, 132, 133, 150, 228, 235, 236, 237, 238, 239, 241, 242, 243, 244, 245

India 7, 23, 24, 54, 59, 125, 129, 133, 148, 169, 200, 244, 280, 325, 326, 327, 328

Iron 161, 162, 258, 268, 277

J

Juice 96, 112, 113, 150, 154, 200, 239, 257, 267, 276, 277, 284, 286, 287

K

Kapha 8, 9, 10, 11, 12, 24, 25, 30, 31, 33, 34, 35, 36, 39, 40, 41, 46, 50, 54, 55, 56, 60, 61, 80, 85, 87, 94, 101, 108, 109, 110, 111, 112, 113, 115, 116, 119, 121, 123, 124, 125, 126, 127, 128, 131, 132, 133, 134, 136, 140, 142, 145, 147, 149, 151, 154, 155, 189, 190, 191, 192, 205, 209, 212, 213, 214, 231, 233, 243, 269, 270, 271, 272, 273, 274, 275, 277, 287, 292, 293

Kefir 254, 263, 273

Kicharee 125

Kidney 31, 99, 133, 144, 150, 152, 153, 168, 196

L

Lamb 169, 254, 264, 274

Lemons 165, 249, 259, 269

Lentils 167, 168, 253, 262, 272

Lettuce 119, 166, 251, 260, 270, 282

Life 1, 3, 4, 5, 9, 19, 22, 28, 29, 35, 36, 37, 38, 39, 41, 48, 51, 53, 65, 69, 72, 77, 83, 88, 93, 97, 98, 101, 102, 104, 114, 118, 120, 122, 123, 130, 135, 146, 157, 177, 181, 185, 188, 191, 198

Life Goals 19

Life Style 1, 5, 22, 31, 87, 146, 157, 160, 188, 190, 191, 197, 198, 199, 201, 202, 204, 216, 217, 236, 249, 296, 298, 308, 326

Light 12, 19, 57, 69, 92, 110, 126, 134, 147, 169, 174, 189, 93, 194, 194, 206, 207, 209, 212, 213, 215, 240, 280, 309

Lima 168, 249, 253, 259, 262, 269. 272

Liquid Food 112, 113

Liquor 154

Live 3, 11, 31, 33, 36, 53, 66, 73, 90, 101, 103, 123, 162, 164, 175, 199, 200, 201, 202, 204, 205, 222, 223, 225, 229, 230, 231, 232, 234, 236, 239, 240, 285, 288, 297, 299, 306, 307, 313, 314, 317, 321

Limes 249, 259, 269

Ligaments 238

Locally Grown Foods 73

Love Relationships 19, 39

Low-Fat Products 132, 284

Lymph 149, 150, 238, 239

M

Mango 165, 249, 259, 269

Maple Sugar 133, 265

Maple Syrup 133, 255, 265, 275

Margarine 133, 136, 138, 141, 195, 255, 265, 274, 280, 284, 288

Martha 101, 102, 103, 163, 198

Material Objects 135

Meats 82, 122, 142, 174, 175, 193, 194, 241

Meditation 207, 208, 210, 211, 212, 214, 215

Melons 81, 82, 250, 259, 269

Menstrual Problems 182, 183

Mental Attitude 66, 67

Mental Nature 17

Mental Problems 34, 71

Metabolism 6, 20, 21, 24, 25, 26, 27, 28, 29, 30, 31, 32, 33, 34, 35, 40, 44, 50, 52, 53, 54, 55, 56, 57, 58, 60, 61, 65, 66, 67, 68, 71, 72, 75, 89, 90, 91, 95, 96, 97, 101, 102, 104, 105, 106, 107, 108, 110, 143, 144, 145, 146, 147, 155, 180, 187, 188, 189, 190, 191, 192, 204, 207, 209, 216, 233, 236, 238, 239, 240, 241, 242, 248, 280, 293, 295, 297, 299, 309, 323

Micronutrient 75, 241
Microwave Ovens 77, 78, 79
Milk 49, 79, 82, 110, 116, 123, 124, 125, 126, 128, 129, 131, 132, 135, 153, 163, 164, 168, 169, 172, 173, 174, 244, 254, 257, 263, 267, 273, 276, 284, 327
Millet 167, 186, 252, 261, 271
Mind 2, 3, 9, 23, 30, 37, 65, 69, 71, 73, 76, 87, 90, 91, 93, 97, 99, 116, 128, 150, 170, 171, 172, 188, 190, 191, 203, 223, 227, 231, 232, 244, 245, 247, 297, 303, 304, 305, 311, 314, 317, 321, 323, 326
Minerals 43, 54, 59, 60, 75, 106, 108, 109, 119, 127, 144, 150, 155, 156, 197, 219, 231, 257, 258, 267, 268, 277, 278, 285, 309, 311
Mint 256, 266, 276
Molasses 255, 265, 275
Money 18, 19, 38, 64, 70, 90, 93, 135, 140, 154, 318
Monounsaturated Fats 137, 138
Molasses 255, 265, 275
Mung Beans 125
Muscle 36, 56, 58, 76, 83, 92, 101, 102, 141, 238, 239, 240, 241
Mushrooms 166, 251, 270
Mustard 166, 167, 251, 255, 256, 261, 265, 266, 270, 274, 275
Mustard Greens 166, 261, 270

N

Nerve Tissue 56, 133, 238, 241
Neurotic Tendencies 19
Nightshade 82, 118, 119, 120, 121
Nutmeg 117, 256, 266, 276
Nutrient 6, 11, 32, 44, 45, 46, 47, 48, 49, 58, 60, 64, 65, 68, 74, 75, 76, 79, 86, 95, 98, 103, 104, 112, 113, 118, 122, 123, 127, 133, 135, 136, 140, 156, 171, 180, 191, 193, 195, 196, 197, 202, 203, 222, 223, 227, 228, 229, 230, 231, 232, 236, 238, 239, 240, 241, 242, 248, 280, 297, 298, 308, 309, 311, 316, 318, 319
Nutrient Assimilation 47, 65, 236
Nutrition 2, 3, 4, 5, 6, 7, 8, 21, 23, 24, 25, 27, 31, 35, 36, 43, 44, 45, 47, 48, 51, 53, 55, 59, 61, 69, 73, 74, 75, 76, 79, 81, 82, 83, 85, 89, 90, 91, 92, 93, 94, 97, 99, 103, 104, 118, 120, 131, 136, 140, 146, 156, 157, 159, 160, 162, 163, 164, 173, 178, 191, 196, 197, 198, 200, 201, 202, 203, 219, 221, 223, 227, 280, 295, 296, 297, 298, 299, 301, 302, 303, 304, 307, 309, 312, 313, 314, 316, 317, 319, 320, 321, 322, 323, 324
Nuts and Seeds 111, 126, 127, 128, 135

O

Oats 167, 186, 252, 261, 271, 284
Ojas 236, 237, 238, 239, 242
Okra 166, 167, 251, 260, 271
Olive Oil 134, 135, 136, 281, 284
Onions 15, 59, 121, 126, 140, 166, 167, 250, 251, 260, 261, 270
Oranges 165, 200, 248, 250, 259, 269
Organic Food 73, 156, 185, 295
Ovum 216, 238, 241

P

Papayas 165, 166, 249, 259
Parsley 166, 167, 250, 260, 270, 276
Pasta 124, 140, 281, 284, 287, 289, 292
Peaches 165, 166, 250, 259, 269
Peanuts 168
Pears 165, 166, 250, 259, 269, 282
Peas 166, 167, 168, 251, 252, 253, 260, 262, 270, 272

Pecans 253, 263, 272
Performance 47, 48, 171, 195, 196, 249
Persimmons 165, 166
Pesticides 74, 75, 91, 92, 117, 118, 141, 174, 184, 185, 299
Ph 2
Physical 1, 25, 30, 31, 32, 33, 34, 35, 36, 37, 53, 69, 83, 85, 116, 120, 144, 188, 197, 202, 235, 238, 242, 245, 304, 305, 306, 312, 314, 328
Pine Nuts 168, 262, 272
Pineapple 165, 166, 201, 249
Pitta Type 10, 11, 26, 29, 31, 32, 34, 35, 38, 39, 40, 41, 56, 85, 89, 90, 96, 106, 107, 110, 111, 112, 113, 115, 116, 120, 121, 123, 124, 125, 126, 131, 133, 136, 140, 142, 145, 148, 149, 151, 154, 155, 189, 192, 207, 208, 210, 233, 248, 259, 260, 261, 262, 263, 264, 265, 266, 267, 268, 283, 284, 287, 291, 293
Pitta/Kapha Type 36, 213, 214
Plasma 93, 99, 106, 133, 144, 149, 150, 238, 239, 240, 241, 242
Plums 165, 166, 250, 259, 269
Polyunsaturated Fats 137, 138
Pomegranates 165, 166
Pork 95, 162, 163, 169, 254, 264, 274
Potatoes 71, 121, 139, 166, 167, 250, 251, 260, 261, 270
Poultry 80, 193, 141, 142, 174, 175, 194
Prana 238, 328
Pregnant Women 152, 181, 182, 316
Preservatives 196, 201, 299, 313
Principle 25, 26, 32, 33, 34, 35, 36, 38, 43, 48, 53, 54, 77, 90, 97, 148, 171, 172, 173, 188, 189, 190, 191, 196, 204, 205, 235, 238, 242, 243, 292, 293, 306, 315, 322
Processed Foods 145, 171, 172, 228, 229, 279, 283, 294
Protein 43, 47, 56, 60, 82, 86, 91, 95, 96, 98, 99, 111, 126, 159, 160, 161, 162, 163, 164, 165, 166, 167, 168, 169, 177, 193, 197, 231, 309
Protein Content 165
Prunes 165, 166, 249, 259, 269
Psychological 6, 18, 26, 37, 38, 39, 40, 52, 53, 64, 91, 98, 216, 243, 310, 316, 321, 322
Pumpkin Seeds 168
Pungent 55, 56, 57, 59, 61, 118, 119, 121

Q

Quinoa 167, 252, 262, 271, 289

R

Radi 166
Radiation 77, 233, 306, 327
Radish 250, 261, 270
Raspberries 165
Raw Food 81, 110, 111, 112, 280, 282, 287
Refined Foods 171, 188, 195, 196, 201, 294, 296, 312, 313
Relationship 19, 39, 40, 44, 199, 203, 216, 306, 307, 308, 309, 310, 315
Reproductive System 178, 241, 242, 243
Reproductive Tissue 178, 238, 242, 243
Rice 123, 124, 125, 126, 153, 167, 186, 252, 261, 262, 271, 282, 284
Ripe 74, 116, 117, 200
Root Vegetables 119
Rotting 49, 50, 122
Rye 167, 186, 252, 262, 271, 289

S

Salads 80, 119, 140, 281, 282, 284, 289
Salt 15, 59, 94, 126, 256, 264, 266, 276, 288, 326
Salty Foods 56
Saturated Fats 138
Seafood 112, 126, 135, 142, 170, 173, 174
Season 66, 67, 73, 74, 88, 91, 109, 111, 116, 117, 118, 199, 200, 201, 202, 249, 292, 293
Seaweed 59, 126, 143, 250, 261, 271
Sensitivity to Environment 16
Sesame Oil 137, 138, 281
Sesame Seeds 168
Sex 178, 179, 181
Skin 12, 28, 29, 31, 57, 58, 96, 121, 135, 136, 147, 152, 155, 183, 189, 283
Skin Temperature 12
Snacks 14, 85, 87, 282
Social Relations 18
Soft Drinks 106, 145, 150, 257, 267, 277, 281, 285, 288
Solid 15, 25, 55, 81, 83, 91, 110, 114, 133, 134, 160, 236, 240, 315
Sour Cream 132, 254, 263, 273
Soy 59, 125, 139, 153, 166, 168, 185, 253, 255, 262, 264, 272, 273, 274, 284, 285, 286
Soybeans 125
Soy Milk 125, 126, 273, 284
Speech Habits 17
Spending 19, 65, 70
Sperm 177, 178, 183, 216, 238, 241
Spices 106, 107, 109, 146, 148, 195, 106, 111, 113, 117, 132, 140, 146, 147, 148, 149, 189, 190, 191, 192, 194, 195, 220, 231, 232, 233, 234, 256, 258, 268, 278, 280, 281, 282, 283, 285, 288, 290, 291, 292
Spicy 10, 14, 57, 107, 121, 285, 267, 287
Spinach 166, 251, 261, 270
Split Peas 168, 253, 262, 272
Sprouts 27, 118, 125, 166, 186, 251, 260, 270
Squash 167, 200, 251, 260, 271
Stimulants 195, 196, 283, 294, 296
Stimulating 60, 116
Stomach 30, 54, 81, 83, 84, 85, 86, 110, 115, 144, 151, 152, 153, 189, 236, 290, 291
Stools 29, 188, 189, 233
Strawberries 166
Strength 14, 16, 30, 31, 36, 48, 53, 56, 57, 59, 113, 123, 128, 133, 135, 170, 181, 192, 199, 235, 236, 243, 245, 326
Stress 5, 9, 10, 11, 37, 89, 101, 188, 197, 202, 203, 204, 207, 216, 226, 227, 228, 235
Sugar 30, 59, 71, 72, 93, 94, 108, 135, 143, 144, 145, 146, 150, 152, 195, 196, 228, 255, 256, 265, 275, 283, 285, 289, 290, 294, 311, 312, 318, 325
Sunflower 139, 253, 255, 260, 262, 265, 270, 272, 274, 281
Sunflower Seeds 168
Sunflower Oil 288
Sweat 15, 209
Sweet 250, 257, 267, 277, 282, 284, 286, 287, 289
Sweet Potatoes 167, 261, 271
Sweeteners 106, 107, 109, 143, 145, 255, 256, 258, 265, 268, 275, 278

T

Taste 55, 56, 57, 58, 59, 60, 61, 75, 76, 84, 87, 88, 90, 121, 126, 129, 148, 150, 231, 248, 280, 283, 286, 291, 296

Tea 32, 83, 153, 154, 191, 195, 232, 257, 267, 276, 281, 282, 283, 286
Teeth 13, 312
Temperature 309
Tissue Levels 239
Tofu 125, 168, 252, 262, 272, 286, 287
Tomatoes 15, 29, 82, 94, 121, 167, 200, 251, 261, 271, 285
Tongue Width 13
Triphala Formula 233
Turkey 169, 254, 264, 273
Turnips 167, 251, 261, 270
Turmeric 232, 233, 256, 266, 275

U

Urination 15, 219

V

Vata Type 9, 11, 28, 32, 33, 34, 37, 41, 55, 56, 61, 80, 81, 83, 85, 90, 96, 104, 105, 106, 108, 110, 111, 112, 113, 115, 116, 120, 123, 124, 125, 126, 132, 135, 136, 140, 142, 145, 147, 148, 149, 151, 153, 154, 155, 188, 189, 192, 205, 206, 248, 249, 250, 252, 253, 254, 255, 256, 257, 258, 280, 283, 284, 287, 292
Vata/Kapha Type 33, 212
Vata/Pitta Type 31, 125, 210
Vegetables 80, 81, 82, 94, 106, 107, 109, 110, 111, 113, 118, 119 120, 121, 123, 137, 161, 164, 166, 185, 193, 194, 250, 251, 258, 260, 268, 270, 271, 277, 281, 282, 283, 284, 285, 287, 289, 292, 313
Veins 12, 238, 284
Vitality 76, 235, 242
Vitamin A 44, 112, 257, 268, 277
Vitamin C 155, 200, 222, 223, 233, 257, 268, 277, 316, 317, 318, 319, 320
Vitamin D 257, 268, 277
Vitamin E 257, 268, 277
Vitamin K 258, 267, 277
Vitamins and Minerals 75, 119, 155, 219

W

Walnuts 253, 263, 273
Water 7, 21, 31, 57, 63, 72, 77, 78, 81, 110, 116, 118, 123, 125, 126, 132, 141, 142, 143, 144, 149, 150, 151, 153, 154, 155, 174, 183, 184, 192, 222, 226, 240, 244, 257, 264, 267, 276, 281, 282, 283, 286, 288, 289, 290, 293, 309
Water Filters 153
Watercress 167, 251, 261, 270
Watermelon 166
Weight Loss 47, 48, 98, 192, 241
Wheat 122, 123, 124, 167, 186, 252, 261, 271, 289
Wheat Allergies 123
White Flour 122, 124
Whole Foods 5, 44, 45, 49, 69, 75, 110, 124, 146, 156, 163, 172, 175, 186, 187, 188, 195, 229, 285, 286, 294, 301, 327
Wine 154, 257, 267, 276, 283, 285, 286

X

Xenobiotic Chemicals 242

Y

Yeast Breads 82, 124, 135, 285
Yoga 114, 206, 326
Yogurt 59, 82, 116, 132, 133, 168, 172, 173, 254, 263, 273, 285

Z

Zelda 198
Zinc 257, 268, 277